ROME OR DEATH

The Obsessions of General Garibaldi

Also by Daniel Pick

Faces of Degeneration: A European Disorder, c.1848–c.1918

War Machine: The Rationalisation of Slaughter in the Modern Age

Svengali's Web: The Alien Enchanter in Modern Culture

Editor, George Du Maurier's *Trilby* (Penguin Classics)

Co-editor (with Lyndal Roper), *Dreams and History: The Interpretation of Dreams from Ancient Greece to Modern Psychoanalysis*

ROME OR DEATH

*The Obsessions of
General Garibaldi*

Daniel Pick

JONATHAN CAPE
LONDON

Published by Jonathan Cape 2005

2 4 6 8 10 9 7 5 3 1

Copyright © Daniel Pick 2005

First published in Great Britain in 2005 by
Jonathan Cape
Random House, 20 Vauxhall Bridge Road,
London SW1V 2SA

Random House Australia (Pty) Limited
20 Alfred Street, Milsons Point, Sydney,
New South Wales 2061, Australia

Random House New Zealand Limited
18 Poland Road, Glenfield,
Auckland 10, New Zealand

Random House South Africa (Pty) Limited
Endulini, 5A Jubilee Road, Parktown 2193, South Africa

The Random House Group Limited Reg. No. 954009
www.randomhouse.co.uk

A CIP catalogue record for this book is available from the British Library

ISBN 0-224-07179-3

Papers used by Random House are natural,
recyclable products made from wood grown in sustainable forests.
The manufacturing processes conform to the environmental
regulations of the country of origin

Typeset in Bembo by Palimpsest Book Production Limited,
Polmont, Stirlingshire
Printed and bound in Great Britain by
William Clowes Ltd, Beccles, Suffolk

To Isobel

General Garibaldi in Rome, 1875

'*Roma o morte*'
General Garibaldi

Contents

SWITZERLAND

SAVOY

TYROL

AUSTRIAN EMPIRE

Bolzano

KINGDOM

Turin   •Milan

FRANCE

PIEDMONT
of
SARDINIA

LIGURIA

Nice

MONACO

Genoa

LOMBARDY-VENETIA

R.Po •Mantua   Padua

DUCHY OF
PARMA

DUCHY of
MODENA

•Ferrara

•Bologna

Udine

•Gorizia

Venice   •Trieste

ISTRIA

CROATIA

•Ravenna

MASSA

LUCCA
Pisa•   Florence•

Livorno•   GRAND DUCHY

Siena•

of TUSCANY

REPUBLIC OF
SAN MARINO

The Marches

Ancona

OTTOMAN
EMPIRE

CORSICA
(to France)

•Ajaccio

Elba

Civitavecchia•

PAPAL

•Perugia

UMBRIA

STATES

LAZIO

•Aquila

Rome•

ABRUZZO

Adriatic Sea

KINGDOM of

SARDINIA

N

MOLISE

Gaeta•

•Benevento

Naples•

KINGDOM

Bari

Cagliari

Salerno•

BASILICATA

Brindisi

Taranto•

Tyrrhenian
Sea

OF   THE

Lipari Is.

•Cotrone

Mediterranean

Palermo•

CALABRIA

Messina• •Reggio

TUNISIA

SICILY

Agrigento•

TWO SICILIES

Catania

•Syracuse

ALGERIA

Sea

MALTA
(to United Kingdom)

ITALY IN 1815
after the Congress of Vienna

0   50 miles

0   50   100 km

GARIBALDI'S FLIGHT
FROM ROME IN 1849

Adriatic Sea

Bologna   Ravenna.
EMILIA ROMAGNA
Forlì.
Cesena.

Comacchio
Magnavacca
3 August

2–3 August

Cesenatico

Musano
1 August
Sogliano
1 August
San Marino
31 July
M. Cerignone
30 July
Macerata Feltria
29 July
San Angelo in Vado
28 July
Bocca Trabaria
27 July
Citerna
24–25 July
Ville
25 July
Arezzo
22 July
Castiglione Fiorentino
21 July
Torrita di Siena
20 July
Lago Trasimeno
Montepulciano
19 July
Perugia
UMBRIA
Sarteano
18 July
Cetona
17 July
Salci
16 July
Ficulle
16 July
14 July
13 July
Todi
11–12 July
Orvieto
S. Gemini
8–10 July
Cesi
8–10 July
Terni
8 July
Configni
7 July
Poggio Mirteto
6 July
Passo Corese
5 July
Civitavecchia
Monterotondo
4 July
Mentana
4 July
Tivoli
3 July
Rome

Florence
TUSCANY

R. Tiber

R. Tiber

L A Z I O

Tyrrhenian Sea

N

0   50   100 miles
0   50   100   150 km

↓ Pontine Marshes

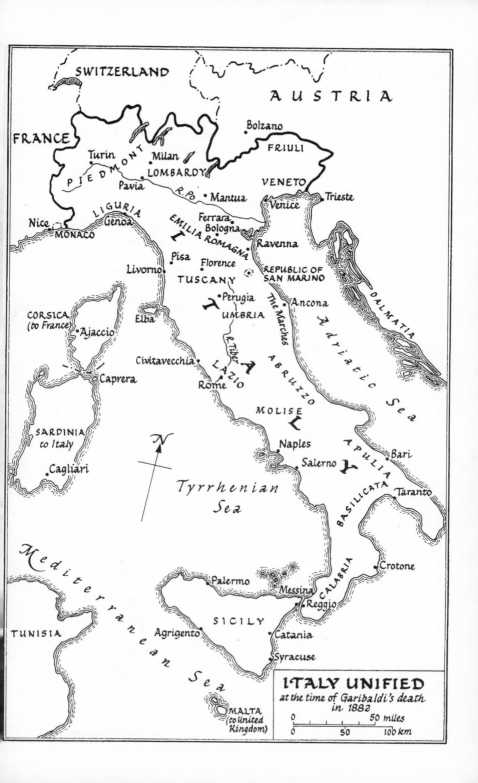

SWITZERLAND

AUSTRIA

FRANCE

Bolzano

Turin

PIEDMONT

Milan

LOMBARDY

FRIULI

VENETO

Pavia

R.Po

Mantua

Trieste

Venice

LIGURIA

Nice

Genoa

MONACO

Ferrara

EMILIA

Bologna

ROMAGNA

Ravenna

Pisa

Livorno

Florence

REPUBLIC OF
SAN MARINO

TUSCANY

Ancona

Perugia

CORSICA
(to France)

Elba

UMBRIA

The Marches

Ajaccio

R. Tiber

Adriatic

DALMATIA

Civitavecchia

LAZIO

ABRUZZO

Caprera

Rome

Sea

SARDINIA
to Italy

MOLISE

Naples

APULIA

Bari

Cagliari

Salerno

Tyrrhenian

Sea

BASILICATA

Taranto

Mediterranean

Crotone

CALABRIA

Palermo

Messina

Reggio

TUNISIA

Sea

SICILY

Agrigento

Catania

Syracuse

MALTA
(to United
Kingdom)

ITALY UNIFIED
*at the time of Garibaldi's death
in 1882*

0   50 miles

0   50   100 km

A Chronology

1807

Birth of Giuseppe Garibaldi in French-occupied Nice.

1814

Abdication of Napoleon. Nice returns to the Kingdom of Piedmont–Sardinia.

1824

Garibaldi sails to Odessa.

1824–33

Works as a sailor in the Mediterranean and Black Sea.

1825

Sails with his father on the *Santa Reparata* to Rome.

1833

Travels to Constantinople on a ship carrying followers of Saint-Simon. At the Taganrog port, on the Black Sea, Garibaldi learns about the ideals of Mazzini's Young Italy movement.

1834

Participates in a mutiny attempt in Genoa, part of a failed invasion of Savoy by the Mazzinians; flees to France. Condemned to death for high treason.

1835

Journeys to Constantinople, Odessa and Tunis, and then to South America where he establishes himself in Rio de Janeiro.

1836

Works as a merchant sailor. As an exile representing Young Europe, Garibaldi's task is to enlist volunteers to go back to Italy and fight for the peninsula's unification.

1836

Rebels, seeking to break free from the Brazilian Empire, proclaim a republic in the province of Rio Grande do Sul. This rebellion, the longest Brazilian conflict in the nineteenth century, endures until 1845.

1837

Garibaldi fights for the independence of the province of Rio Grande do Sul. Unable to put into Brazilian ports controlled by the imperials, arrives in Gualeguay, a port town in Argentina, where the local governor, Major Leonardo Millán, captures and tortures him.

1839

Garibaldi meets Ana Maria de Jesus Ribeiro (Anita), at Laguna.

1840

Birth of Anita and Garibaldi's son, Domenico (known as Menotti), at Mostardas, Rio Grande do Sul.

1841

Death of Garibaldi's father, Domenico Antonio. Disillusioned with infighting among his Brazilian commanders, leaves Rio Grande do Sul for Montevideo with Anita, Menotti and nine hundred cattle. Works as a shipbroker and as a teacher of mathematics and history.

1842

Garibaldi is appointed a naval commander of the small Uruguayan fleet. His task is to fight against the former Uruguayan president Manuel Oribe, now leading the opposition and allied with the Argentine dictator, Juan Manuel de Rosas. In March, he marries Anita in a Catholic church in Montevideo.

1843

Garibaldi becomes the commander of the newly formed Italian Legion. Birth of Rosa (Rosita), Garibaldi's first daughter.

1845

Birth of second daughter, Teresa (Teresita). At the end of the year, Rosita dies.

1846

Garibaldi fights his most important South American land battle at San Antonio del Salto. His fame spreads to Europe. Named a general by the government of Uruguay; takes charge of the defence of Montevideo. Election of Pope Pius IX on 17 June.

1847

Together with a comrade, Garibaldi writes a letter offering his services to Pius IX. At the end of the year, Anita, Menotti, Teresita and Ricciotti (their recently born second son) leave for Nice.

1848

Insurrection in Milan against the Austrians. Garibaldi sails to Italy with sixty-three legionaries (and his daughter Rosita's remains). Offers his services to the King of Piedmont, Charles Albert. Commands a volunteer unit, fights against the Austrians at Luino and Morazzone; retreats across the frontier to Switzerland. Murder of Count Pellegrino Rossi in Rome. Pius IX and his entourage flee to Gaeta, in the Kingdom of Naples.

1849

Establishment of the Roman Republic. Garibaldi leads the resistance to a French military attack on the Janiculum Hill but his forces are overwhelmed. Rome surrenders and Garibaldi is forced to flee. He leads a few thousand soldiers through central Italy, avoiding combat with the French and Austrian armies. Disbands his men in San Marino; chased by the Austrians; Anita dies on 4 August, at Mandriole, near Ravenna; Garibaldi makes his escape.

1849–53

Exile.

1850

Pius IX returns to Rome. Garibaldi works as a candlemaker in New York. Giovanni Battista Cuneo, who had fought alongside Garibaldi in South America and in Italy, publishes his biography.

1851–4

Garibaldi travels extensively, visiting Panama, Peru, Tasmania and the Far East.

1852

Death of Garibaldi's mother, Rosa Raimondo. Count Cavour becomes Prime Minister in Piedmont.

1853

Mazzinian rising in Milan. Death of Angelo, Garibaldi's elder brother, born in 1804.

A Chronology

1854

Garibaldi returns to Italy. Buys part of the island of Caprera, off the Sardinian coast.

1855

Death of Felice, Garibaldi's younger brother, born in 1813.

1856

Visits Cavour in Turin. Attempts unsuccessfully to secure the release of political prisoners held by the Bourbon king of Naples.

1858

Travels to Turin again to meet Cavour. Offered the rank of major general in the Piedmontese Army.

1859

War breaks out against the Austrians; leads his *cacciatori delle Alpi* (Alpine huntsmen) into conflict. Captures Varese and Como. The Villafranca armistice puts an end to the dispute. Acquisition of Lombardy by Piedmont. Garibaldi's plan to invade the Papal States overruled by King Victor Emmanuel II, ruler of the Piedmont-Sardinian Kingdom. The first edition of Garibaldi's autobiography is published in New York. Battistina Ravello gives birth to Garibaldi's child, Anna Maria, known as Anita.

1860

Marries the eighteen-year-old Giuseppina Raimondi, but abandons her within hours of the marriage. Rare appearance in the Piedmontese parliament to protest the cession of Nice by Cavour and Victor Emmanuel to France. Official annexation of Nice and Savoy to France. Without government backing, Garibaldi and his thousand Red Shirts sail from Quarto in Liguria to Sicily. In the name of Victor Emmanuel, Garibaldi proclaims himself dictator at Marsala.

Defeats the regular army of the King of Naples at Calatafimi. Captures Palermo. Wins the Battle of Milazzo. Crosses the Strait of Messina and marches through Calabria. Enters Naples and proclaims himself 'Dictator of the Two Sicilies'. With 30,000 men under his command, wins an extraordinary military victory on the Volturno River, north of Naples. Meets Victor Emmanuel at Teano; hands over his powers to the King. Victor Emmanuel makes a triumphal entry into Naples, with Garibaldi sitting beside him in the royal carriage. Garibaldi leaves for Caprera. Alexandre Dumas the Elder's *Mémoires de Garibaldi*, based on the General's original manuscript, with commentaries by George Sand and Victor Hugo, is published in Brussels.

1861

Proclamation of the Kingdom of Italy; Victor Emmanuel assumes title of King of Italy. Death of Cavour. Abraham Lincoln offers Garibaldi a Union command in the American Civil War. A Garibaldi biography, *Denkwürdigkeiten*, by Marie-Espérance von Schwartz, under the pseudonym of Elpis Melena, is published in Hamburg. Publication in Paris of *Les Garibaldiens: Révolution de Sicilie et de Naples*, by Alexandre Dumas the Elder.

1862

In an attempt to march on Rome, Garibaldi is seriously wounded and arrested by Italian troops at Aspromonte, in Calabria. His famous catchphrase of the time is 'Rome or death'. Granted an amnesty by Victor Emmanuel.

1863

Resigns from parliament.

1864

Visits England and receives huge public acclaim.

A Chronology

1865

Italian capital moved from Turin to Florence.

1866

Italy secretly sides with Prussia against Austria. Wounded again at the Suello Battle, in the Trento area. In a second war of independence, Garibaldi and his volunteers engage the Austrians at the Bezzecca Battle. '*Obbedisco*': Garibaldi agrees to obey after receiving a telegram from Victor Emmanuel II, in which the King orders him not to pursue his military campaign. Austria cedes Venetia to France which, in turn, concedes it to Italy. Death of Michele, Garibaldi's youngest brother, born in 1816.

1867

Plans to invade Rome, but Garibaldi's forces are routed at Mentana, where he is arrested by the Italian government. Set free in Florence; returns to Caprera. Birth of Clelia, Garibaldi's first daughter by Francesca Armosino.

1869

Birth of Rosita, Garibaldi's second daughter by Francesca.

1870

Italian troops invade Rome; Rome and Lazio annexed to the new Italian state by plebiscite. 29 December: Exceptional flooding of the Tiber.

1871

As a general in the French Army in the Vosges, fights in the Franco-Prussian War. Elected a deputy in Paris but soon resigns. Commission of inquiry into flooding appointed. Rome becomes the capital city of Italy.

1872

Mazzini dies in Pisa. Garibaldi's memoirs published in Italy.

1873
Birth of Manlio, Garibaldi's first son by Francesca.

1874
Menotti's land-restoration project at Carano (a disease-infested expanse of about nine hectares later renamed Carano-Garibaldi), in the Agro Romano, results in the construction of schools, churches and simple health centres (*stazioni sanitarie*).

1875
Garibaldi arrives in Rome and declares his plans for the diversion of the Tiber. Attends parliament. Submits his proposals for the preservation of Rome from flooding. Government agreement to finance studies of various schemes for the defence of the city against inundations. The commission approves a project put forward by the engineer Canevari; Garibaldi's project turned down. Further modifications are made to the Canevari plan. Death of Anita, Garibaldi's daughter with Battistina Ravello.

1876
The government contracts the first round of building works on the Tiber.

1878
Death of Victor Emmanuel II and succession of Umberto I. Close of correspondence on the Tiber.

1880
Garibaldi's twenty-year-old marriage to the Marchesina Raimondi annulled by the Court of Appeal. Marries his third wife, Francesca Armosino.

1882
Garibaldi dies at Caprera. Publication of Giuseppe Guerzoni's

biography, *Garibaldi*, and Jessie White Mario's *Vita di Giuseppe Garibaldi*.

1889

Publication of a further version of his autobiography in English, with a supplement by Jessie White Mario.

1900

Exceptional flooding of the Tiber. The banks, close to completion, succeed in containing much of the flood. Appointment of a further commission of inquiry results in additional building works and fortification of embankments and bridges. Death of Manlio Garibaldi.

1903

Deaths of Teresita and Menotti Garibaldi.

1924

Death of Ricciotti Garibaldi. Introduction of Mussolini's radical bill on 'integral land reclamation', the start of a new campaign to conquer marshland. In the Pontine Marshes, south of Rome, work begins to transform thousands of hectares into villages and small farms.

List of Illustrations

1 Roman Fever

'Let us turn to Italy: the fairest portions of this fair land are a prey to this invisible enemy, its fragrant breezes are poison, the dews of its summer evenings are death. The banks of its refreshing streams, its rich and flowery meadows, the borders of its glassy lakes, the luxuriant plains of its overflowing agriculture, the valley where its aromatic shrubs regale the eye and perfume the air, these are the chosen seats of this plague, the throne of Malaria.'

William North, *Roman Fever*

Towards the end of January 1875, General Giuseppe Garibaldi, the popular hero of Italian unification, left Caprera, his austere island retreat in the Mediterranean, on a journey to Rome. The old man proposed to enlist support for a civic mission that had become his personal crusade: to divert the course of the River Tiber away from the Eternal City. His ambition was to overcome flood and malarial fever, drain marshes and provide irrigation for rural land, make the river navigable, create docks and fill in the water channel through the Eternal City, building over it a Parisian-style boulevard, which he anticipated would be a wonder of the modern world.

Word of the General's imminent arrival on the mainland quickly spread and a vast surging crowd (a 'human ocean', said one contemporary observer) gathered to see him step ashore at Civitavecchia.[1] Many who now observed Garibaldi were struck by his aged appearance – he was by then in his sixty-eighth year. He made no secret of his intention to undertake a last great adventure that would fittingly mark, as he wistfully declared to assembled well-wishers, 'the sunset of my career'.[2] Every assortment of dignitary was there to greet him, as were representatives of the Italian and foreign press. A musical fanfare had been arranged, courtesy of the National Guard's own band.

The trip began promisingly enough and was undertaken in typically eye-catching fashion. Garibaldi's style was, as ever, spectacularly understated – his flamboyance of purpose in seeking the resurrection of Rome was in stark contrast to his humility of manner and vulnerability. The General's rejection of fripperies, worldly wealth and stuffy manners was always among his most captivating public gestures. He appeared decidedly frail in health – brought low by arthritis and rheumatism – and required the steadying arm of his oldest son, Menotti.[3] Even Garibaldi's increasingly exhausted appearance as the day wore on added to public approbation, graphically suggesting the fortitude that was so central to his reputation. It was well known that Garibaldi did not seek to puff himself up as one of the 'great and the good'. Onlookers were excited to see that he had donned his famous red shirt and had a poncho casually spread over his shoulders – costume that recalled his rough military adventures.

After refreshments and rest, Garibaldi stepped calmly through the throng, as though he was merely an ordinary passenger taking the train to Rome.★ In this period, there were three classes of carriage available to the railway traveller;

★ For the papacy, the existence of this railway (any railway) had been extremely contentious. Pope Gregory XVI (elected in 1831) had opposed such newfangled inventions outright. 'There is storm in the air,' he declared anxiously in 1846, shortly before his death, 'revolutions will soon break out.' Banning railways had been part of a broader strategy to keep malcontents – and their incendiary ideas – out of the Papal States. Were not railways the work of the Devil? Indeed, '*chemin* it was a measure of the General's relaxed attitude to such social hierarchies and gradations of comfort that newspaper reporters expressed no astonishment when he took the modest option.[4] He was a celebrity renowned for the fact that he eschewed the accoutrements of pomp and power. Even the journey had its symbolic resonance: it took Garibaldi through the Roman countryside (the Campagna) in which he had previously fought and suffered for the Italian national cause, and across the Tiber, on a modern iron bridge, itself a sign of changing times. The railway timetable for this route was notoriously prone to cancellation due to river flooding, but nothing went wrong that day.[5]

GARIBALDI A ROMA

Veduta della Piazza della Stazione al momento dell'arrivo.

Garibaldi's tumultuous reception before Termini railway station in Rome, January 1875

de fer, chemin d'enfer' was a notorious papal quip. The Pope who succeeded him, Pius IX, was to prove, by contrast, somewhat more amenable to the introduction of new technology and modern locomotion, and sanctioned the lines that in due course would transform access to central Italy. Pius inaugurated this particular railway route, between Rome and Civitavecchia, in extravagant fashion. His ornately gilded carriage was made in Paris and included a drawing room, dressing room and an oratory (De Cesare 1909, pp. 131–2). The contrast with Garibaldi's approach to the journey could hardly have been greater.

3

When the train finally pulled into the railway station in
Rome, there was loud applause. He was greeted by music
and the welcoming cheers of working men's associations.
Garibaldi was now wearing a blue cap embroidered with
gold. Some tried to touch or kiss him; among these overeager
admirers, an Italian journalist drily observed, were a number
of swooning English ladies. The police were out in force,
although the army was confined to barracks. The atmosphere was generally relaxed on the streets, if not in government circles or the Vatican. The Pope was said to be terrified
that Garibaldi was intent on fomenting further anarchy and
revolution.[6]

The triumphal procession moved slowly through the
cheering crowds. Garibaldi ordered his carriage to halt at
his hotel earlier than expected, expressing concern about
public safety. He rested briefly, but soon reappeared on the
balcony, to make an emotional address to the throng below.
He told the Romans how moved and proud he felt to be
among them once again. At 8 p.m. that same evening, he
made a brief visit to the residence of Menotti, near the
Pantheon, but there was little time for private retreat.
Everybody wanted access to him, and even the empty
carriage was pawed over: it was taken to the Gianicolo (the
hill that had been the scene of his famous exploits a quarter
of a century earlier, on behalf of the Roman Republic,
against the invading French Army) and, amid chaotic celebrations, was accidentally smashed on its way down the steep
descent.[7]

News that Garibaldi planned to attend parliament the next
day led to a flurry of interest; entry entitlements were a
prized possession for the well-connected few.[8] His power of
attraction remained considerable: right through the period
of his Roman residence, and even in the sweltering heat of
an exceptionally warm May, Garibaldi's parliamentary appearances led to crowds of well-wishers queuing for admission.[9]
To much approbation, he addressed his colleagues on the

environmental task that lay ahead. Many public figures were keen to appear as his devoted ally, or at least as his admirer: within days of his first arrival he had been presented with more than three hundred visiting cards by members of parliament, of very diverse political persuasions.[10] Meanwhile, poetry was penned to mark the event of his arrival in the Eternal City, and to bless his project for the Tiber.[11]

Notwithstanding his precarious physical state, Garibaldi quickly embarked on a round of appointments. He visited the scene of his earlier campaign of 1849, met old combatants, delegations of workers and numerous politicians.[12] But he was not to be distracted for long by reminiscences about the past; his concern with future flood measures, rural reclamation, irrigation and flow rates remained at the front of his mind. He spent much time studying the precise nature of the building work required along the Tiber; he summoned his kitchen cabinet of experts and went about jockeying for influence, as best he could, with senior members of the government. He vigorously pursued his objective over the months that followed, pitting his energies against the deadly floods, the decrepit river banks and the 'Roman fever' that was generally thought to result from exposure to the invisible 'miasmatic' vapours rising up out of the contaminated earth.

Before the General could accomplish the regeneration of Rome and its region, he knew he had to persuade the politicians that his plans were viable. He intended finally to claim the parliamentary seat that had been his for the taking for many years. At the time this story begins, Garibaldi was internationally famous and, at least in liberal eyes, perhaps the most widely admired living person in the world. It would be hard to exaggerate the degree of public excitement that his long-postponed trip aroused. For decades, he had been a household name, known to millions in Europe, and beyond, as an enormously attractive figure and as his country's most extraordinary foot soldier, the very 'personification of Italy'.[13]

Rome or Death

News of Garibaldi's arrival in the Eternal City had been the worst-kept secret of the year so far. For months, he had made it clear to various confidants that he was in earnest about making the journey, and using all his might to help free Rome from the dangers of the Tiber. He was prepared to lobby tirelessly to promote the cause of the city's physical revival, and to advocate ways to stem the floods and the fevers that were thought to be linked with stagnant water. Disappointments would soon follow, but, at the outset, he appeared wholly confident that fundamental changes could be made, to sanitise Rome and restore its glory.

To say that the General was temporarily preoccupied with the issue would be a gross understatement. He wrote numerous letters discussing the problem of Rome and the Tiber. In the months and years to come, he continued to study the river's currents, depths and angles. As soon as he was in the city, he gave speeches, pressed politicians and

Garibaldi and his advisers on the Tiber in 1875

even the King for their support, took exploratory boat trips downstream, addressed parliament, proposed legislation, endeavoured to establish a public fund to accept the investments of members of the public (modelled on the Suez Canal scheme) and actively sought the advice of engineers and financiers from Italy and abroad.

Garibaldi pointed out the benefits that a sanitised Tiber and a navigable route would hold for future generations. Even the microclimate might be changed by grand engineering and landscaping. Freed from the dangers of flood, dampness and decay, he promised, young Italians might be spared malaria; scrofula, arthritis and various other diseases of blood and nerves might also be eased. He urged scientists, sanitary experts, archaeologists and artists to support his plans. These engineering proposals were cast as a war for Civilisation against Anarchy. The General described a future waterway pulsing with economic life rather than spilling dirty refuse and exuding the mysterious vapours of fever and death. He was adamant that an 'internal' solution – that is mere river-bank constructions – would be insufficient; 'external' measures were vital as well, although the precise nature of these measures kept shifting. Rome's future required that a definitive solution be found to the crisis of bursting banks; all that must become a thing of the past. Garibaldi's designs for the city took their place amid a plethora of other contemporary schemes for urban change, the modernisation of infrastructure and the public commemoration of national unification.[14] Among his entourage of supporters, plans for new canals, locks and ports proliferated.[15] His critics complained that while his schemes certainly had a grand sense of vision, they would require an immense investment and, even then, might not be practicable.[16]

The General grew impatient when, as he saw it, others fretted excessively over details. He wanted immediate action, suggesting, for instance, that priority be given at once to the plan, envisaged by some of his supporters, to excavate a grand canal to the east of Rome. Frustrated by the slow progress of political deliberations in the city during 1875 and 1876, he and his fellow enthusiasts proposed that to speed things up the work could be undertaken with the support of a hundred earth-moving machines of English design. Much discussion of machinery, steam-powered ploughs, locomotives, new bridges and so forth took place, as Garibaldi sought to keep things moving, and maintain the political initiative. A stream of visitors arrived to consult him at the villa he had been loaned in Rome and that was to form the hub of his Tiber campaign.[17] He retained an extraordinary charisma, and yet still now (perhaps especially now, as his powers faded) he was perceived as acutely gullible, sometimes even as something of a simpleton. The General, declared *The Times* some years later, in a poignant obituary, had been 'pounced upon by an army of sharp contractors and dreamy projectors, and bewildered by plans and schemes for the very surveys of which the funds were not forthcoming'.[18] Increasingly dispirited by the grind of Rome, as weeks turned into months and the project remained unresolved, he had moved back and forth between his 'rocky hermitage' off Sardinia and the political fray in the capital, only to face further setbacks and disappointment.

Garibaldi wanted not only a navigable but also a clean waterway.[19] Understandably so, since many of his contemporaries condemned the Tiber as a foul and squalid sewer generating untold human infections, a sorry fate for a river which in ancient times had been renowned for its purity, and as an exceptional source of fresh fish. The antique splendour of the river, when the banks were (supposedly) beautifully maintained, was regularly contrasted with the feeble structures and facilities that now existed.[20]

What more disgusting and dangerous contrast with the limpid beauty of the Eternal City bathed in a serene light than the unsavoury reality of stewing waters, seeping downstream, pervading the rotting underground systems, giving off foul gases that rose up through the permeable layers of the soil? In addition to catastrophic surface floods, there were known to be unidentified, stagnant pools, lurking beneath Rome. Expert commentators drew attention to the concealed waters and sewage that lay under the buildings and the thoroughfares of the city. These dangers were considered no less urgent for being out of sight.[21] From these depths, it was thought, miasmas circulated, festering through the toxic soil, incubated in the muddy water, borne through the air, then generating the fevers that made Roman life so notoriously precarious, as though all that was most disgustingly solid melted perniciously into air.[22]

2 Engineering the Future

'There was talk of draining and planting [the Roman Campagna]; much futile discussion on the question whether it had been fertile in the days of the old Romans; and even a few experiments were made; but, all the same, Rome remained in the midst of a vast cemetery like a city of other times, for ever separated from the modern world by that *lande* or moor where the dust of centuries had accumulated.'

Émile Zola, *Rome*

Garibaldi's mission to tame the Tiber was swept along by powerful currents of passion and myth. No project could have been more 'down to earth' than the General's improbable venture into civil engineering, and yet a kind of 'metaphysical magnificence' hovered over the scene.[1] This river carried an extraordinary surfeit of cultural and historical meaning, as did the beloved hero who had now descended so dramatically upon the capital. Garibaldi was drawn by Rome's artistic and historical stature, insisting on its predestined role as world capital of the future,[2] but he was also a connoisseur of urban decadence, a passionate critic of the city's sclerotic, backward-looking administration and an anxious diagnostician of its deadly illnesses. Nobody grasped better than he did the mysterious malaise and the portentous symbolic significance of the Eternal City for the future of Italy and civilisation at large. 'One hour of our life in Rome is worth a century of life elsewhere,' he had written to his wife, as the Roman Republic was collapsing around him in 1849.[3]

After the completion of the first and most dramatic stage of national 'liberation' in 1860, Garibaldi had returned to his humble home and liked to speak of himself as a simple farmer, an '*agricoltore*'. During the following fifteen years, he had oscillated between active military engagement and rural retreat. He appeared to shun the ordinary business of government. Indeed, this great martial hero made no secret of the fact that he loathed the political 'talking shop' and would be content to remain away from parliament – to which he was, nonetheless, frequently elected – cultivating his garden, aloof from the fray. His place in history was already secure, his life's work apparently done. Anyway, he was seen by many of his peers of the right and moderate left as far too radical to hold senior office in the governments of the post-unification period.

Yet despite this stance, Garibaldi chose to leave his island at the start of 1875, to return to Rome and tirelessly lobby politicians for the sake of his Tiber scheme. Something about this task clearly captivated him and he felt personally responsible for the conduct of the campaign. How did this burning concern of his old age link with his earlier celebrated adventures as army commander and revolutionary activist? How far were the painful losses he had endured in his most immediate family – most notably the calamities that befell his wife Anita and several of his daughters – the determining factors in his latter-day obsession with public health and sickness? In short, what really lay behind the General's belief that the moral and physical transformation of the capital and its hinterland would provide a fitting final chapter to his life's work? Rome was seen by many nineteenth-century visitors as peculiarly linked with death and desire. What was it that led so many commentators to agree on the city's morbidity, erotic allure

11

and dynamic effect on unconscious mental processes? And how was the tale of the General's final Roman mission related to the history of Italian unification and its troubled aftermath?

From one point of view the explanation is not obscure and involves consideration of such burning contemporary concerns as public health, agricultural improvement and economic development in the new state. But to understand Garibaldi's intense personal investment in these issues necessarily draws us into deeper biographical enigmas and psychological puzzles, particularly concerning guilt, mourning and reparation. This book examines the myriad of social, cultural and political connections between health, corruption and the Eternal City in the Victorian age, and it also asks how far we can piece together the hidden jigsaw of Garibaldi's own motives for reclaiming Rome. To answer these questions entails exploring several different types of evidence – from the tribulations and traumas described in Garibaldi's own writings to the political ideals set out by Giuseppe Mazzini (1805–72) and other visionary architects of national union; from statistics about death rates in Rome and the Campagna to the collective fantasies of nationhood in which the General's story took pride of place. Garibaldi possessed immense moral authority and charisma, and he became a scathing critic of the new governments that ruled Italy after its political integration: at times it appeared that he thought no better of the 'new regime' than the 'old'. To be sure, he was addressing chronic and acute social, economic and medical difficulties that plagued nineteenth-century Italy, but he also sought to transform the symbolic and spiritual meanings of Rome. The timing of one particular Tiber flood – in 1870 – was to have an especially acute significance, but it was not the only occasion on which the unruly river wreaked havoc, and precipitated from Catholic priests and secular nationalists a flurry of moral judgements and alarming predictions about the fate of the new Italy.

Engineering the Future

In 1870, when Rome was incorporated into the recently created Italian nation,★ it was by no means the country's largest city. Its population was exceeded by that of Naples, Milan, Genoa and Palermo.[4] It was generally seen as an economically unproductive place, conservative, backward-looking and self-indulgent − a parasite − and yet it was also perceived as essential to the Italian future. Its vast historical shadow and its aesthetic fascination were widely described, but so too was its potential value in the new state. To repossess Rome and to bring it back to life became frequent refrains of Italian nationalist thought. It was Garibaldi the soldier, above all others, who had represented that drive to lay hold of the Eternal City and make it, once again, a colossus. He spoke of Rome as a beloved woman, the great 'matron of the world', who had to be saved from tyranny and corruption, and coaxed back to health and strength.[5]

This was a time of remarkable Western advances in science and technology. It was a period in which anti-clerical and materialistic views circulated widely in radical intellectual and political circles, including in Italy, but also in which there were extraordinary signs of spiritual revival and religious counter-attack. The story of Garibaldi's military and

★ At the time of national unification, 1860, the city of the Popes had been left out of the Italian state, much to Garibaldi's disappointment. 'Rome or Death' became his rallying call in the 1860s, as he tried, vainly and repeatedly, to secure what he regarded as the natural capital and thus to complete the ambitions of the Risorgimento. In 1870, international events conspired to remove a hitherto insuperable obstacle to Rome's assimilation in the national state. The Franco-Prussian War put paid to the Emperor Louis Napoleon's regime and his protection of the papacy. On 20 September of that year, Italian troops entered the Eternal City, and a new era began. Sidelined from that final conquest and from the centre of power in the new state, Garibaldi soon turned his attention to a potential technical feat that could change the physical and moral landscape of Italy.

political exploits played its part in wider ideological battles over religion, science and nationalism. The General sought to purify and control the Tiber, but also to reverse the moral and physical putrefaction which he and many others associated with the Church. He had long sought to break the Catholic stranglehold on politics in central Italy, and yet quickly found himself at the heart of a new cult which acquired many elements of the religious system that he sought to defeat.

Garibaldi's Roman project brings to light fascinating inconsistencies in his character and image, the ambiguity of his desires – conscious or otherwise – and the contested nature of his symbolic role in Italian and world history. He spent much of his life plotting and fighting: during his long exile from Italy in the 1830s and 40s, he had become a remarkable soldier and sailor – already a folk hero in Latin America before the extraordinary saga of Italian unification began. The passion – even obsession – that he revealed in old age evoked memories of his earlier campaigns to capture and protect the Eternal City, and the personal triumphs and tragedies that had ensued. Thus this curious episode of the General's struggle with the Tiber brought 'the hero of two worlds' back to the centre stage of politics: Garibaldi's much trumpeted return to Rome reminded his contemporaries about the inimitable achievements and style of a man who had mutated into a national icon.

As the General entered Rome, he harked back to the larger successes and failures of the Risorgimento, the diffuse movement for Italian national awakening and self-rule that had gradually spread its optimistic message through nineteenth-century culture and thought, and that had come to a climax with the achievement of unification. Through his clamorous efforts to bring science, technology and enterprise to the capital, he drew attention not only to the region's economic stagnation, environmental problems and lack of entrepreneurial activity under the often hidebound policies of the Vatican, but also to the remarkable web of myths, fantasies and desires that shaped his own life and the wider history of nationalism.

In Garibaldi's battles, the personal and the political were inevitably fused together. His campaign to modify the air and water of Rome was no exception. The details can be gleaned from his correspondence, contemporary reports, the footnotes of biographies and some mouldering unpublished papers in the Italian state archives.[6] Opening these files is like lifting the lid on a once animated family feud. Behind the technical drawings, old newspaper cuttings and notes sent to and from the General and his acolytes lie the traces of passionate feelings, exalted ambitions and intense grievances. His visit to Rome was billed as but the latest triumphant chapter in a life filled with eventful excursions; but it was also to prove the start of a further frustrating odyssey that took Garibaldi slowly and painfully into an administrative labyrinth.

The reforms that this reluctant politician thought necessary to rejuvenate Rome could not be executed with the same boldness and swiftness that he had sometimes found possible in war. His endeavours ran up against strong opposition, leading him to express (not for the first time) his outrage with career politicians. He hurled accusations of sloth and sleaze at 'Rome', and drew attention to the plight of the peasants who eked out so miserable a living in the Roman Campagna, and not uncommonly died before their time on its notoriously malaria-ridden land. There was certainly nothing fanciful about the picture of suffering and mortality that he conjured: both poverty and disease were powerfully and inescapably real.

Garibaldi presented himself as the quintessential man of action; yet no less intriguingly the Tiber affair reveals him as a stern moralist: his practical deeds, shining reputation and hostile judgements were inextricably entwined. The

General's insistently modest style, radical proposals and withering speeches were all uncomfortable rebukes to those in power. When in splendid surroundings himself, he appeared to be distant from them, uninterested, as if to make clear that it was a matter of small importance to him either way, like some saint for whom the trappings of this world are ultimately insignificant. During his great military campaigns, he had slept in palaces, huts and in the open air, with the same composure. An English devotee noted how he had lived in a restricted, austere space, even within his palatial residence, when he became the ruler of Naples in 1860.[7] Yet he was an appealingly inconsistent ascetic, with his own touching foibles and predilections for the good things in life, and for display: thus he would occasionally don a rather gaudy embroidered cap, or insist that he be served excellent coffee on the eve of combat.[8]

Throughout much of Garibaldi's adult life, political admirers and critics, fellow campaigners, journalists and artists had scrutinised and commemorated his work. Inevitably, there was an element of conscious performance – playing to the gallery – in many of his actions. At times it is difficult to disentangle the casual from the contrived features of the General's behaviour or to separate substance from style. Indeed, style *was* of substantial importance. Undoubtedly, Garibaldi and the other central players in the struggle for Italian unification were aware that they played out their allotted roles in a live *theatre* of politics. Garibaldi, and the so-called 'prophet' of the Italian nationalist cause, Mazzini, no less than the Pope, were required to dress and act their part. In war and in peace, the Risorgimento was nothing if it was not a battle of images. The stories and histories that were written about it were inevitably partisan. As the key events of the national struggle in the Italian peninsula unfolded, the exploits, conduct and rhetoric of the protagonists were subsumed into political folklore. Even the manners and costumes of the leaders were powerfully emblematic: against the blatant splendours of the papacy,★ for instance, who could forget the appearance of Mazzini, attired in sombre black clothes, or of Garibaldi in his poncho, leading the 'Red Shirts' on behalf of a different, more austere and honest Italy?

No doubt, as Garibaldi faced the adoring crowds in Civitavecchia and Rome in 1875, the continuing public expression of love for his person and collective admiration for his past activities shaped his self-perception as the man of destiny. The line between biography and autobiography had long been blurred, thanks in part to the contribution of various star-struck participant-observers, including the French author Alexandre Dumas, who helped Garibaldi to chronicle and romanticise the great adventures of his life. As the General's historical reputation and political significance had grown larger, so the weight of his every word and action became heavier. 'Being Garibaldi' must have become an increasingly onerous task, albeit one that he continued to perform with remarkable aplomb. His charisma would be difficult to exaggerate. Notoriously, women of all ranks fell for him, sometimes with such warmth as to cause the normally unflappable champion embarrassment. No shortage of men became besotted as well. On occasion, so it has been said, Garibaldi had to protect his hair from the scissors of souvenir hunters.

★ The French novelist Émile Zola memorably, if tendentiously, captured this flamboyance of Church ceremonial and costume in his anti-clerical novel of the 1890s, *Rome*. Here a visitor witnesses the glittering empty procession of Rome's holymen, as though glimpsing 'the splendid skeleton of a colossus whence life was departing'. '[T]he processions and *cortèges* [displayed] all the luxury of the Church amid operatic scenery and appointments. And he tried to conjure up a picture of the past magnificence – the basilica overflowing with an idolatrous multitude and the superhuman *cortège* passing along whilst every head was lowered; the cross and the sword opening the march, the cardinals going two by two, like twin divinities . . . and at last, with Jove-like pomp, the pope, carried on a stage draped with red velvet, seated in an armchair of red velvet and gold, and dressed in white velvet, with cope of gold, stole of gold, and tiara of gold.' (Zola 1896, pp. 168–9).

Some went all the way to the General's remote house, in the hope of being offered a lock of hair or an old shirt. If he was the object of a cult, he was also the unwitting instrument of a brisk commerce; even his uniform was eventually sold off to an Englishwoman by one of his labourers, to whom it had previously been given as a present.[9]

Thus the historical importance of Garibaldi lay not just in material achievements but in the symbolic sphere. His every gesture and pronouncement were taken to be pregnant with cultural and political meaning. As the living embodiment of the ordinary citizen's mistrust of government corruption, hatred of tawdry compromises and impatience with stultifying conventions, he could be relied upon to create, by his mere presence in Rome, a combustible atmosphere. For some contemporaries, the General personified the energy, dynamism and courage that were now required by the nation; for others, his vaguely costed projects, airy rhetoric, unconventional lifestyle and bluff, martial approach to life were symptoms of – rather than solutions to – Italy's very considerable difficulties. Garibaldi hoped to surpass the achievements of ancient engineering, not least all of those astonishing accomplishments of drainage, sewage disposal and water transportation undertaken by the Romans themselves. Surely, he argued, with modern science and enough political will, the challenge of creating a new, vibrant Rome, a fitting capital for modern Italy, could be met.[10]

During Garibaldi's lifetime, civil engineering was indeed dramatically altering the landscape, the speed of communication and the ease of trade in many parts of the world. By the late nineteenth century, new canals, railways and roads were increasingly integrated into networks in the more advanced economies such as Britain, Germany or the United States. Such developments were widely celebrated as the culmination of several centuries of technical innovation and gathering entrepreneurial ambition. In proposing to tame the elements, regenerate the city and facilitate the free movement of goods and capital across large swathes of hitherto inaccessible rural territory, Garibaldi sought to help Italy 'catch up' with its fast-changing neighbours and rivals.

New means of constructing hard-wearing, fast-draining carriageways, already pioneered in eighteenth-century France, had been quickly emulated elsewhere on the Continent, presaging further technical advances in the nineteenth century, not least by British engineers, such as J. L. McAdam and Thomas Telford, who set new standards for both road and canal design. In the 1850s, the first reinforced concrete house was built in Paris, and the material was soon to be used in many major infrastructure projects. Isambard Kingdom Brunel's Clifton Suspension Bridge (1830–63) was a sign of the times, as was his vast ship, completed in 1858, the *Great Eastern*. Originally called *Leviathan*, it boasted the first double iron hull, and played a crucial part in achieving a further transport coup: the laying of the first successful transatlantic cable. Closer to home for Garibaldi, it was announced in Rome in 1875 that a telegraph cable would soon be laid on the sea floor, between Sardinia and the mainland.

Vast areas of hard rock were now routinely blasted aside by gunpowder and, increasingly, by dynamite, a new explosive, patented in 1867 by the Swedish physicist Alfred Nobel. The pioneer contractors who burrowed their way through Mont Cenis in the 1860s inaugurated various spectacular Alpine tunnelling projects. This was the period, too, in which old proposals (dating back at least to Napoleon) to dig beneath the Channel were dusted off and revamped: plans for a subterranean railway between England and France were put forward by a company, formed for the purpose in the 1880s – a source of much anxious and excited literature.[11]

In water supply and sewage disposal, civil engineering achieved outstanding advances. This was the era that witnessed a dramatic turnaround in the state and appearance of the Thames, with the creation of remarkable new embankments, concealing vast new east–west sewers, able to deal effectively with tens of millions of gallons of waste. Source of the notorious 'Great Stink' of 1858, the river became the stimulus for a massive public building project, which led to much of the city's sewage being diverted well downstream of London and then dispatched far out to sea. The chief engineer, Joseph Bazalgette, orchestrated dozens of contractors and their huge contingents of labourers, who excavated millions of cubic yards of earth, and laid hundreds of millions of bricks through more than eighty miles of new sewers, at a cost of over £4 million. First inaugurated in 1864, the full extent of the enterprise became apparent six years later, when the final section of new embankments was opened. Londoners were offered a state-of-the-art system, stretching along the northern side of the Thames, from Blackfriars to Westminster.[12] How much Garibaldi knew of this is uncertain, but he was no stranger to the English capital. He would, no doubt, have had chances enough to sniff out London's problem for himself on his occasional visits in the 1850s and 60s, and to hear of the proposed remedies at first-hand.

Large-scale dams as well as long-distance piping and pumping were transforming land and living conditions in the Old World and the New. In America, the Erie Canal, 363 miles long with eighty-two locks, from Albany on the Hudson to Buffalo on Lake Erie, was an important early example of the daunting scale of civil engineering that was now viable. Built by the state of New York between 1817 and 1825, it greatly enhanced the ease of trade to and from the Midwestern prairies. Whereas only about one hundred miles of canals had been dug in 1800, by the end of the century, America possessed more than four thousand miles of artificial waterway open to barge navigation. Lakes and rivers were being tamed, linked and exploited in ever more ambitious schemes. In the 1880s, for instance, a waterway was planned that would link the south branch of the Chicago River with the Des Plaines River at Lockport, Illinois. This would involve reversing the river flow away from Lake Michigan in order to halt pollution of the lake by the city's sewage. Construction of the canal was to involve the largest ever earth-moving operation undertaken in the United States.

In Greece, a deep ship canal was created at the Isthmus of Corinth, connecting the Aegean and Ionian seas. Built between 1881 and 1893, it was bounded by almost vertical rock cliffs rising to more than 259 feet above water level in the canal's midsection. During the later nineteenth century, enormous drainage schemes were planned and undertaken in the Low Countries.[13] By this time, all of Europe's major rivers had already been partially reshaped by human intervention; no longer multi-channelled, expansive and diffuse, they increasingly followed precise and defined routes.* Often 'canalisation' had been undertaken, at least to an extent, through the creation of embankments. Water management and landscape transformation went hand in hand through many parts of the Continent.[14]

Italy was brought into being in the second half of the nineteenth century, but in the eyes of General Garibaldi and many other commentators this achievement had quickly palled. The new nation fell short of the dreamy aspirations that preceded it, giving birth to a 'politics of nostalgia' within years of its creation. Garibaldi was far from alone in his lamentation of collective deficiencies, past and present. Indeed, he came to articulate, and even to personify, a far more extensive attitude of intellectual and political dissatisfaction. The state was seen

---

* In *The Communist Manifesto* of 1848, Marx and Engels had paid tribute to a bourgeoisie, whose entrepreneurs, scientists and industrialists had shown so remarkable an ability to subject nature's forces to human designs. '[M]achinery, application of chemistry to industry and agriculture, steam-navigation, railways, electric telegraphs, clearing of whole continents for cultivation, *canalisation of rivers*, whole populations conjured out of the ground – what earlier century had even a presentiment that such productive forces slumbered in the lap of social labour?' (Marx and Engels 2002, p. 25; my italics.)

as inadequate to his private yearnings, to Risorgimento visions and, later, to the strident nationalist ideology of redemption that ominously flourished in *fin-de-siècle* culture and politics. As the General mournfully recalled, 'It was a very different Italy which I spent my life dreaming of'; 'not this "humiliated" Italy, governed by the worst elements of the nation'.[15] His passion for the Eternal City and his deep concern with the physical and spiritual regeneration of the nation can be closely linked with the wider anxieties and desires of his age; but they cannot just be explained away in those larger social and historical terms.

Garibaldi's character was full of powerful and puzzling contradictions. He was the defender of the free, scourge of slavery, supporter of universal suffrage. He was a commander who had shot mutinous subordinates without hesitation, but who had scruples about killing priests, despite declaring that he despised them above all others; or at least most of them (some priests had conspicuously helped him in the past, or even joined forces with him). As his biographers have observed, Garibaldi had a reputation for tenderness and tolerance, but also for unflinching severity. He could express great affection *and* callousness towards certain members of his own family, and, still more, towards recalcitrant underlings, over whom he ruled as an army commander. He was deeply fond of animals, yet showed a red-blooded indifference to killing. He presided over the first international pacifist congress, but agreed with the maxim that 'war is the true life of man'. As a child, his sentimental attachments were notable (he had on one occasion, for instance, been inconsolable at the fate of a dying grasshopper); as an adult, he was said to have been capable of ordering a man to be shot without putting down his cigar. In his youth, he demonstrated how to kill a turtle with his bare hands, although he could not stand to eat a lamb that he had nursed.[16] He became a tough soldier and an uncompromising nationalist who nonetheless urged European governments to work towards a single state of

Europe, in the belief that spending on the army and navy could then be greatly reduced, and huge sums of money released to deal with poverty, advance industry, build roads, construct bridges, dig canals and so forth.[17]

A secular figure in one sense, Garibaldi was also, for many people, akin to a religious martyr. Some portraitists and essayists explicitly likened him to Christ. When a book of adapted Garibaldian 'catechisms' appeared in Naples in 1865, the text was in the form of brief questions and answers for young people in what scrupulous Catholics could only consider a grotesque imitation of religion.[18] Willing to compromise when

A nineteenth-century portrait, likening Garibaldi to Christ

nobody expected it of him, proud at times of his pragmatism, he also supported questionable ventures such as schemes for national expansion to the north east. Above all, he was known as the battle-hardened military genius whose astonishing victories played a central role in the struggle to unify Italy. During his many cross-country treks, notably in the Campagna, he became well acquainted with the hard lot – the sweat and tears, dreams and fevers – of the peasantry. Garibaldi's sympathy for the poor, his natural assumption of authority and his daredevil adventures were celebrated far and wide in a flourishing literature aimed both at children and adults: the emerging 'Italians' of the newly created

Garibaldi leading his men into battle

nation. Details of his less than conventional domestic circumstances, his children out of wedlock, mistresses and petitions for divorce were an embarrassment, but these were usually forgiven as the idiosyncratic behaviour of a man who, despite it all, was morally unassailable, a figure who had written his own 'larger than life' script.

3 Stagnation and Salvation

'What the flaming sword was to the first Eden, such the malaria to these sweet gardens and groves. We may wander through them, of an afternoon, it is true, but they cannot be made a home and a reality, and to sleep among them is death. They are but illusions, therefore, like the show of gleaming waters and shadowy foliage in a desert.'

Nathaniel Hawthorne, *The Marble Faun*

Corresponding to the territorial limits of the Commune of Rome in the Middle Ages, the Roman Campagna is an area of about two thousand square kilometres, traversed by the Tiber and Aniene rivers as well as a number of minor waterways.[1] Also known as the Agro Romano, the Campagna's plain extends along the Lazio shoreline and is limited in the south by the Alban hills and the gulf of Terracina, in the north by the Tolfa and Sabatini mountains and in the east by the Sabini mountains, part of the Appenine chain.★

★ In *The Marble Faun*, Hawthorne memorably described these circumscribing heights, 'which have gleamed afar, to our imaginations, but look scarcely real to our bodily eyes, because, being dreamed about so much, they have taken the aerial tints which belong only to a dream. These, nevertheless, are the solid frame-work of hills that shut in Rome, and its wide surrounding Campagna; no land of dreams, but the broadest page of history, crowded so full with memorable events that one obliterates another; as if Time had crossed and recrossed his own records till they grew illegible.'

Rome or Death

Malaria afflicted this region across recorded history, although its virulence has not been constant.[2] At the end of the first millennium, the enigma of fever in and around Rome remained a source of much perplexity and anxiety. As St Peter Damian, Bishop of Ostia, put it in a letter to Pope Nicholas II in the middle of the eleventh century: 'Rome, devourer of men, tames the erect necks of men: Rome, fruitful in fevers, is very rich in the harvest of death. The Roman fevers are faithful to a constant law. Once they have assailed a person, they seldom leave him while he is still alive.'[3]

Some regarded fevers as punishment: the medieval poet, Petrarch, thought that they might be caused by the absence of the Popes from Rome. Malarial illness lurked in the margins – sometimes at the centre – of Italian life and its image frequently entered literature. Quartan fever (one of the forms that malaria might take) is described, for instance, in *The Divine Comedy*.[4] Such references in Dante, or for that matter in Shakespeare, who offered various passing comments on the morbid climate of Rome, were assiduously noted by some early twentieth-century specialists on malaria who were interested, as a sideline, in documenting the folklore and literary history of their subject.[5]

Any such compendium of cultural observations on the curious sickliness of Rome and the eerie deadness of its environs would necessarily be extensive. A few examples may serve to set the scene. Montaigne in 1581: 'The approaches to Rome, almost everywhere, have for the most part a barren and uncultivated look.'[6] The French visitor found it strange that an area this close to the great city could appear so unproductive and be so thinly populated. In the eighteenth century, as he pondered Rome's decline and fall, Gibbon did not neglect to depict the signs of environmental desolation: 'But the great part of the Campagna of Rome is reduced to a dreary and desolate wilderness; the overgrown estates of the princes and clergy are cultivated by the lazy hands of indigent and hopeless vassals; and the scanty harvests are confined or exported for the benefit of a monopoly.[7] The very danger and desolation became, in romantic eyes, attractive in the extreme. Byron spoke of the 'old Tiber' moving through a 'marble wilderness' and of Rome as the 'city of the soul', 'mother of dead empires'.[8] In the title to a sonnet he wrote in the 1830s, the Roman poet Giuseppe Gioacchino Belli described the Campagna's physical menace and emptiness as 'The Desert'.

Although much of the Campagna evoked gloom and even dread, some areas were extolled for their exceptional beauty and serenity. Frascati, outside Rome, was renowned for its pure running streams, blooming almond trees, clear skies, vibrant colours. A few locations, such as Tivoli, with its extraordinary Villa d'Este, its miraculous landscaped gardens and fountains, were celebrated far and wide for their charm and elegance. But in general the region was understandably regarded as a pestiferous nightmare.

In the time of Garibaldi, the Roman Campagna retained some residual romantic associations, but it also came to be seen as the symbol of the wider crisis facing modern Italy, a crisis that encompassed issues such as emigration, poverty, disease, agricultural under-investment and lack of education. Increasingly, it became the testing ground for the latest scientific and medical inquiries into malaria; various information campaigns and medical projects were undertaken to help protect the peasantry from the ravages of disease. History, science and myth were nowhere more confusingly blurred than in this remarkable corner of the country – an area whose sparseness of population and development was in inverse proportion to its wealth of meanings and associations. Through words and images, the land was seen to be haunted by the ghosts of a now remote world, and herein lay part of its fascination. There were ruins enough to bring the spectres of ancient Rome vividly back to life. Yet whether extolled or feared by the aesthete, the territory was in dramatic economic and agricultural decline.

An appreciation of the intense scientific anxiety and political gloom associated with the state of the Eternal City itself can also be gleaned from an account by the French psychologist and historian Hippolyte Taine, who visited in 1864. Having studied Rome's civic problems, he concluded that the squalid and disease-ridden streets were breathtakingly perilous; they were nothing short of an abomination.[9] Taine offers a memorable counterpoint to all those famous 'grand tour' eulogies of Rome as art capital, heart of Christianity, centre of the ancient world or even delightful erotic playground for the Italophile. His account of the city is permeated by images of filthy lanes, hovels, slimy corridors and disgusting smells. Inside this hellish labyrinth, he describes an array of aimless vagabonds and crowds of 'dog-like' waifs, relieving themselves in the streets. For Taine, few more desolate places could be imagined on this earth: he found Rome dark and lifeless, a giant site of death. With its bad air, water and soil, and, above all, its bad management, Rome now represented all that was inimical to the modern age, to good health, vigour and economic enterprise, and to a progressive culture, open to rational enquiry.

There was little sign here of any playful or voluptuous dimension to the image of Rome or the Campagna; nor much pleasure taken in the picturesque or the sublime. Taine could appreciate and admire some of what he saw, but he also struck a tone of dismay, as though he was not going to be seduced by the enticements and mysteries of the region. Classical glories could not conceal contemporary horror. His was a very different rendition from that offered by earlier artists such as Poussin or Claude, or even by more recent painters who were still drawn primarily by Rome and the Campagna's beauties and charms.[10] Taine's dominating impression was of an offensive and sinister milieu, a kind of 'deathscape', albeit with occasional pleasing enclaves. He doubted that either the will or means existed to redeem Rome and make it, or its region, a fit and salubrious place for further development. The emphasis was on intransigence, decay and failure. In the course of his wanderings Taine had been horrified by the state of the river, which he described as yellow and diseased. He likened the Tiber to a ghastly snake writhing through a desert of corruption.* The banks were infected by vermin, their brickwork breaking open, while the crazy old tenements virtually tipped into the water, amid unmentionable refuse.[11]

Commentators outdid one another in marvelling at the aura of devastation and tracing their own emotional reaction to vivid scenes of natural and historical decay.[12] Malaria evoked considerable apprehension, even terror, as it had done for bygone ages. The periodic onslaughts of such fiery illnesses had once been likened to the powers of a goddess or the breath of a dragon. Modern archaeologists, using forensic scientific techniques, have exposed ancient Roman burial sites, in which the corpses of children who had suffered

---

* Towards the close of the nineteenth century, the great naturalist writer Émile Zola amplified Taine's earlier descriptions, making the putrid Tiber a powerful symbol of the city's chronic stagnation and the fatal difficulties of the new state. His fictional exposé, *Rome*, described the sinister and sad waters of the once glorious Tiber now flowing with a 'sluggish senility' and bringing 'nought but death' (Zola 1896, p. 451). During a visit to Rome, undertaking background research for his book, Zola learned that to sanitise and reclaim the countryside, and to make the Tiber navigable, as it had been in ancient times, would cost colossal fortunes and involve vast public works. In his view, the poor prospects for bringing such a project to fruition highlighted the incapacity of the nation at large. Zola suggested that it might prove impossible to effect real material transformation here (diary entry, 8 November 1894, in Zola 1958, p. 186). The romance of the past distorted the needs of the present. In the words of Orlando, a well-intentioned 'Garibaldian' veteran, who features in Zola's novel, Rome 'was a purely decorative city with exhausted soil, she had remained apart from modern life, she was unhealthy, she offered no possibility of commerce or industry, she was invincibly preyed upon by death, standing as she did amidst that sterile desert of the Campagna' (Zola 1896, p. 551).

malaria were held down by weights, in order to prevent the demons of the fever escaping and affecting the healthy.[13]

Folklore and religion provided numerous explanations, prophylactic measures and consolations, and continued to dominate popular understanding of the disease throughout the nineteenth century. For many, fever was just an unavoidable, grim fact of life. The novelist Giovanni Verga, a committed devotee of naturalistic description, gave a memorable picture of the Sicilian peasants' hopeless battle to stay healthy, in his story 'Malaria'. It was first published in 1881, but conveyed the dismal experience of countless generations, dispersed through fever-ridden environments.[14]

The phrases 'Roman fever' and 'malaria' were often used interchangeably, as a panoply of specialists speculated about the causes of the high death rates that bedevilled the city and its environs.[15] Many would-be experts pondered the best means of preventing the debilitating bouts of sickness that ravaged the victim at set intervals. Malaria had its distinct tertian and quartan varieties. That indispensable late nineteenth-century traveller's handbook, by Baedeker, gave firm health advice on how to avoid chills and heatstroke, fevers and other locally occurring indispositions. The visitor was told not to drive in an open carriage after dark, for fear of malaria (to say nothing of brigands in remoter parts).★

Tourist visits had to be carefully routed to minimise the

★ As they had fought their way through undergrowth and bogs, in the years of the Italian campaigns, Garibaldi and his men had had no time for such niceties. Tough they may have been, but many of them had also inevitably caught the fever. Advice and help were increasingly available in the last three decades of the century, at least for the leisured classes. Baedeker suggested safe times and routes through rural terrain, as well as advice on the clothes, umbrellas and goggles (the best were of grey-coloured glass) that might serve as appropriate accoutrements. In Rome, blue veils were declared useful accessories for ladies. Recommendations of where to procure an extensive medicine chest before departure from London were also detailed in the meticulous tourist handbook. For stomach bugs and other health hazards that lurked in the various parts of the country. Many travellers no doubt took to heart the advice of Augustus Hare, whose late-nineteenth-century classic *Walks in Rome* was into its twentieth edition by 1913. Hare warned that it was a mistake to think of Rome as possessing a mild climate: if it could be enchanting, it could also be surprisingly severe and carried many dangers for the unwary. 'Violent transitions' from the hot sunshine to the cool shade and back could prove fatal to the uninitiated, he warned. Insalubrious areas were to be avoided, particularly at dusk. To linger at the wrong time of day, at the wrong time of year, near certain sites, such as Roman excavations, was 'inordinately imprudent'. This 'insidious ague-fever' was always on the lookout for its next hapless prey. Hare listed so many danger spots for the tourist to avoid between July and November that the reader might well conclude that it was best to avoid the city and region altogether in those months.[16]

Incautious tourists ran risks, but it was the peasants on the land who endured the most chronic torment, and who died in the greatest numbers. Although malaria was by no means restricted to the poor, there were many reasons why the peasantry suffered the most. A certain type of mosquito carries malaria to human populations, and often the peasants were

---

minor indispositions it was deemed best to seek out a local Italian doctor and rely on tried and tested local remedies (Baedeker 1909, p. xxix, and *passim*). Roman drinking water was declared palatable, although strongly impregnated with lime, thereby considered unsuitable for those suffering gout or constipation (Baedeker 1886, p. xxvi). The problem of malaria, however, was a more serious matter, and to avoid it required great care. The guide provided what geographical advice and climatic understanding it could. The names and addresses of English, or at least English-speaking, physicians and pharmacists in Rome were provided. Those afflicted by fever were especially recommended to see an eminent medical man, Dr Nardini, who was available to receive new patients daily, between 3 and 4 p.m., in his private consulting room by the Piazza Venezia (Baedeker 1869, p. 88).

quite unable to avoid being bitten. Netting was by no means universally available, and in the Lazio region, it was common practice for families to sleep in the fields to guard their crops from thieves.[17] Malnutrition and gruelling living conditions hastened death; well-fed and comfortably-off sufferers were of course more likely to survive. Much uncertainty still surrounds the history of the virulence of malaria across the ages, but there is some evidence that nineteenth-century modernisation of transport made the conditions for the disease still more acute in parts of rural Italy. It was noted for instance that the incidence of fever sometimes increased along the routes of railway lines. Excavations might create the potential for new stagnant ponds; cuttings might also interfere with drainage patterns and alter the water table, in turn affecting the habitat of insects.[18] Some building projects reduced the availability of surface water, others increased it. But what is clear enough is that in the later nineteenth century, when Garibaldi turned his attention to the plight of the region, a majority of the population of Lazio still suffered from malaria. Sixty-six per cent were afflicted, according to an estimate of 1886.[19]

Not all of the territory of the old Papal States was in the same desperate condition as the Campagna – there were areas of the Marches and Umbria that offered good yields of corn, fruit and vines, but much land, even there, was poor and unproductive. In the area surrounding Rome, some buffalo, horses, sheep and goats were raised; there was small-scale market gardening close to the city and some production of grain, although attracting labour for the harvest was no easy task, even given the desperate unemployment that afflicted so many parts of the country. Largely owned by absentee landlords (a common problem through much of rural Italy, especially in the south), the Campagna had fallen into ever greater disrepair during the eighteenth and nineteenth centuries. But whatever the variations in the conditions of agriculture in the region at large, there was precious little evidence of the plans for rural development or the confident investment that was apparent in parts of Lombardy and Tuscany during the second half of the nineteenth century.[20] After unification, there were to be new schemes to encourage cultivation and a commission was appointed, leading to a report, in 1872, which held landlord absenteeism responsible for many of the area's social and economic problems. Garibaldi advocated a new, redistributive justice, and he also focused on the material neglect of the land itself. In May and June 1875, he presented the details of his land–reclamation proposals to parliament, focusing, as we have seen, on river diversion, soil improvement, agricultural reform and drainage.[21]

Given its location near the centre of that extraordinary ancient empire, the Campagna was never perceived as some insignificant rural backwater; it remained famous (or infamous) for many reasons. It was a ruined space that you traversed, en route to the Eternal City, the site of innumerable classical and Christian splendours; here, for many, was the most coveted destination of the 'grand tour'. With the establishment of Rome as the capital of the state of Italy, many thousands of newly created 'Italians' travelled to the city for the first time, to take their place in the swelling government ministries, the burgeoning service industries and the booming building trade. They joined growing hordes of foreign pilgrims and holidaymakers. Travelling nervously along the Campagna's great Roman roads, visitors looked out and glimpsed a world of decay and abandonment. Words such as 'malign', 'fetid', 'insect–ridden' and 'hostile' were frequently and spontaneously invoked in the Pontine Marshes (a vast stretch of land, lying between Rome and Terracina, to the south) and in the Roman Campagna.★

★ A measure of the misery of the Campagna's population, eking out a living in the remote shadows of a once great city, can be gleaned from an account by a novelist and traveller, Charlotte Eaton, in *Rome in the Nineteenth Century*, published in 1820. Eaton encounters the feverish, broken inhabitants who subsist at Ostia,

Rome or Death

Significant tracts of land close to the city, which, in the seventeenth century, had been bursting with vines, fruit trees and vegetables, were left to rot during the following two centuries. Many drew the conclusion that the Campagna,

---

the ancient port of Rome. Glancing around, Eaton identifies a few pathetic dwellings, but no gardens or modern amenities; she walks through the debris, eventually meeting a bony, gaunt woman to whom she asks, 'Where are all the people of the town?' 'Dead!' comes the mournful reply. A handful of male and female workers, two priests and some convicts ('whose lives it is found convenient to shorten' by living here) remain. It is a strange experience, remarks the visiting author, to approach Rome from such a desolate site: 'it is melancholy to reason and humanity to behold an immense tract of fertile land in the immediate vicinity of one of the greatest cities in the world, pestilent with disease and death, and to know that, like a devouring grave, it annually engulfs all of human kind that toil upon its surface' (Eaton 1852, vol. 2, p. 386, and vol. 1, p. 63). Compare this depiction by an English visitor to Ostia half a century later: 'Melancholy sits brooding in the solitude, with Miasma and malaria by her side, fed with the consuming fires of slow fever and shivery ague' (Davies 1873, p. 19).

The Pontine Marshes became virtually synonymous with the horrors of heat, fever and death. That patchwork of swamp, denuded open terrain and dense forest was something near phantasmagoric to behold, as a traveller, Tito Berti, made evident, when he risked a journey there in the summer of 1884. He recalled how 'the Pontine forest creates fear and horror. Before entering it cover your neck and face well, because swarms of large, blood-sucking insects are waiting for you in this great heat of summer, between the shades of the leaves, like animals thinking intently upon their prey.' He went on to speak about a sinister, even nauseating zone, in which thousands of insects were constantly moving around, and thousands of marsh plants grew abundantly, in the hazy heat. Others stressed the beauty of the land (a sea of flowers in May and June) and drew attention to a covert deadliness belied by surface appearance. Hans Christian Andersen travelled through the Marshes in 1846 and described much of beauty and luxuriance. What struck him was the disparity between the aesthetically appealing and fertile landscape, and the desperate state of the peasants who dwelt there – pale and sick, with yellowing skin (Sallares 2002, pp. 169, 170, 176).

once blessed as a fertile land, was now cursed, thereby throwing a ghastly pall over Rome, Italy and even over Western civilisation itself. In fact, some of this commentary provided a rose-tinted view of the past; for even in the ancient world, the region of Lazio had been closely associated with problems of flood and fever. Indeed, many of Rome's leaders had sought to improve the parlous state of the land: Julius Caesar planned to drain the Pontine Marshes, but the scheme did not get very far;[22] the Emperor Nero planned to drive a canal through to Lake Avernus from the Tiber delta, connecting all the coastal lakes in Latium, but this too came to nothing.[23]

In some areas of rural central Italy, travellers found extremely arid conditions (often referred to as a desert); in others, repellent bogs. Water was rarely available in the right quantity, and to farm in parts of the Roman Campagna was to play a version of Russian roulette. In the 1860s, a series of measures had been attempted to improve agricultural conditions in the region, but reports of failure remained more common than of success.[24] The story was told, for instance, of a group of French Trappist monks who began reclaiming land on a farm in the Campagna, in 1868, offered to them by Pope Pius IX. Out of this group of twelve pioneers, ten fell ill, and of these four died. Six returned to France. Undeterred, in 1873 the same community established an agricultural association and obtained the whole farm on permanent tenure. Here is a description of their fate: 'Within eight years there died every year on the average, twenty to twenty-two monks. Thirty-five had to leave Rome on account of the fever.'[25] To aid the languishing Trappists, 162 convicts were consigned to them as labourers 'but these also died in large numbers and the project was eventually abandoned'.[26]

After the government's confiscation of extensive Church estates in the 1870s, some peasants from other parts of Italy were bribed or otherwise induced to work land in the

Campagna that had been newly acquired by farmers, profiteers and entrepreneurs. Despite the promise of quinine,★ good dwellings, clean drinking water and so forth, the conditions they found on arrival remained devastatingly dangerous, as one appalled observer, a certain Dr Giusti, made clear in his bleak report: 'The inspectors no longer know what to do, for the people, who can no longer stand on their feet, are unable to do any work. Every day a cart takes the fever patients to the Roman hospitals, every day many patients die there from pernicious fever – a real hecatomb.'[27]

★ Rome had been one of the first places in Europe to receive a mysterious Peruvian bark, given the name cinchona. This wonder product, containing quinine, had first been brought back to Europe after legend had it that the Countess of Chinchón, wife of the Viceroy of Peru, had herself been cured of fever through its remarkable properties. The first samples of Peruvian bark reached the Papal States in the 1630s, via Spain. Trials were conducted at the Santo Spirito Hospital in Rome. Jesuits were prominent in spreading news of the bark in other parts of the world. Pietro Puccerini, apothecary of the Jesuit-led Collegio Romano, had given instructions for its use in 1649 that became widely influential. The bark became famous after very high-ranking sufferers, including Cardinal Chigi in Rome, had been treated with it. Only in the early twentieth century, however, did it become a widely used prophylactic measure, whose distribution was orchestrated by the state. In 1901, the provision of quinine was made a state monopoly in Italy. Thereafter, the government made the drug more readily available. Laws passed in 1902 and 1904 provided for its public distribution. This was the culmination of years of inquiry, regarding the science and social reform required to combat malaria, a process of investigation that had been enormously stimulated by unification. Nonetheless, the existence of quinine in central Italy may already have had some limited impact in containing the ravages of malaria in the Campagna during the eighteenth century. The malariologist, Angelo Celli, claimed that the region 'was saved by this wonderful remedy from an inevitable and complete decay. If [quinine] had not been introduced at the very moment of the outbreak of the terrible malaria pandemics, the surroundings of Rome would undoubtedly have been transformed into a desert worse than those which we find in Central Africa.' Celli 1933, p. 158; cf. Celli-Fraentzel 1931, p. 2; Celli-Fraentzel 1934, p. 385; Rocco 2003.

From January to June each year, lamented the eminent malariologist and professor of comparative anatomy at Rome University, Dr Battista Grassi, the countryside beckoned like 'the promised land', only to fall back into its desperate fever-ridden state thereafter.[28] Standing before the Queen of Italy in 1900, he appealed for a 'new Risorgimento', aimed at this 'other Italy' where malaria reigned. Only with the defeat of fever could such condemned land truly become a fitting part of a modern, viable nation.[29] In the Campagna and throughout many parts of Italy, poverty and want led peasants to leave the land in droves, heading for the cities, and often away from Europe altogether, if they could afford the journey, in search of more favourable circumstances. More than 370,000 people emigrated from Italy between 1872 and 1881, and over two million left between 1882 and 1901.[30]

Garibaldi relied, loosely, upon the idea of 'miasma', and drew particular attention to the way the waters in the lower parts of Rome, so polluted by organic material, created a sordid dampness. The great Roman sewers had fallen into complete disrepair, adding to the crisis of pollution and 'bad air'. The fetid earth, he believed, gave off gases, contributing to malaria and many other forms of sickness. How could the government stand idly by, he asked, while the citizens were forced to inhale this dubious brew?* In Garibaldi's view, the explanation of any such administrative or political failure lay in a deeper and more entrenched historical corruption. Garibaldi often suggested that Italian vigour had been sapped

---

* National honour, no doubt, also came into the calculation. This was an age in which northern travellers often prided themselves on their superior cleanliness. Baedeker's *Handbook for Travellers* would provide, a few years later, the flavour of this condescension: 'The popular idea of cleanliness in Italy is behind the age, dirt being perhaps neutralized in the opinion of the natives by the brilliancy of their climate' (Baedeker 1886, p. xxi).

by centuries of oppression, inertia and venality. For instance, in one of his long-forgotten novels, *Cantoni il volontario*, published in 1870, the General offered a chapter entitled 'Italian Physiology'. Here he differentiated the healthy and the sick forces that were spread out across the land. Every region had its moral degenerates – he referred to 'failures', 'cripples' and 'deformities' – and foremost among the parasitic and useless sector of society was the legion of hypocritical priests.[31] Moral corruption and physical sickness, it seemed, percolated together through this insalubrious land. A spirit of decadence, it was argued, had led to the progressive abandonment of agriculture, industry and military prowess, or vice versa.[32]

Miasmatic theories can be found from the classical age onwards, set out most famously in ancient Greek thought by Hippocrates. In *Airs, Waters and Places*, Hippocrates had considered a range of environmental factors (such as wind, soil, water, temperature) in human health. His ideas were still widely influential during the Renaissance and came to be explored in the work of important physicians, such as Girolamo Fracastoro, author of an important work on contagious diseases in 1546. Seventeenth-century medical men continued to develop ideas about fatal vapours, adding to a constellation of beliefs about the pernicious effects of marshlands. Noxious vapours were thought to rise up from open sewers, churchyards, slaughterhouses, butcher shops, burial grounds, cesspools, and innumerable other pits of decay.[33]

Increasingly, it was argued that dangerous lands might be ameliorated by enlightened rulers, rather than be simply avoided. During the seventeenth and eighteenth centuries, a variety of medical engineering projects were canvassed in Europe, in which health concerns and major landscaping initiatives converged. Both the countryside and towns could be medically improved.

In England, rivers were sometimes said to 'vomit forth

ill ayres'. Ideas about disease and the role of emanations given off by standing water were explored here by famous seventeenth-century commentators, including the great physician Thomas Sydenham and the highly influential natural philosopher Robert Boyle. In Italy, Bernardino Ramazzini, who was professor of medicine at the University of Modena between 1682 and 1700, noted that malaria epidemics in the region where he worked were linked with floods, stagnant waters, 'acid particles' in the air and prevailing north winds.[34] The Roman anatomist and clinician Giovanni Maria Lancisi, who produced a treatise entitled 'the noxious effluvia of marshes' in 1717, believed that swamps caused malaria in two ways. They carried pathogenic matter to people, in the form of fluids, and they produced emanations that infected the atmosphere. Lancisi speculated about the role of mosquitoes, but this was largely neglected in favour of the miasmatic theory in which he and other doctors believed.[35]

Advocacy of drainage, ventilation or street cleaning was not unprecedented,[36] but powerful economic and health arguments for the political importance of large-scale environmental intervention were increasingly to converge. There was a growing belief that it was possible to alter dramatically the face of the land, and thus to change fundamentally the relationship between human populations and disease. New hygiene and land-reclamation initiatives in the eighteenth century often did cause a real reduction in rates of illness by altering the conditions that allowed the agents of a particular malady to flourish, even if the theory upon which such action was based has since been disproved. Keeping houseflies at bay really could affect the likelihood of typhoid and dysentery, for instance, even if nobody knew precisely why.[37]

Garibaldi, like many of his Victorian contemporaries, was convinced that miasma brought fever. The name 'malaria' (bad air) indicated the widely shared assumption

39

about how fever symptoms came about.[38] As one specialist observed in a study of murky vapours in 1870, 'everybody agrees that the periodic increase in fever is principally caused by miasma'.[39] That particular commentator on patterns of disease in Italy had traced the fatal effects of miasma on the populations of towns and cities, from Milan to Brindisi. To claim that there was universal agreement was a slight exaggeration, however, for the miasmatic theory had long had to compete with other hypotheses, such as those relating to the existence of mysterious minute creatures, '*animaletti*', which penetrated human blood and wreaked havoc.[40]

Scientific ideas about infectious and contagious diseases were in dramatic transition during the second half of the nineteenth century; specialists vigorously debated, in the light of their own theories, the appropriate 'hygienic' measures that should be adopted to safeguard people against dangerous air or poisonous drinking water. The 'microbial revolution' associated with the work of such remarkable chemists and experimental scientists as Louis Pasteur (1822–95) and Robert Koch (1843–1910) was to transform many aspects of public health policy. The foundations of the science that came to be known as bacteriology were laid between 1870 and 1885, although how much Garibaldi knew of any of these arresting scientific hypotheses and empirical details, we cannot be sure. '*Pasteuriser*', meaning to pasteurize, entered the French language in 1872 (and was to be found in English by 1881), to describe a system of germ destruction (sterilisation) by Pasteur's method. An Italian translation of the term came into use within a few years. A landmark event occurred in France in 1885, with the introduction of new administrative procedures for the bacteriological analysis of water, although even then older miasmatic theories hung in the air, still providing a richly suggestive general image of lurking impurities and hovering dangers.[41]

In the study of malaria, miasmatic theories of the disease's transmission remained widespread at least until the advances made by the French doctor and pathologist Charles-Louis-Alphonse Laveran (1845–1922). Autopsies of victims in Algeria led Laveran to identify the specific parasites that were responsible for malaria.* He announced his important findings in 1880, travelling from his laboratory in Algeria to Rome soon afterwards, to bring these glad tidings, and to share in and contribute to the work of Italy's own impressive group of malariologists. Such *esprit de corps* was to give way, however, to some divisive splits, rivalries and squabbles among Europe's cutting-edge scientists and researchers: narrow nationalism was often to overcome public protestations that such crucial applied science could not be constrained by personal vanities or political chauvinism.

Even after the discoveries of Laveran and other pioneering malariologists of the 1880s and 90s, some public commentary about malaria continued to be conducted in terms of miasma.[42] For many centuries, the towns and the countryside of Lazio had been mapped according to their potential for emitting such poisonous vapours. Dotted around Lazio were notorious swamps that continued to be dreaded as 'reservoirs of miasma'.[43]

Whatever the precise explanation for malaria, cholera, typhoid and other diseases, it was not surprising that Garibaldi was convinced that Rome's waterway constituted a major hazard. Crumbling old pipes spewed forth waste in wanton disregard for public health. The river had become nothing but a disgusting sewer. These critical views came not only from Garibaldi, but also from others, such as Angelo Vescovali, an engineer with a senior post at the Roman municipality and not a man easy to ignore.[44] But this concern was not simply medical and hygienic: 'fetid corruption'

---

* Laveran was awarded the Nobel Prize in 1907.

'Malaria' (oil on canvas) by Ernest Hebert, 1850

connoted the physical *and* the moral quality of the city.
Garibaldi and many of his contemporaries repeatedly drew
public attention to this horrifying conjuncture. Rome
appeared, at every level, to be sick.

In many cultures, wetlands have symbolised despair and
despondency. Swamps, those sludgy 'blackwaters', have
repeatedly been cast as more or less synonymous with hopeless, death-breeding decay and moral rottenness. In the eighteenth and nineteenth centuries, the word 'stagnation' (from
the Latin *stagnum*, meaning pool) could be used to imply
an unhealthy absence of economic activity or a lack of
energy in a given population, not just to characterise a
natural morass. As we have seen, images of marshes and
descriptions of miasma featured widely in travel writing
about Italy. Equally, they were deployed in social and political commentary in Victorian England, often with a self-
conscious reflection back to the 'slough of despond' explored
in the religious literature of an earlier time. Swamps have
suggested sin, despair and lethargy through many historical
periods, but they were also increasingly perceived in the

nineteenth century as breeding grounds for so-called degenerate families.

Swamps could stand as metaphors for the perils of nature or of civilisation, the recalcitrance of the past, or the pathology of the future. Marshes were sometimes divided into benign and malign forms, according to their salinity;[45] on other occasions an undifferentiated swamp was presented, more a suggestive figure of speech than a real geographical location. They featured abundantly, for example, in the work of that influential Victorian social critic Thomas Carlyle. Here, seething 'raw' nature in barbarous lands and the polluted cities of modern England were pictured alike as noxious swamps. Take Carlyle's notorious 'Occasional Discourse on the Nigger Question', published in 1849, where the reader encounters the Caribbean as a disturbing primeval world of bogs, sickness and moral backwardness. There was apparently *only* fever and swamp before the superior white man brought his 'civilisation':

> For countless ages, since they first mounted oozy, on the back of earthquakes, from their dark bed in the Ocean deeps, and reeking saluted the tropical Sun, and ever onwards till the European white man first saw them, some three centuries ago, those Islands had produced mere jungle, savagery, poison-reptiles, and swamp-malaria . . . Swamps, fever-jungles, man-eating Caribs, rattlesnakes, and reeking waste and putrefaction.[46]

Carlyle's *Latter-Day Pamphlets* (1850) described those migrating to the English capital in scarcely less dismal terms. The people were said to have oozed-in upon London, from the stygian quagmire of British industrial life. He pictured the metropolis as a cesspool that could never be cleaned and the incoming hordes as waste currents of human ruin.[47]

Before long, images of and arguments about the mire of moral backwardness and political disorder were deployed by

medical commentators, and by evolutionists and degenera-
tionists, who saw certain lands as a breeding ground for
idiocy, or worse, creating a spiral of pathology, across generations. In France, the doctor and psychiatrist B.A. Morel,
author of an influential treatise on degeneration of 1857,
considered the alarming relationship between human
pathology and a noxious environment such as marshland.
In England, Dr Thomas Southwood Smith, the prominent
campaigner for public health and sanitation measures, put
the risk of miasmatic emanations as follows: 'Nature, with
her burning sun, her stilled and pent-up wind, her stagnant
and teeming marsh, manufactures plague on a large and
fearful scale.'[48] Another influential doctor and public admin-
istrator, William Farr, developed the theory that marshy coasts
and flood plains produced a people who lived sordidly,
without liberty, poetry, virtue or science. To live in such
lands was to degenerate.[49] The fens in East Anglia (once a
site of malarial fever, albeit of less virulent form than in
Rome) were to arouse substantial biomedical concern of
this type.

In Italy, too, malaria-infested land was to become linked
with fears of moral and biological degeneration. Tainted
constitutions and immorality, it was thought, led ineluctably
to one another. In a survey in the 1920s, focusing on the
chronic impact of malaria on the population of the peninsula, a Glasgow-based physician, William K. Anderson,
regarded the natives of the south of Italy as prone to libertinism, drunkenness, want of religion, gross superstition and
murder (often by poisoning). Malaria played its part in
producing 'a deformed, degenerate and idiotic people'.[50]
Anderson cited contemporary Italy as an example of the
high price a civilisation paid for its historical exposure to
this disease. Moving from the general to the particular, he
pointedly suggested that malarial fever among the Calabrian
poor was the cause of paralysis on the Italian railways, since
employees were so unreliable.[51] Many Italian malariologists,

in the late nineteenth and early twentieth centuries, took a similar view about the moral incapacity induced in families exposed to fever. Set against this background, it is easy to see how the scientific campaign to defeat malaria in Italy came to be fought not only on behalf of patients themselves but of their nation: fever-ridden citizens were incompatible with a vigorous 'race'.

Occasionally, artists and environmentalists have sought to beautify swamps or to see muddy ooze as rich and fecund rather than deadly.[52] But the vocabulary that surrounds the description of boggy land characteristically highlights unproductive labour, dismal scenes, monotony, rank and barren decay, solitude, dreariness, gloom, even nothingness. Recent commentators on the cultural history of wetlands have particularly noted the frequent association of swamps with images of illness and depraved womanhood. The concept of 'swamp' came to be linked with a threatening, feminised wilderness, even a primeval slimy backwardness, while modern technology (all those dredgers, pumps and dykes) tends to be linked with 'civilised' masculine triumphs.[53] The contrast between 'good' flowing water and 'bad' stagnant pools is not only a common-sense assumption in all hygiene movements, and to be found expressed in many quarters throughout the history of medicine, it is also a fundamental organising principle to be found in our conception of nature and of society. The link between environmental stagnation, moral corruption and political petrification was supported by powerful new medical and scientific theories during the nineteenth century – in many accounts it went without saying that unimpeded flow (of blood, water, air, goods or ideas) was benign and healthy, while obstructions and impediments to movement were reprehensible and unwholesome.[54]

Garibaldi's mission to save Rome in 1875 took place before the decisive series of breakthroughs into the science of malaria by Laveran in Algeria, Battista Grassi in Italy and

Ronald Ross in India. As we have seen, theorists of disease had not been shy to speculate before the systematic modern study of malaria came of age around 1880. What made the field so confusing was not the dearth of explanation, but its superabundance. There had been, for centuries, a bewildering proliferation of semi-plausible hypotheses. It is hardly surprising, therefore, that Garibaldi's own ideas about the causes and effects of malaria were less than crystal clear: dozens of explanations had jostled for public attention in the eighteenth and nineteenth centuries.*

Some feared that winter waters were noxiously trapped in the ground. With warmer weather, fermentation would take place, bringing dire results. A small amount of summer rain was thought quickly to produce further miasmatic emanations. In the city, the problem was imagined to be less severe than in the country, because the earth's fumes were held back by the built environment. But even the city was dangerous enough, since only certain streets, squares and houses were sealed off from the ground with hard, man-made surfaces. Even if total hygiene was impossible, regular street cleaning was viewed as a sensible precaution, reducing the scope for pollution. Some specialists advised house-dwellers to repair holes in basement floors in order to exclude harmful, subterranean gases.

Despite perceptions to the contrary, Rome and its environs were in fact no more dangerous than many other parts of the country. Indeed, once records were compiled, late in the nineteenth century, it became clear that Lazio's death

---

* In a wide-ranging discussion of Roman malaria in the 1790s, a pamphleteer had taken into consideration factors such as wind, polluted rain, seaweed, deforestation, geology, reptiles, bad air, underpopulation, agriculture (or the lack of it), stagnant water and insects. Like Lancisi before him, this author came tantalisingly close to the real causes, as he wondered whether the worms and mosquitoes that bred prolifically along the Tiber might be relevant. But of one thing he was sure: fetid evaporations from the soil were bad for human health (Anon. 1793, pp. 59, 61).

rates from fever were not as bad as those in much of the south and the islands. The physician, scientist and social reformer Angelo Celli, writing in 1910, provided a retrospective survey of malaria-related mortality figures in the various regions of Italy. In 1887, for instance, there were 883 deaths in Lazio, 526 in Piedmont, 504 in the Veneto, 440 in Lombardy, 303 in Emilia, 270 in Tuscany, 68 in Umbria, 55 in the Marches and 37 in Liguria. On the other hand, there were 1,345 in Basilicata, 1,883 in Campania, 1,912 in Abruzzi and Molise, 2,234 in Sardinia, 2,448 in Calabria, 2,721 in Puglia and 5,404 in Sicily. Admission rates in Rome's general hospitals for malaria and other serious fevers were cut from 390 in 1877 to 34 in 1908, a decrease due in some part no doubt to the various safety measures that were introduced to reduce contact between human populations and mosquitoes, but above all due to the wider distribution of quinine. Death rates fell over the same period from 77 to 17.[55]

Considerable uncertainty surrounds the accuracy of such estimates and it should be borne in mind that systematically recorded statistics on mortality rates only emerged in the 1880s. According to these, malaria killed 21,033 people in Italy in 1887, 15,987 in 1888 and 16,194 in 1889. Between 1890 and 1898, they ranged from about 10,000 to about 20,000 per annum. Another significant yardstick was the incidence of malaria in the army. Between 1877 and 1899, over 300,000 soldiers were reported to have fallen sick with the disease.[56] By the early twentieth century, death rates from malaria had been dramatically reduced; in 1909 they had fallen by more than three-quarters compared with twenty years earlier.[57] What gave Roman fever its special urgency, its unique atmosphere of crisis, owed more to culture, politics and history than to the sheer virulence of the disease or the frequency of death.

Although death rates in and around the capital were not in fact so exceptional, discussion of the malarial problem

here was more heated than anywhere else in Italy. Some
linked Rome's ills to vices inherited from the ancient past.
Others speculated about the failure of Italy to produce, in
Northern European fashion, a true religious Reformation.
Identifications of moral pathology, racial weakness, economic
incapacity, spiritual impoverishment and geographical curse
proliferated. Alongside social, economic and political diagnoses, the strange emanations of the soil, wind and air were
anxiously discussed in the context of strategies to boost the
fortunes of the capital and its region. Thus did debates about
physical health and sickness, cultural well-being and moral
corruption become entangled.

In late-nineteenth-century Italy, some 15,000 deaths per
year were the norm for malaria. This was out of a total
population, according to the national census of 1871, of
nearly 27 million. It is true that cholera, TB and typhoid
rates were sometimes higher than those for malaria,* but if
the latter killed 15,000, its debilitating effects were felt by
vastly more, perhaps by as many as two million people a
year.[58] Small wonder then that malariology loomed so large
as a political and scientific priority in post-unification Italy,
that the Campagna was much discussed, and that the debate
over causes and effects seemed at times to acquire a febrile
and desperate tone in its own right. The terrain was mapped
and explored; remedies were ritually announced and
denounced; and by the start of the twentieth century, some
intrepid researchers were to be found experimenting with
their own bodies, by setting up temporary dwellings in the
Campagna, to see what would become of them, as they
tested out the latest device to protect the flesh against the
mosquito.

---

* Cholera rates, for instance, varied considerably, in this period, but 50,000 deaths
or more were not unknown, as occurred for instance between 1884 and 1886;
typhoid killed 27,000 in 1887 alone and TB was said to have killed 63,000 between
1887 and 1889 (Clark 1996, p. 20).

The variety of malaria common in Rome and the Campagna turned out to be falciparum, the form most deadly to humans.* Scientists made a series of critical advances in understanding the disease and its transmission, in the late nineteenth century, identifying the mosquito, the four main varieties of plasmodia that afflict us and much besides. Important work was undertaken in Italy. In 1898, for instance, three Italian researchers, Battista Grassi, Amico Bignami and Giuseppe Bastianelli, succeeded in proving that the malarial parasite was transferred by mosquitoes to human beings. We now know that malaria results from a plasmodium, a single-celled parasitic organism, and that it can be carried and passed on to people, by a particular sub-variety of mosquito, known as the anopheline type. Single-celled parasites invade the blood and reproduce by asexual division until they split open the host cell that they have entered. They then return into the bloodstream, infiltrating new cells until finally this prompts an immune response in the body, and the appearance in the sufferer of those telling symptoms such as severe sweaty fevers, chills and headaches.[59]

In the wake of this revolution in understanding, malaria was, eventually, to be decisively checked in Italy, using DDT against mosquitoes. Some impact was made by the chemical 'Paris Green' against mosquito larvae, but it was above all the use of DDT after the Second World War that constituted

---

* Although about two hundred varieties of malaria have now been identified, four species affect human beings, 'those belonging to the genus *Plasmodium*: *P. falciparum* (malignant tertian), *P. vivax* (benign tertian), *P. malariae* (quartan), and *P. ovale*, a fairly mild type of malaria [that] was not endemic in Mediterranean countries' (Sallares 2002, p. 9). The last major outbreak of malaria in England occurred between 1857 and 1859, during two extremely warm summers, although there were some later more minor outbreaks, for instance in parts of Kent during the twentieth century. Crucially, England was afflicted by the milder form of the disease, vivax, rather than the falciparum variety that was the scourge of Italy (Sallares 2002, p. 153).

the decisive breakthrough.[60] This is not to say that in the twentieth century the science of malariology was ever fully successful or that malaria was eliminated worldwide – far from it. However, in the case of Italy, at least, the material success of such operations is clear enough: the last case recorded in the country occurred in 1962, but for the most part, it had been eradicated by 1950, despite some awful setbacks, including the endeavours of the retreating Nazis to sabotage drainage efforts in the Pontine Marshes, in the latter stages of the Second World War.[61]

Malaria remains a massive health problem in many parts of the world today, and perhaps, with the disease's growing resistance to modern drugs, even a problem of gathering intensity; nonetheless much is now known for certain that in Garibaldi's day remained a source of only the vaguest speculation. In 1875, Roman fever was indeed a mystery and public discussion of the illness linked the language of medicine with issues such as private morality, historical corruption and racial decay. In earlier times, warring theologians had furiously debated the route to perdition and salvation. Disputes about the best way to regenerate the Church, and the people, had divided Guelphs from Ghibellines, Jesuits from Jansenists. In the late nineteenth century, doctors debated, hardly less heatedly, the best way to purify the land and sanitise the living conditions of the population. Quarrels over who had first understood and explained the real relationship between malaria and the mosquito were shot through with personal emotions. One notorious dispute eventually hardened into lifelong hostility between two illustrious researchers from Italy and England.* The idea that something specific to the locality of Rome produced a profoundly

---

* The argument over scientific credentials and priority led to a spectacular falling-out between two of the giants of malariology, Ronald Ross and Battista Grassi – a feud that endured for a quarter of a century. The Englishman bitterly challenged the Italian's claims, accusing him of plagiarism, indeed of 'Roman piracy'. Each made numerous public protestations of his innocence, and complained about the

diseased and depraved culture was nothing new, but the terms of reference were gradually shifting from an overtly religious towards a scientific and materialist perspective; evidently, whatever its pretensions to neutrality and objectivity, the language of late-nineteenth-century medicine, science and anthropology (materialist or otherwise) was by no means value-free.

Garibaldi insisted on the historic stature of his project. He drew attention to other contemporary initiatives such as the Suez Canal and gestured towards past Italian triumphs. Solutions to the Tiber's floods had been discussed since ancient times. Although historically prone to inundations, Rome was also famous, after all, for its management and

---

bad faith of the other. Unlike the pioneering investigators, Laveran, Koch and Ross himself, Grassi never received the Nobel Prize to which many at the time felt he was entitled. Ross went to considerable lengths to ensure that Grassi was not awarded the highest accolades. In one particularly acerbic note, Ross compared his own supposed intellectual maltreatment at the hands of Grassi with the persecution and malice that had once been directed at Copernicus, Bruno and Galileo. Ross also likened his fate to that of Edward Jenner, who discovered a means of preventing smallpox by vaccination, whereupon 'a number of ingenious people discovered that they had discovered it first'. And that was not all: Ross's pain was compared to that of Prometheus, who gave fire to men and was punished for ever by being bound upon a frozen crag where a vulture fed itself on his liver. Socrates also sprang to mind: the philosopher was poisoned at the instigation of his enemies for expressing his opinion on various philosophical matters. 'Then there is the sublime case of Christ who gave us the highest of all philosophies and who was crucified for doing so.' Ross acidly summed up his complaint with the words, 'After years of labour I succeeded in finding the malaria parasites in mosquitoes; but immediately after my results were published some Italian gentlemen succeeded in finding the same thing "*independentemente da Ross*"' (Ross 1924, pp. 1–2). Another characteristic swipe appeared the year after: '[Grassi's] dialectic is exactly that of the "informers" of Ancient Rome described by Tacitus, every sentence contains a truth and a falsity so closely woven together that the victim must spend pages in extricating and exposing them' (Ross 1925, p. 319).

control of water. The ambition to alter the course of the Tiber made Garibaldi the heir of Julius Caesar, declared *The Times* approvingly, as it traced the genealogy of his noble idea.[62] Although the Tiber had never been tamed, nonetheless in ancient Rome's aqueducts, baths and fountains lay the built record of so many aesthetic and practical triumphs over the anarchy of the elements. As early as the second century before Christ, a twenty-four-metre arched bridge had spanned the Tiber.[63] By the fourth century after Christ, there were over 1,350 public fountains in the Eternal City.[64] As the power of Rome had moved towards its zenith, so its ability to transport large volumes of water across the land had grown ever more astonishing. Garibaldi was not alone when he indignantly wondered how Rome – of all places – could be enslaved by raging water in the modern age.

The ruins of the great aqueducts stood as a powerful impetus to later engineers. The achievement was immense and so too the sense of pride it engendered. Pliny the Elder, who lived in the first century AD, viewed the construction of Rome's sewers as among its greatest achievements and the aqueducts as a wonder of the world.[65] He marvelled at a system that enabled water to flow through urban dwellings, public buildings, country villas and gardens, and which had involved such feats of tunnelling, bridging and levelling.[66] Ancient Rome had evidently achieved an astonishing command of water and its well-functioning sewers and waterways were a symbol of its wider civic achievements. On the other hand, critics of Roman corruption and dissipation often made analogies to failing sewers or even to disordered guts.* In 1425, new information about the ancient Roman system had become available, with the

---

* As one historian has recently observed: 'Cicero's city of Rome in crisis is like a constipated gut stuffed with citizens' bodies, which, as soon as they are dead, become so much garbage in a gut bleeding at its outlets, the Forum and the Tiber' (Gowers 1995, p. 28).

discovery, in the Monastery of Monte Cassino, of Sextus Julius Frontinus' *De aquis urbis Romae* (c.97 AD).[67] The Church had sought to become a fitting heir, producing in turn a surfeit of ideas and initiatives, above all during the Renaissance, for the reclamation of ancient edifices and impressive blueprints for new fountains, pipes and canals.[68]

Many civic plans concerning possible building works in Rome during the Renaissance aimed to rectify the old struc-tures – to deal with the defects, for instance, of the city's sewage system and to dredge and clean out the Tiber.[69] The restoration of clean flowing water was both a practical mission and a spiritual ideal; such works of renewal and improvement were increasingly seen as an indication of the power and achievement of papal reformers.[70] During the reign of Leo X (1513–21) ambitious but unrealised reclama-tion projects were drawn up by Bramante; some other proposals for agricultural reclamation and repopulation of the Pontine Marshes were implemented later in the century.[71] One plan put to Paul IV (1555–59) in 1560 envisaged the creation of a massive artificial water reserve that would prevent the Tiber overflows from affecting Rome, while irrigating the Campagna at the same time.[72] Gregory XIII (1572–85) carried on the policy debate about reclamation; various engineering projects were approved, and some were even put in place, only to be destroyed by the floods of 1598. Paul V (1605–21) endeavoured to improve the navigability of the Tiber, under-taking works along the banks and on the coast, but the revival of river traffic was short-lived.[73] In other words, rulers had not always ignored the difficulties of navigation, flood, fever and irrigation that so cruelly afflicted the people of the region. But success was partial at best, chimerical at worst.

Decay was to prove in many ways irreversible. The gradual disintegration of that ancient system of aqueducts, sewers and fountains symbolised the decline of an entire civilisa-tion, and there was no shortage of speculation about the relationship between such crumbling structures and the history of human disease. Commentators had long wondered about the connection between the overflow of the Tiber and rising death rates due to local fevers.[74]

Garibaldi did not offer any precise examination of illustrious past schemes for any of Italy's great rivers. Whether he even knew, for instance, of Leonardo da Vinci and Machiavelli's plans, developed in 1503, to move the Arno and make it navigable is not apparent.[75] A more immediate inspiration, no doubt, was to be found in the nineteenth century itself, with the canal and other transportation projects associated particularly with the radical social ideas and political philosophy of a remarkable French aristocrat, Henri de Saint-Simon, who died in 1825. Garibaldi, who encountered the work of Saint-Simon's devoted followers during the 1830s, was impressed by the group's belief that science, engineering and capital could be harnessed in the interests of progress and enlightenment, and specifically on behalf of the poor and needy. The General's advocacy of Roman canal construction was in several ways a reflection of Saint-Simon's insistence on the economic, political and social importance of fostering new means of commerce and communication.*

---

* This influence had extended, very notably, to canal construction at Suez and, later, Panama. Both these projects owed a considerable amount to the enthusiasm and imagination of Claude-Henri de Rouvroy, Comte de Saint-Simon (Saint-Simon 1975, pp. 15–16). He had visited Mexico in the 1780s and presented the Viceroy with a blueprint for a canal across the Isthmus of Panama, linking the Pacific and Atlantic Oceans. Although the plan was rejected, this did not put paid to Saint-Simon's long interest in transportation and communication. In 1787, he offered his services to the Spanish government in its endeavour to create a canal linking the city of Madrid with the Atlantic Ocean. Working with the chief architect of the project, Francisco de Cabarrús, director of the Banco de San Carlos and chief financial adviser to King Charles III, he drew up fresh plans. Saint-Simon proposed to take responsibility for putting together a workforce of six thousand men. The outbreak of the French Revolution scuppered these designs,

Garibaldi was adamant that if holes could be cut through mountains, huge trenches dug from sea to sea — as at Suez, where, to widespread public admiration, a canal had opened in 1869 — it would be shameful in the extreme if the Italian government failed to implement his plan for the salvation of Rome. His river project was thus conceived as a decisive reckoning for the new Italy; it was presented as a struggle for enlightened reform against blind reaction, science against superstition, life against death.[76] And lest anyone think this rhetoric was far-fetched or the aspiration silly, all he had to do was remind them of an embarrassing water-borne environmental disaster that had befallen the city four years earlier, only months after Rome was so controversially seized from the Pope.

---

and Saint-Simon returned to France at the end of 1789. Other initiatives followed, in which Saint-Simon or his disciples advanced the case for a new communications system as a means to promote industry and trade. Ambitious plans for industrial progress, including a comprehensive network of railways, rivers and canals, were set out by Michel Chevalier in the Paris newspaper, *Le Globe*, which followed a Saint-Simonian agenda: its subtitle was 'Journal of the Saint-Simonian Religion'. Chevalier, who was to become professor of political economy at the Collège de France, influenced various European bankers, financiers and industrial entrepreneurs, particularly railway enthusiasts. Suez also bore the hallmarks of Saint-Simonianism. Indeed, the venture had been strenuously advocated by Chevalier in 1832, as a major plank in a new *système de la Méditerranée*. This project had got off the ground when another of Saint-Simon's disciples, Barthélemy-Prosper Enfantin, founded a *Société d'études pour le canal de Suez*, whose preparatory work paved the way for the start of construction on the canal in 1854. In 1879, Ferdinand de Lesseps (a French diplomat, noted follower of Saint-Simonian ideas and active participant in the earlier Suez Canal scheme) formed a company to build a canal in Panama. The scheme went through numerous vicissitudes and cost many lives before the waterway finally opened to traffic in August 1914.

4 Flood

'Let Rome in Tiber melt and the wide arch
Of the ranged empire fall! Here is my space.
Kingdoms are clay; our dungy earth alike
Feeds beast as man.'
                    William Shakespeare, *Antony and Cleopatra*

In her *Diary of an Ennuyée*, published in 1826, a visiting
writer, Anna Jameson, recorded the experience of
reaching Rome, under sinister, impenetrable clouds that
covered the whole Campagna. The clouds soon burst, and
Rome suffered a deluge: 'We have had two days of truly
English weather; cold, damp, and gloomy, with storms of
wind and rain.' The diarist added: 'I know not why, but there
is something peculiarly deforming and discordant in bad
weather here; and we are all rather stupid and depressed.'
By contrast, warm weather, when it came, was said to be
heavenly.[1] But the climate of Rome was not simply a topic
of conversation: winter and summer could bring very real
dangers to the entire population. Rome's changing seasons,
and in particular the menace of its floods and fevers, were,
as we have seen, imbued with complex cultural and political meanings, and also had a profound material impact on
the city and its people. To view such practical consequences
and metaphysical fears at their starkest, turn to 1870, Italy's
annus mirabilis (or, from another point of view, *horribilis*). In

the autumn, Rome had been unified with Italy, but the event that most immediately affected the lives of the city's inhabitants at the year's close was a flood.

The Tiber makes a journey of about 370 kilometres from its source in the Apennines to the sea. 'It goes seething through the Campagna like a boiling cauldron,' observed one awed English visitor in 1873. In its turbulent waters, he observed, a thousand ancient memories roll past, and the murmur of history itself is 'written on its turbid wrinkles as they flow down to the sea'.[2] The river's most famous stretch takes it winding through the centre of Rome, where it periodically overflowed, at times disastrously. In winter, the water level of the Tiber had to be carefully noted by prudent residents who lived close to the banks; bulletins were sometimes provided in the press, with the same anxious vigilance that might characterise a physician monitoring the mood swings of a potentially violent patient. At the start of 1870, *The Times* correspondent had walked along the Tiber and noted the dangerous speed of the current and the large volume of water churning through, but in that instance no ill effects followed.[3] There were many occasions, however, when the waters did indeed spill over, deluging Rome's streets and buildings. Demands for action to tame the river had a long history, but so also did a sense of the city's helplessness before God, or the gods.[4] Roman floods in the winter also exacerbated the risk of malaria the following summer, since the residual waters left behind offered new breeding grounds for mosquitoes.

There had been much uncertainty and speculation about the causes of the frequent Tiber floods that battered ancient Rome. In the early period of Christianity, its followers were much blamed for the flooding, as for many other natural disasters.[5] At different points, across the centuries, Christians as well as non-Christians would find themselves held responsible for such 'punishments'. Natural disasters were sometimes attributed to human folly and lapses of morality, or rather to the displeasure of the deity in the face

Piazza Navona during a flood, from a seventeenth-century print

of those transgressions. So often in Roman history, dramatic political and social events had been mysteriously linked with the Tiber's surging waters: from the violent death of Caesar to the election of the unexpectedly liberal Pius IX in 1846.[6] But however fantastic the explanation of its rising levels, the damage the Tiber could cause to the city was not in doubt.

In one sense, then, there was nothing so surprising about the arrival of yet another flood at the end of 1870.[7] Nonetheless, for many the specific timing *was* rudely shocking: that Rome should be deluged, at the end of the year that had sealed Italian unification with a final political triumph over the papacy, was highly unsettling. That the flood followed so close on Christmas only added to the argument that this was no mere accident. That year saw the culmination of a military and political process that had trampled over the authority of the Vatican.[8] What more unpropitious sign for the fledgling nation could be imagined than this evidence of an angry Tiber? It was remarked, often enough, by the end of the nineteenth century, that the years since unification were a sad and sorry period in Italy, not only because of financial crisis, hunger and poverty, brigandage, corruption and emigration, but also because of river flooding, hurricanes, earthquakes and the volcanic eruptions of Vesuvius.[9] Italy was reeling from both natural and political events in these years. Cholera outbreaks (such as that in Naples in 1884), military reverses (such as that suffered by the Italian Army at Adowa in 1896), or earthquakes (such as that endured in Sicily and Calabria in 1908) were to evoke anguished calls for national 'self-examination'. Some saw political or spiritual shortcomings behind each disaster. Were such events, in reality, ominous communications, full of deeper meanings and warnings? Cholera was thus to be understood by some influential Catholic authorities as a divine punishment.[10] Flood and fever provoked the same enquiry and sometimes the same conclusion. Small wonder if the uncontained Tiber that now swamped the city in December 1870 quickly rose up the political agenda. This latest misfortune prompted the creation, in 1871, of a high-level government-led commission of inquiry into the state of the river and the sewers. This paved the way for major public works in the last two decades of the nineteenth century, a practical and necessary response to the inconveniences of 'Nature'.

The invasion of Rome and the integration of the city with the new state in 1870 had occurred despite, not because of, the wishes of the Pope. The flood was thus evidence of retribution, insisted more than one Catholic paper in the immediate aftermath.[11] After all, the Bible itself was crammed with examples of the elemental punishments inflicted by a disappointed God, and the 1870 flood was conceived in exactly these terms. Such religious claims provoked much outrage in newspapers sympathetic to the national cause: editors berated the prelates who were exploiting the event to prey upon the guilty consciences of those Roman citizens who had welcomed the arrival of Italian troops.[12] In turn, the Catholic press angrily repudiated the charge of fomenting hatred.[13] The message that the flood was retaliation for the secular overthrow of Church rights first instigated by those three architects of unity, Mazzini, Cavour and Garibaldi, and culminating in the invasion of Rome on 20 September 1870, was for many at the time a persuasive and provocative one.[14] It also concentrated the minds of those in favour of secular control, spurring them on to solve the Tiber problem once and for all, and thus not lay the city open to such superstition. Either way, the symbolic stakes of the 'natural' disaster were clear.

Rome was not the only city, nor 1870 the only year, in which serious floods had caused social disruption and theological debate in nineteenth-century Italy. There were other comparable instances at hand: the Po and the Arno had burst their banks often enough. Florence had been affected by a serious flood in 1869. Pisa suffered again in 1872, as the Arno once more failed to contain itself. In the same year the Po overflowed dramatically, affecting many tens of thousands of people. Such occurrences were, if not routine, at least periodic dangers. Rivers were potential mass killers – through drowning some of those unfortunate enough to be in the vicinity or through the effects of water-borne diseases – and destroyers of houses, cattle and crops.[15]

What particularly marks out the Italian flood problems of the early 1870s was the conjuncture of political and natural events, and the cultural and social shock waves that emanated from the crisis of church and state in Rome. According to a recent historical account of the north Italian floods of 1872, 'a thirst for miracles' found, as it were, liquid replenishment in all the disaster reports. Unruly waters served as a grim reminder of the dangers of impiety and were quickly taken up in sermons and other religious counter-offensives against the arrogant state. No surprise that images of the Virgin Mary should soon be placed at the sides of these turbulent rivers by a desperate peasantry – no surprise in the sense that the tenacious Catholic beliefs of the population of rural Italy had often been remarked upon and had caused raised eyebrows on many earlier occasions.[16] The great French writer Stendhal, author of *Promenades in Rome* (1829), had observed that the people of the Campagna were so steeped in a primitive form of Catholicism that, in their eyes, no natural event ever occurred without a miracle.[17] Or consider this description of the lives of rural folk, offered by an Italian historian early in the twentieth century:'The most laborious, most unhappy, most resigned, and least exacting of this population were the labourers of the Campagna and the vine cultivators. They visited Rome on Sundays, dressed in their primitive costumes, their faces showing traces of malaria; they assembled in the piazzas to buy provisions, to get their letters written by the public letter-writer, or to be shaved, sitting under [an] umbrella.'[18] Even after the First World War, medical specialists lamented that peasant ignorance and false beliefs severely hampered educational efforts in the so-called national 'war on malaria'. Folklore and an 'industry of miraculous cures' were still being used as prophylactics, despite being completely useless, complained one seasoned campaigner, Guido Cremonese, in 1924.[19]

In the 1870s, accounts of all these Italian floods and their potentially divine meaning had travelled beyond the areas immediately affected. News spread more quickly in the new state; not only by word of mouth or through sermons, but also in a burgeoning urban and regional press. Debate about the ideological and spiritual exploitation of flood became vituperative in the

Portrait of Pius IX, 1875

extreme. Thus was the Tiber caught up in the rhetoric of Catholic grievance and secular defiance.

Pope Pius IX had made his extreme disapproval for the taking of Rome evident enough. Ever since the earlier crisis of 1848–9 (of which more later), he had been offering warnings against secularisation and impiety. This was an age in which new ideas very much at odds with traditional religious explanations of the natural world were gaining ground in Italy, as elsewhere in Europe. Ideas about social and moral authority drawn from positivism, materialism and evolutionary theory circulated, at least within the educated, professional middle class, that made up an increasingly prominent constituency. Italian and foreign commentators who advanced fiery arguments about science and politics, counter to Church teaching, punctuated the intellectual conversations of the new state. In Rome, opinion was sharply divided over a proposal, first hatched among students in 1876, to erect a statue to the heretic Giordano Bruno, who had been burned at the stake in 1600. Extensive controversy and political manoeuvring ensued, before the monument finally appeared in Campo dei Fiori thirteen years later.

Many nationalists had looked to earlier famous 'men of conscience' as an inspiration, and also used them as a stick with which to beat the Church. Garibaldi made it clear which side of the ideological fence he was on, when he declared his admiration for Copernicus, Galileo and Kepler (all of whom had notably challenged the orthodox religious thinking of their day). New accounts of the materialist basis of life were emerging and offered little if any quarter to the biblical version of human development. The ideas of Jacob Moleschott provide a case in point. A Dutch doctor and scientist, he was appointed to a chair of physiology in Turin in 1861 and developed a brand of militant materialism much admired in certain Italian scientific milieu. He influenced, among others, the founder of Italian criminal anthropology, Cesare Lombroso, who began publishing his studies of 'criminal man' in the 1870s to much disapproval from the Church. Darwin's *Origin of Species* and Huxley's *Man's Place in Nature* had both been translated into Italian during the 1860s. But this was also a period of significant Catholic renewal and critique of science across Europe: the Pope had staked out his intransigent opposition to such scientific tendencies, above all in a fierce counter-offensive entitled *The Syllabus of Errors* (1864).★ The Church, he made clear, was not going to be cowed by liberalism (or worse); rather, it was on the march against the swelling currents of materialism, evolutionism and moral uncertainty.[20] Reinvigorated cults, linked with the Virgin Mary, the Saints, new sites of pilgrimage, and widely supported claims of miracles at places such as Marpingen and Lourdes, gave the lie to claims that materialist science was carrying all before it.[21]

There were few more powerful metaphors of social instability and political foreboding in this period than noxious air, brackish waters, black clouds or severe storms. In England, Dickens had made the ubiquitous fog a compelling opening metaphor for London in *Bleak House* (1852–3). In 1885, Richard Jefferies wrote a terrifying tale in which the capital disappeared for ever under a flood. Its ominous title was *After London*. Here the reader was to imagine London as a vast stagnant swamp, which no man dare enter, since death would be the inevitable fate.[22] A year earlier, John Ruskin's *Storm Cloud of the Nineteenth Century* had brought together images of industrial devastation, moral pollution and political dereliction of duty in a massively charged representation of England's threatening black skies. In various writings, Ruskin

---

★ *The Syllabus of Errors* attacked many aspects of liberalism and progressive thought. Freedom of conscience and the press were called into question, while socialism and rationalism were sharply criticised as modern evils. The Pope gave notice that he felt under no obligation to make his peace with such movements and beliefs. Science was to be placed under the aegis of religion not vice versa (Mack Smith 1959, pp. 90–1).

had spoken of 'miasmas' induced by human corruption, indus-
trialisation and greed, for instance as he looked on aghast at
the course of the Franco-Prussian War.[23]

Meteorology and miasmatic theories of disease offered a
rich vocabulary for prophets and critics of liberalism and
utilitarianism. In Italy, they were also to be deployed in angry
polemics against the airy mystifications and baleful influence of the Church. Ruskin's references to miasma alert us
to the specific and pervasive medical hypotheses which had
been influential since ancient times. Miasma-based theories
still dominated the understanding of malaria in the nineteenth century; commentators stressed the fatal mix of gases
and saw them as the products of a noxious environment. As
the great historian of Renaissance civilisation Jacob
Burckhardt put it in 1860, 'the whole horizon of Rome
was filled with vapours, like that leaden veil which the
Scirocco drew over the Campagna, and which made the last
months of summer so deadly'.[24] As was described earlier,
the causes and consequences of miasma divided writers, but
few doubted the existence of a potentially fatal effluvium.

Burckhardt described the doubtful joys of summer, but
now, ten years on, and in midwinter, heavy dark clouds were
closing in with a vengeance. The weather over central Italy
had been far from clement around Christmas. On Monday
the 26th, the rain, accompanied by violent thunder and
lightning, came down in torrents, especially in the
Apennines. Gradually but unstoppably, the Tiber's water
seeped through Rome, flowing across banks that had been
left in a crumbling and derelict condition by previous administrations. One clap of thunder was so loud that houses shook
as though it was an earthquake. Lightning struck the Vatican,
passing through the roof of the Pope's chapel and destroying
a picture at the altar.[25] Despite all this, and the meteorological observations made at the Jesuit centre of instruction,
the Collegio Romano, and at the Capitol, little was done
and no general alarm was raised.[26]

With strong winds blowing, melted snow coming down from the mountains and the clouds black, a few astute observers may have guessed it was time to batten down the hatches, but most residents were taken completely unawares by the scale of the flooding that occurred, especially since so much of the damage was done in the middle of the night. By 26 and 27 December, the situation was dangerous and the river levels were still rising. On those days, the waters crept up, eventually seeping through the Jewish ghetto, Trastevere, the Pantheon and other low-lying areas. By the morning of the 28th, in some parts of the city, the waters had swamped the lower floors of *palazzi*. The elegant Via del Corso, Via dei Condotti and Via Giulia looked like canals, and the city was said to resemble Venice more than Rome.[27] Both Piazza Navona and Piazza del Popolo were submerged, more like lakes than squares.[28] Many people woke from their slumbers after the festive season to find their houses infiltrated, water seeping under doors.

Not very many deaths resulted directly from this inundation: far fewer, in fact, than on some earlier occasions in the Tiber's own brimming history of mishap. But at the time it was viewed as a major disaster.[29] Estimates of fatalities varied from three to seventeen, and some newspapers had to withdraw early reports about multiple deaths that later proved unfounded.[30] Nor was the direct social dislocation as severe as in some of the previously mentioned floods of the Po and the Arno. The Po flood of 1872, for example, led to much wider upheaval: according to one estimate, 20,000 families were made homeless.[31] And certainly no Italian or foreign reader of the press would have imagined that what had befallen the city in 1870 was historically unprecedented in Rome or elsewhere. News of anarchic rivers sweeping lands at home or abroad, across Europe and sometimes still further afield, was not infrequently reported.

Yet public dismay in Rome at the beginning of 1871 was not simply a function of water damage or death rates, real or imagined; rather it reflected acute embarrassment, even mortification, that a moment intended to have been a national triumph was washed out by the Tiber. The river had come 'like a thief in the night', complained one chronicler of the flood.[32] Another bemoaned the increase in theft and looting as the waters receded.[33] When a newspaper referred to the entire city grieving for its loss and described a people in mourning, it was not far wrong. The disaster was understood as a psychological as well as an environmental crisis. A certain groundswell of anger was also soon apparent. Was it not a case of criminal neglect, a wanton disregard for the urban fabric that besmirched the good name of Rome? The idea of the Church's direct responsibility for these problems, or even the suspicion that it had a malign secret strategy to produce flood and fever, still remained current in these years, indeed well into the twentieth century. The image of a vast and secret centre of moral and physical corruption, emanating from the papacy, remained influential, in anti-clerical thought, providing a powerful counterpoint to the Church's own language of moral appraisal and denunciation.

The doctor and malariologist Angelo Celli felt he had to counter this kind of anti-clerical 'clamour' against Church wrongdoing. Certainly the Vatican had something to answer for, but Celli debunked the wilder myth, fostered, apparently, by some anti-clerical polemicists, that the papacy had wilfully brought on the catastrophe of the soil, the neglect of the river and the misery of the people. Could it really be, as some suspicious anti-papal commentators thought, that the swamps of the Campagna, the floods of Rome, the pathological conditions of the entire region might reflect a malevolent design? There were, apparently, still critics of the Church who complained not only of its complacency or 'blind eye', but of a precise, destructive calculation and it was thus necessary for Celli, writing in the inter-war period, to repudiate the idea that the Popes had *desired* to transform whole areas of the Papal States into desert or marshland in order to enhance the glory of the Church in Rome. Such rumours about the intent of the Vatican, he wrote, were ridiculous and entirely baseless.[34]

In some accounts, the Church was not seen merely to have neglected the Roman Campagna, but rather to have aided and abetted its physical destitution for the most perverse 'spiritual' or 'aesthetic' purposes. Garibaldi had rather relished such tales of clerical malice and had himself accused the Pope and his underlings of contriving to produce environmental and social neglect.[35] He railed against the cruel indifference shown to the plight of the rural people. The priests, he complained, look stupidly to the past or the hereafter, averting their eyes from the practical tasks of the present, thereby obstinately barring development. For Garibaldi, the Campagna was a painful monument to historical decline and the people's suffering. In his novel *Clelia*, he gave characteristic expression to his dismay at the unhappy changes brought about in this environment.

> That country once so populated and fertile, is now all barren and deserted, indeed, it would be difficult to find another spot on earth that presents so many objects of past grandeur and present misery as the Roman Campagna. The ruins, scattered on all sides, give pleasure to the antiquary and convince him of the prosperity and grandeur of its ancient inhabitants, while the sportsman finds beasts enough to satisfy him, but the lover of mankind mourns over it as a graveyard of past glories, with the priests for sextons.[36]

The novel, released in English and Italian editions in 1870, contained scattered references to the Campagna as a land of death and desolation, a malarial hotbed, where beautiful old orchards and villas had collapsed, to be replaced by pestilential marshes and disease. The Tiber and the land were shown to be monstrously neglected, ruined by a papacy that constituted nothing less than a cancer in the Italian body politic. In the same spirit, newspapers sympathetic to the national state acidly described the way the priests, faced by the flood in December 1870, had thought only of their damaged churches, never concentrating on the wider infrastructure of the city. Thus the flood was cast not only as a disaster, but was also, specifically, linked with debates about Church selfishness and malice, enervated will and the *humiliation* of Italy.

Various efforts had been made by previous administrations to deal with the Tiber's threat. In 1805, Napoleon (by then the ruler of Rome) had briefly revived the same question and delegated the responsibility for flooding to a trusted subordinate.[37] Around 1850, Pope Pius IX commissioned an engineer to assess current needs and undertake a further spate of works. Yet as the 1860s wore on, it was still clear that all such endeavours had failed, and far more was required than had been accomplished in any past civic-building project, if Rome was ever to become secure. New measures to deal with the Tiber were urged upon the Pope before the city was taken from him in 1870. One French observer, Hippolyte Dieu, who had worked as a diplomat in Rome, insisted on the necessity of practical action, but also complained that his very efforts to explain the danger to the Church were diverted and lost, mysteriously falling foul of the Vatican censor's 'arrogant scissors'.[38] As everyone could see in that fateful December, urgently expressed advice had been more abundant than practical action.

The Tiber, enthused Monsieu Dieu, in his pamphlet of 1870, needed to be restored to its former glory. If the Suez Canal, nearly two hundred kilometres long, could be built, so new canals and river-dredging operations could be undertaken to relieve the risk of flooding and improve trade in the thirty kilometres or so that separated Rome from the sea. Renovation works for the Tiber were costed at the relatively modest level of 57 million lire.[39] He concluded that taming the river's anarchic behaviour would revitalise the city and the countryside. Surely the Vatican should press ahead with this venture, he argued, thereby confounding the view that the papacy was scientifically backward. He ended his plea with a description of a future Rome replete with a vast port, a navigable canal and reclaimed marshes. Blessed with these advantages, it was said, the city would enjoy greater international support and admiration, and hence the Papal States would be armed with better protection against the rapacity of the new Italy.[40] But by the autumn of 1870, the Pope was a fading power: no longer the relevant authority to whom one might appeal for action on the Tiber.

The disaster came sooner than that particular petitioner may have anticipated. By the end of 1870, Rome was once again a sodden mess. The water had been metres deep in some places and as it started to retreat, it left behind a morass of stinking mud and slime. It was as though Rome's river had defecated on the new Italy. The flood generated a sense of injury, of anticlimax and foreboding, of damage done to the very spirit of the new polity. No wonder that in the early 1870s Garibaldi fretted about the state of Rome, and took an interest in the river that had so demoralised its population.

These social and cultural circumstances are, of course, relevant in explaining Garibaldi's programme for urban renewal. He was sensitive to the plight of the people and passionately opposed to the apathy and fatalism that had befallen the city. Faced with so immediate a calamity, Rome's inhabitants were hardly of a mind to offer a resounding endorsement of modern progress as they remained trapped in their homes or were busy repairing their dank property. It was a moment of national integration that had been envisaged quite differently by the visionaries and planners of the new state. Meanwhile, the crisis continued: collections for the poor and needy were organised at various points in the city and throughout the country.[41] A number of press articles indignantly reported the contemptuous attitude of the

Church and complained that the priests failed to contribute manpower when the citizens needed every able-bodied person to fulfil their duty. The King and the Pope each eventually offered some funds directly for the relief effort, although it was noted in some quarters that the Vatican dispensed money in such a way as to deprive the inhabitants of the Jewish ghetto of any help. Some criticised the way the Church administered its aid secretly and separately, to avoid mixing up religious donations with contributions derived from people who had been excommunicated.[42] Certain journalists caustically remarked on how Vatican apologists were trying to put a good gloss on the Pope's own feeble efforts to provide succour.[43] By contrast the troops were widely praised for their patriotic endeavours to bring comfort to the flood's many victims. Responsibility for emergency works was placed in the hands of a military commander. Many privately owned horses and carriages were requisitioned, although patriotic individuals sometimes volunteered such resources unasked.

A few intrepid mariners succeeded in bringing their boats from the coast to Rome. Travel through the city was difficult and wider communications with other parts of Lazio and beyond were disrupted. At one stage, Rome's famous thoroughfare, the Corso, had to be traversed by boats, rafts or pontoons. The central post office was closed for sixty hours and the city was left in darkness on 28 and 29 December, owing to the flooding of the gas works.[44] Candles were placed in windows to help illuminate the dismal streets. One newspaper, unable to sustain publication throughout the days of the disaster, was forced to republish old reports from a previous issue when it reopened for business, begging the patriotic indulgence of its readers at this time of public emergency.

With the streets awash, Rome was also preparing to receive, for the first time, its nervous new monarch. The visit had already caused much confusion – it had been publicly announced, only to be put off, time and again, through the previous autumn. As Victor Emmanuel II hesitated, the politicians became increasingly impatient, begging their northern monarch to put in an appearance and raise morale now that this dismal blow had befallen the city. The King vacillated, for he would arouse Catholic disapproval if he entered the city, nationalist disdain if he kept away. He was anything but keen to make the journey, let alone stay in Rome, at this doubly inauspicious time − beset by the bitterness of the Church and now, it seemed, by the Heavens.[45] Some loyal observers urged him to be bold and spoke of his presence as that of a comforting angel.[46] Fervent supporters of the Vatican, however, made no secret of the fact that they regarded his visit as a gross affront: that he would dare to set foot in Rome before any agreement about its future had been made with the Pope, struck them as outrageous.

Public reports indicating that a conciliatory letter from the King to the Pope had been brusquely deposited in the Vatican archives without a reply, did nothing to improve the feverish and bitter atmosphere. Anecdotal evidence in the newspapers also suggested that when Victor Emmanuel did finally arrive, cheering well-wishers had sought to enter the Church of Santa Maria Maggiore, only to discover its doors had been barred by clerics who no doubt suspected the crowds were malevolent and intended to smash the place up.

Any atmosphere of celebration was muted: the tense political stand-off and the natural disaster were doubly constraining. Sensitive to the immediate physical misfortunes that had befallen so many of his new subjects, Victor Emmanuel urged the authorities to redirect the money that had been reserved for the celebration of his visit, to deal with emergency relief. Contemporary reports described the square in front of the Quirinal, crammed with the vehicles of Roman nobility, and noted the appreciative lines of people spread out along the procession route as the King's three carriages, along with soldiers on horseback, made their way past.

The Monarch's affection for the city was by no means strong at the outset. And the state of the river and the streets did little to allay anxieties, not only about the future fate of Rome, but also about the personal price the King might have to pay for the city's forceful seizure. He arrived at three in the morning during the night of 30 December, spent the day on a tour of the centre, expressing sympathy and distributing alms, but insisting that he be en route north by 5 p.m. Some of his subjects muttered about his unseemly haste to depart – the visit was just a few hours long, one paper sulkily complained. As a contemporary French diplomat, who had observed the head of state at close quarters, drily but incontrovertibly put it, Victor Emmanuel had managed to enter Rome, but had contrived not to sleep there.[47]

The civic mood had remained sombre as the royal vehicles headed past the Coliseum and the Forum. Talk of dead bloated bodies floating downstream can have done little to lighten the atmosphere or reassure Victor Emmanuel's party.[48] Moreover, there were many strange signs that could be taken as wonders. What anecdotal news of the many indignities suffered by Rome's inhabitants may have reached the cosseted King or the faraway Garibaldi (at this time fighting for the French republic against its Prussian invaders) is uncertain, but it would be surprising if newspaper reports of these urban horrors escaped either of them entirely.[49] Tales of mud, muck and general disgrace circulated; observers reported seeing luxurious items, carpets, silks, velvets and other costly fabrics bobbing along on the water or beached up in some filthy corner. Many shops had been unexpectedly hit by the flood at a time when they were closed for the holidays. Much merchandise was ruined. Sharp-eyed traders quickly saw an opportunity to purchase such objects at knock-down prices or else to steal them. There was soon a brisk market in soiled second-hand goods, to say nothing of a minor crime wave as intruders forced their way into abandoned premises.

Fortuitously, the King had been invited to celebrate the

new year in Florence and so made his excuses and departed. By then, anyway, the worst of the flood was over. It had already started to subside on 29 December and, by the end of the year, the water was once again flowing along its ordinary bed. In early January 1871, a phalanx of engineers and state administrators sat in meetings, trying to decide what to do. Despite declarations about the urgency of the task, the wheels of power turned slowly; some years would elapse before much substantive action was taken, although compared with other endlessly postponed public projects in Rome during these years, such as the notoriously prolonged planning and construction of the Vittoriano Monument, it was perhaps remarkable that work was carried out at all before the century was out.[50] Various schemes were canvassed.[51] The robust and pragmatic views of Vescovali, the chief engineer from the technical office of the Roman administration, about the need for raised embankments were to form the centre of debate. He compared the Tiber's condition with that of rivers in Vienna and Paris, Lyons and Bordeaux, eventually proposing, among other things, the

A late-nineteenth-century view of the Tiber as it passes the Isola Tiberina in Rome

construction of very high banks made of stone.[52] These proposals and committee outcomes – the eventual products of which visitors to Rome will immediately encounter as they walk along the river – were a far cry from the Tiber scheme that Garibaldi brought to the capital at the start of 1875. The General made clear that the flood of 1870 was never to be repeated; no longer should the Tiber be allowed to 'invade' people's homes.[53]

The Tiber seen as it passes the Isola Tiberina in the twentieth century, after the construction of embankments

But Garibaldi was interested not only in flood barriers, artificial channels and river depths, but in the moral and spiritual purification of Rome and Italy. His feelings about the stagnation and salvation of the city and the state were complicated in the extreme, and to grasp why, it is necessary to consider his personal history and ideas, and also the complex position that Rome and its Church occupied in Risorgimento thought.

5 Hopes of Italy

'At Rome shall we proclaim the Kingdom of Italy. There only can we sanctify the family compact between the free and enslaved sons of the same soil. As long as in Italy there are chains to be broken, I shall pursue my path or strew it with my bones. I will never sheathe my sword until Rome is proclaimed the capital of United Italy. Rome or death.'

General Garibaldi, *Autobiography* (speech of 1862)

Admiring biographers and enthusiastic cheerleaders have had no difficulty in making of Garibaldi's life a modern epic. Who can deny that it took an astonishing and heroic course? His path was always strewn with obstacles, and the saga of his deferred military triumphs and political defeats endured many years. Garibaldi's adventures and achievements were easy to present in celebratory national histories, paintings and souvenirs, but the nature of his character was less immediately apparent and in many ways lent itself to contradictory representations. Some praised the General's lack of malice in the face of adversity. Others noted that there were certain slights and disappointments he could never forget or forgive. He nursed a burning sense of indignation, yet at the same time cultivated a style in which he could remain both intimidatingly aloof and dauntingly benign towards his foes. Seen from one angle he seemed fascinatingly deep, from another, remarkably and lovably simple. *The Times* described him thus:

> Garibaldi had the ideal lion nature in him, all the dignity and gentleness, the sudden flash of anger, the forgiveness, the absence of all rancour, malice, or uncharitableness. Even the brute Leonardo Millan, who had struck, racked and imprisoned him without reason . . . was suffered to go unscathed, the only vengeance of Garibaldi being limited to fixing his look into his face so as to give him to understand that he was recognised, but deemed utterly beneath a man's resentment.[1]

Through the twists and turns of his life, some detected a master of improvisation, while others saw a pawn. Looking backwards, Garibaldi himself would always seek to find continuities, as though the fragmented episodes of his existence had to be seen as connected chapters in the central unfolding story of national liberation. He constantly endeavoured to keep faith with the dead, paying homage both to soldiers who had fallen willingly in 'the cause' and to those who had died prematurely in their beds, sadly robbed of their time. Family names were often explicit acts of remembrance. The names of his children commemorated those who had had their lives cut short by natural causes or political oppression. Garibaldi's son Domenico had the same name as his grandfather; the one that he came to be known by – Menotti – recalled an earlier nationalist hero who had sacrificed his life. The name of his brother – Riciotti – was in homage to another political 'martyr'. Garibaldi's daughter Teresita was named in memory of Garibaldi's sister, who had died at the age of two. The General's own *nom de guerre*, Borel, was drawn from a Frenchman who had sacrificed his life in a failed revolutionary mission organised by Mazzini in the 1830s.[2]

For Garibaldi, it was a matter of honour to keep the dead alive in one's mind. He expressed often enough his painful sense of loss, even his melancholic desire to sacrifice his own life, and thereby join those who had paid the heaviest price. At other times, he seemed intent on exonerating himself completely from imagined accusations that he had betrayed the dead by virtue of his very survival. The complexity of his attitude to his own successes and failures, and particularly to the fact of his own endurance, amid so many fatalities, is well captured in a section of his *Autobiography* that he had penned in Tangier during the spring of 1859. Here Garibaldi discusses the deaths of two dear companions in a dreadful shipwreck just off the coast of South America, in 1839. Garibaldi was in charge of an overladen ship that capsized in an appalling storm. Sixteen men died, including Luigi Carniglia and Edoardo Mutru, both of whom he describes as very close friends. Garibaldi

Garibaldi, shipwrecked in 1839, tries in vain to save his comrades

survived while others drowned. Despite his best efforts to rescue his fellow sailors, the sea swallowed them up. He lists those who died in the disaster, only to become preoccupied by a missing name – one man whose identity he is unable to recall. The failure of recollection evidently bothers him and leads into a flurry of self-accusations and exculpations:

I ask pardon of my country for having forgotten it [the

name of the dead man] . . . I know that during that time many events otherwise more terrible than that I have just related have passed in my life; I know that I have seen a nation fall, and that I have vainly endeavoured to defend a city [Rome]; I know that pursued, exiled, tracked like a wild beast, I have deposited in the tomb the wife who had become the heart of my heart; I know that scarcely was the grave closed, when I was obliged to fly like the damned of Dante, who walk straight forward, but whose twisted heads look behind them; I know that I have no longer an asylum; that from the extreme point of Africa I look at that Europe which casts me out like a bandit, me, who have never had but one thought, one love, one despair – my country! – I know perfectly well all this, but it is not the less true that I ought to remember that name. Alas! I do not remember it![3]

After his many escapades and battles in South America, he had returned to Italy in 1848, intent on contributing to the armed insurrections whose goals of political liberation and national unification were once again in prospect in Italy. He sent Anita and the children ahead to Nice, following soon after. It looked to be the beginning of a new era inside and outside the peninsula. The creation of a single Italy – whether through the federation or centralisation of its various states – was becoming an ever more prominent European talking point. Although Garibaldi did not trouble himself overmuch with the niceties and nuances of doctrines, it is important to note how complex and confused was the political and ideological background to his plans.

'Italy' was not simply an invented nineteenth-century construct: it had some geographical and political meaning in ancient times and in the Renaissance. Dante and Machiavelli, for example, had thought of it as an entity long before polit-ical visionaries sought to revive its prospects in the 1830s and 40s. Campaigners for national self-rule and moral regeneration not only identified in the work of some great artists and writers from the past a shadowy, embryonic notion of Italy, but also suggested that therein lay glimmers of the ideology of nationalism itself.[4] Some wished to present Dante as the true ancestor of the Risorgimento; more plausibly, precursors were identified in the eighteenth century, for instance the remarkable Neapolitan historian and theorist Giambattista Vico.[5] While such genealogies of nationalism and patriotism were often fanciful, the eighteenth century had indeed provided some reasoned and sentimental enquiries into the nature of political bondage and division, well before Napoleon's unsentimental conquest of Italy showed, in lightning fashion, the real possibilities of integration under a strong ruler.

The year 1815 had brought the final defeat of Napoleon. Italy could not be restored precisely to its position before the French Revolution, but the political map of the country had once again been broken up and reconstituted in a manner that suited the interests of the victorious European powers, above all the Hapsburgs. Hopes of a decisive breakthrough for the nationalist idea of a self-ruled and united state in the 1820s and 30s were repeatedly dashed, but by the 1840s its supporters felt that they really had something to be optimistic about: the prospect of a sea change in the fortunes of the cause.

In the period between the final defeat of Napoleon and the 1848 'year of revolutions', several clandestine organisations emerged, seeking to negotiate, plot or blast their way to freedom and national unity. Some pursued a militant, secretive and violent line of action in confronting the traditional ruling powers, not least the papacy, whose reactionary political administration represented, for followers of Enlightenment and French Revolutionary ideas, a particularly galling thorn in the flesh. In fact, Rome seemed relatively impervious to local insurrection, enduring far less political disruption than many other areas in this period. Although the wish to revolutionise Rome was keenly felt by many intellectuals, nationalism was not a mass cause; it was only ever the passion of a minority, for the most part, students, administrators, doctors, lawyers, journalists and teachers. Occasionally, disgruntled clergy, wistful aristocrats or politically inspired artisans joined the various insurrectionary movements on offer.

The peasants were by no means always sympathetic to the old regimes, but where they arose in rebellion, for instance in Sicily in 1860, they were not fighting for anything as remote and abstract as 'Italy'. The vast majority, at the time of unification, did not use 'Italian' (it is generally reckoned that a mere 2 per cent of the population spoke the national language); very few thought of themselves in terms of anything as large as a region, let alone a nation. Nonetheless, this minority of Italian nationalist dreamers and revolutionaries could draw, of course, on a whole European tradition of thought and practice. Some brought back from France the lesson that bloodshed would always be indispensable in the overthrow of tyrannical governments. French Jacobinism was to find expression in Italy in the ideas and practice of Michelangelo's descendant, Filippo Buonarroti (born in Pisa in 1761), who had been actively involved in revolutionary conspiracies and uprisings in Paris in the 1790s and had suffered imprisonment. Later, he established a secret sect in northern Italy, a revolutionary organisation colourfully named the 'Sublime Perfect Masters'. Its intricate, tiered internal organisation was used to keep its goal – communism – closely under wraps. It was almost a secret society within a secret society, one of several such entities to gain strength and gather enthusiastic recruits in the first decades of the nineteenth century.

Although there were radical conspirators of the Buonarroti type, most of the visionaries of the new state adopted a more moderate approach to the regimes who ruled post-Napoleonic Italy. Some of these luminaries looked particularly to the papacy to lead a new moral crusade. One result was to politicise directly, or at least to 'nationalise', the fraught endeavour, already undertaken by various theologians, to reform the institutions of the Papal States themselves and to seek a more enlightened social and political outlook from the Pope. But senior clerics who sought to effect reform of the culture and policies of the Vatican in the nineteenth century were to experience intense frustration, or worse, as notably occurred when Hugúes Félicité Robert de Lamennais, an illustrious liberalising presence within French Catholicism, sought change, through dialogue, with the Pope.

Lamennais had sought to accommodate the spirit of the French Revolution, while also calling for Catholic renewal across Europe, but faced ever more disheartening obstacles to his plans in the Vatican. During the 1820s and 30s, he became increasingly dismayed by the obdurate reactionary stance and worldly corruption of the papacy. It was hard for Lamennais and his followers not to conclude that the Pope was 'a cowardly old imbecile' and the papal court 'the most dreadful cesspit . . . the great sewer of Tarquin itself would have been incapable of dealing with such a mass of filth'.[6] Once again the language of physical and moral corruption would flow together, converging in one horrific image of Roman foulness, presided over by a venal hierarchy. Lamennais was neither the first nor last reformer to wait in vain for the call to come for an audience with the Pope. He bided his time at a monastery in Frascati; week after week he hoped to be summoned for a meeting with the head of the Church, but the word never came. Disappointed, he finally left on 9 July 1832.★[7]

In the 1840s, many of the most influential proto-nationalist thinkers in Italy remained devout Christians, who sought the integration of Italy under the aegis of the Church. Among the notable political declarations of this decade, for

---

★ After a further turbulent period of rebellion against and reconciliation with Church authority, Lamennais renounced his allegiance to Roman Catholicism four years later and remained for the rest of his life unreconciled. On his deathbed in 1854 he refused to see a priest.

example, was Cesare Balbo's *Hopes of Italy* (1844), which reflected a frankly religious aspiration; unification, he argued, would accomplish, among other things, the rejuvenation of the papacy.[8] Balbo hoped to revive what he called the 'dream' of a united kingdom of Italy. Even more importantly, the marriage of Catholicism and nationalism had been the aim of an influential reformer, Vincenzo Gioberti (1801–52), to whom Balbo had dedicated his book. Gioberti, one-time chaplain to the Savoy royal family, was a philosopher, theologian, historian and patriot. His views about contemporary Italy and his criticism of the country's abject subservience to foreign masters struck a powerful chord. He longed for the day when decisions about Italy's destiny would no longer be made in Vienna or Madrid, Paris or London, but rather in Rome. A country that had endured so many invasions across the last two thousand years could perhaps now govern itself. He insisted on the historical legitimacy of national unity and on the inevitably central role of the papacy in any new national undertaking.[9] Although he himself wrote complex high-minded philosophical texts, his work was, rightly, deemed incendiary and potentially subversive.

Gioberti's views, however circumspect, had led him into political hot water and by 1833 he was already in exile. In Brussels, ten years later, he published his most famous and controversial work on the moral legitimacy and pre-eminence of the Italian cause, *Il Primato*. In this and other books of the time, Italy was held up as a shining cause, a state that would become its own master, free of despotism and foreign interference, happily governing its own affairs in enlightened fashion. Gioberti's book unexpectedly chimed in with developments at the centre of power in Rome. In 1846 and 1847, with the new Pope, Pius IX, installed, it looked to many (surprised) observers as though there was growing tolerance, even sympathy, in very high circles for such reformist ideas, but events once again turned the argument upside down.

Garibaldi was no more a political theoretician than he

was a theologian, but like so many others who watched Pope Pius IX's hesitant lurch towards the liberal light, and his unexpected offer of blessings 'to Italy', he sensed a new national dawn. Garibaldi had his eye on the main chance and had no objection to fighting for this new Pope, if he was now truly on the side of the Risorgimento. The General had sailed to Italy in 1848 to take up arms, although under precisely whose authority remained in doubt. Prone from a very early age to be hostile to the clergy (unlike his more devout parents, especially his mother), he now fervently hoped the Vatican might join in the national awakening that had been promoted by intellectuals and activists.

Garibaldi had returned to the old country with considerable military credentials, an object of veneration and fear. Admiring tales of his exploits in Latin America had circulated far and wide, long preceding his own return to Italy. Five years earlier, in 1843, he had taken command of the Italian Legion in Montevideo (herein lay the basis of the extraordinary, casually clad volunteer forces that came to be known under the shorthand term of the 'Red Shirts'). In 1847, still in distant exile, he made overtures, through intermediaries from the Legion, to the Vatican, offering to return to Italy, and provide his services in support of the Pope's growing dispute with the Austrians (who continued to treat central Italy as an open corridor for the movement of their own troops), but he received the disappointing reply that his help would not be welcomed.[10] After his return to Italy, integration or collaboration with the armies of the Piedmontese and Tuscan regimes initially proved equally elusive. Garibaldi's request that a death sentence (passed on him by the Piedmontese government years earlier as punishment for his participation in the Mazzini-inspired political revolt in Liguria during 1834) be cancelled continued to fall on deaf ears. That was eventually revoked, but his proposal to lead his 'irregulars' on behalf of the forces of progress was treated gingerly by that ambiguous and vacillating ruler Charles Albert, head of the House of Savoy, ruler of Piedmont and Sardinia; once again Garibaldi was rebuffed. Snubbed by regular army elites, he and his volunteers went on to fashion their own inimitable contribution to the practical realisation of the Risorgimento.

In 1848, as the old order tottered and fell in many European cities, Garibaldi's offer to fight for 'liberty' was finally taken up; the provisional government in Milan made some use of him, after the eviction of the city's Austrian rulers. But the north of Italy was itself hopelessly divided and there was often little coordination, and outright conflict, between activists in different regions; the plans and aspirations of monarchists and republicans, regulars and volunteers frequently collided. Charles Albert hoped to capitalise on the Lombard rebellion, but while the ensuing Piedmontese invasion of Lombardy was construed by some as liberation from Austria, others saw it merely as the imposition of a new oppression. A measure of the problem facing those who sought to unite Italians against the Austrians could be seen when Lombard peasants deliberately opened up river walls and dykes to flood the countryside and thus thwart their Piedmontese 'liberators'.[11]

These were politically uncertain times and Charles Albert was no staunch ally of the Risorgimento. At one point Garibaldi was defiantly holed up with a thousand men at Lake Maggiore, still intent on taking the fight to the Austrians, only to be told by the King to demobilise, as the diplomats once again changed tack. Amid much confusion and dismay, an armistice was agreed; Garibaldi's ragged troops gradually melted away, while their leader slipped into Switzerland, dazed by fever.[12] Eventually he made his way back to Nice, and his family. He had any number of plans for further actions, ranging from Venice to Sicily, but it was in fact to be his involvement in the defence of republican Rome that made Garibaldi a household name abroad.

Rome was profoundly affected by the hothouse atmosphere of 1848. In that year, insurrectionary rumblings in the Eternal City turned, de facto, into revolution. The Vatican's unpopular conservative chief minister, Count Pellegrino Rossi, became a particular symbol of oppression, and a specific target for the grievances and death threats of various secret societies. On 15 November 1848, Rossi was on his way to the Legislative Assembly when an assassin leapt at him and plunged a dagger into his neck. He died soon after. This assassination served as the catalyst for wider revolutionary activities. With the failure of Austrian-led punitive measures in support of the old order and the appearance of ever more threatening crowds on the streets, the Pope himself became increasingly nervous. He fled, with the aid of sympathisers, including the Bavarian ambassador Count Spaur and his intrepid wife.*

Leaving pandemonium behind, the Pope ended up at Gaeta, in the Kingdom of Naples, under the protection of Ferdinand II, the ruler of southern Italy.[13] The vacuum was soon filled. By the end of December 1848, a provisional government had been set up in Rome; elections followed, in the new year, that formed the basis for a constituent assembly which in turn established the legal framework of the republic that lasted only from February to July of 1849. A giddy mood of political possibility, even of utopian transformation, briefly captured the city. *La Battaglia di Legnano* – the latest opera by the great composer and nationalist sympathiser Giuseppe Verdi – had its premiere in Rome in January.† Garibaldi and Mazzini were both in the audience

---

* The ambassador's wife, the beautiful Countess Spaur, was the daughter of an Italian dramatist of French descent, Count Giovanni Giraud, and the widow of the English traveller and writer, Edward Dodwell, who had died in 1832 after an illness apparently contracted during an ill-fated journey from Rome to the Sabine Mountains two years earlier.

† The rousing choruses to operas by Verdi such as *Nabucco* and *Ernani* provided a continuing, much appreciated musical echo of Risorgimento hopes and hatreds. The thinly disguised references that Verdi made to contemporary politics (all those allusions to 'tyranny' and 'liberation') were widely understood, and the music became a significant cultural rallying point of nationalist sentiment and ambition.

for the first night, and no doubt savoured chorus lines such as '*Viva Italia forte ed una*'. By March, a triumvirate made up of Mazzini, Aurelio Saffi and Carlo Armellini had taken control of the government.

Before long, however, the Pope's urgent appeals that outside Catholic powers should restore his temporal authority were answered. Ferdinand quickly moved his army north to the frontier; the Austrian emperor, whose forces had by now defeated those of Piedmont, also sent troops towards Rome, while, most seriously of all for the Republic, French forces were dispatched by Louis Napoleon, in order to aid the restoration of the Church to its natural seat (or as cynics saw it, in order to curry favour among French Catholic voters back home in France). Nine months after the Roman Republic fell, the Pope, escorted by French troops, returned in state. A new age of reaction began, and Mazzini never forgave the Pontiff, or the French who had turned their backs on the Italian nationalist cause.★

★ In Mazzini's account of the political 'tragedy', the sequence and responsibility were described as follows: the Pope deserted the cause of reform and fled to Gaeta. A government commission which he had instituted refused to act in a manner that could effect a reconciliation between Pius and the new de facto rulers of the city. Two deputations entreated the Pope to return, but he refused. The republic was thus declared on 9 February 1849, offering to put an end to anarchy and civil war. Italian republicans were falsely accused of being foreigners in Rome, but the republicans truly belonged there and were the real martyrs of the affair. They were the ones who were made to wander the globe, bearing the cross for their honest beliefs. Meanwhile, France, Mazzini claimed, had been guilty of making a grubby bargain for Catholic votes. The French government thereby corrupted the ideal of liberty and sullied the international image of itself as '*la grande nation*.' He accused France of committing an unforgivable crime, having by 'falsehood, by the materialism of promotions and by the examples of their chiefs, corrupted the soldiers of France, making them executioners of their brothers, in the name of the Pope, whom they despise; and by the side of Austria, which they abhor; of having degraded to a meaningless symbol – to a material idol, to be blindly

For Garibaldi, Catholicism itself was now on trial. This new political setback deepened still further his suspicion and visceral disgust with 'the priests'. They became an object of detestation and an ever more conspicuous target for his rhetorical attack. The papacy was seen to embody every imaginable vice, crime and human betrayal in history. For Garibaldi, to reclaim Rome was to prise it away from this deeply loathed Church that was in turn linked to historical decay, depravity and death. He declared in his *Autobiography*: 'In all my writings I have waged open war against priestly influence, which I have always believed to be the prop of every vice, despotism, and corruption to be found on this earth.' He continued: 'The priest is possessed by a lying spirit – the liar is a thief, the thief is a murderer, and an endless series of infamous corollaries might be deduced from the same starting point.'[14] The celibacy of priests was a disguise for their libertinism, he complained, and one of the first duties of the new Italy would be to liberate the nuns.[15] Garibaldi presented the clergy as the very epitome of malevolence: the priest was 'a thing in black' who betrayed every virtue supposedly guaranteed by his cloth.

Mazzini was no less aghast than Garibaldi at the Pope's supposed infidelity towards the moral revolution of the Risorgimento. Mazzini never ceased to stress the sacred value of the Italian struggle and the essential nature of the fight against corruption and tyranny. Purity and health were

---

followed wherever it may lead, a banner which is the sign of an idea, of a faith; of having sown the seeds of a hatred which will be slow and difficult to uproot between two nations which everything tended to unite in the bonds of affection, between the sons of fathers who have taken together the sacrament of glory and suffering upon all the fields of Europe; of having brutally given the lie to the holy dream of the brotherhood of the peoples, and afforded the enemies of progress and humanity the ferocious joy of seeing France degraded to be a bully and the executioner of their designs . . .' Mazzini 1849, pp. 13–14.

crucial designations of the revolutionary spirit, and Rome remained the holy city, and the dream city, of this fervent nationalism. 'Rome was the dream of my young years, the religion of my soul,' Mazzini wrote. 'I entered the city one evening, early in March [1849], with a deep sense of awe, almost of worship . . . as I passed through the Porta del Popolo, I felt an electric thrill run through me – a spring of new life.' Before the republic was ignominiously overthrown, he had declared to the assembly that 'Rome shall be the holy Ark of your redemption, the temple of your nation', and then added:

> Just as to the Rome of the Caesars, which through action united a great part of Europe, there succeeded the Rome of the Popes, which united Europe and America in the realm of the spirit, so the Rome of the People will succeed them both, to unite Europe, America and every part of the terrestrial globe in a faith that will make thought and action one . . . The destiny of Rome and Italy is that of the world.[16]

Having initially hoped that the Church would lead the struggle, he came to the conclusion by the 1850s that it was past redemption. The papacy, he repeated again and again, was dead, as a consequence of its unholiness and its corrupt alliances (so much 'fornicating with princes', as he put it).[17] The integrity of the Church had been destroyed by the inquisition and medieval schisms, and by the Pope's desertion of 'the people' in the nineteenth century.[18] Nonetheless, however moribund the institutional form of the faith might be, Rome, he always argued, was 'the city in which broods the secret of our future religious life'.[19] Mazzini sought to reclaim the concepts of holiness, purity, cleanliness and morality *from* orthodox religion. Democracy should mould itself to these ideas and to the mission of a holy collective life. The highest virtue in this cause was self-sacrifice.[20] Even as he denounced the existing Church, Mazzini drew upon religious language, speaking of the apostles of the Italian campaign, of heresy, the soul, the sacred, sacrifice, faith, the perils of corruption, egotism, vice, fatalism, individualism and tyranny, the necessity of virtue and the holy alliances of peoples.[21]

In the late 1860s, Garibaldi had turned to the writing of fiction, and here his hatred of the Church and his desire to purify Rome remained much in evidence. Melodramatic in mood, sentimental and acerbic by turns, his tales attacked the Church so fiercely and were developed so crudely that some of the General's most ardent supporters were embarrassed, even begging him to reconsider his wish to publish. The story that he called *Clelia* and that was translated into English as *The Rule of the Monk*, in 1870, reflected the General's consistent loathing for the class of fawning courtiers and lackeys who congregated in Rome, and, above all, his enduring contempt for the 'Vicar of Christ' himself.[22]

The flavour of the story can be suggested soon enough. Clelia is the daughter of Manlio, a sculptor, who struggles to remain independent in this impossible, 'priest-ridden country'. His wife has become frail due to the various privations of Roman life, but her angelic heart has been passed on to her daughter. They reside in that popular and plebeian quarter of the city that lies across the Tiber; indeed, the gorgeous Clelia is known to all as 'the Pearl of Trastevere'. The family live on a street ascending the Gianicolo (the hill on which Garibaldi had staged, in vain, his eleventh-hour defence of the Roman Republic in 1849). They are a virtuous, hard-pressed family, living a true spiritual life. In contrast, Garibaldi sketched the secret, unnatural world of the papacy. The Pope and cardinals live amid enormous wealth, abusing their power, indulging in every languid form of luxury and hideous vice. Unfortunately, the beauty of Clelia attracts the eye of Cardinal Procopio, one of the most important prelates in the Vatican, and one close to His Holiness. Procopio sends an agent, Gianni, to bring Clelia to him. He pretends he wants to commission statues from Manlio for his oratory, but in fact his designs are purely sexual.

As the historian Christopher Hibbert observes, Garibaldi rather lacked '*chiaroscuro* in his vision'; his certainty was 'unclouded by doubt'.[23] Issues of right and wrong, innocence and guilt, it seems, were absolutely clear to him in this novel, as so often in his pronouncements. Yet at the same time, the sheer excess of the writing, the passionate tone, the horror-stricken appeals, the unstoppable lament, suggest that more was at stake than the standard requirements of political propaganda. A tremendous array of crime is put on display, the basis for a massive anti-clerical accusation.[24]

Meanwhile, Garibaldi describes how a young peasant girl, Camilla, is betrothed to a good man Silvio, who, sadly, is stricken by malaria, which leads to the postponement of the marriage plans. She takes fruit to sell in the Piazza Navona, only to be entrapped and seduced by the cardinal. Their union produces a miserable child, put to death by one of the cardinal's henchmen. Camilla loses her mind and is secretly immured inside a madhouse (from which she later escapes). Eventually, Silvio is reunited with Camilla. In these intolerable social and political conditions, a revolutionary plot gradually develops in Rome, led by various noble spirits. The conspirators meet in that 'sublime ruin', the Coliseum. Throughout the novel, they use various ruins, ancient, labyrinthine tunnels and secret shelters for their urgent meetings. And so it goes on.

Garibaldi evidently had no time for Church apologists. Others would take a more sympathetic view of the Pope's vacillations and misfortunes in the 1860s and 70s, portraying with some compassion his humiliation as the 'avaricious' Italian state finally closed in on the spoils of Rome. Onlookers described the compelling spectacle of the old Church in crisis and sought to convey the emotions stirred up by the prospect of the Catholic hierarchy's reduced worldly power in the new state. Many wondered how far Rome would really be transformed for the better, and how far Italy would be 'Romanised' – that is to say, damaged by the old forces of corruption and pathology. In Rome, that most symbolically complex location for the new Italian capital, Risorgimento campaigners pinned their darkest fears for the future, and their greatest hopes of national redemption and purification. Against this utopian city, projected into the past or the future, but never 'here and now', the painful nature of modern social and political reality came to be gauged.

Rome was as much a spiritual ideal, a private shrine, a public aspiration, as a real urban space, a city, with a physical form. Garibaldi himself acknowledged as much when he spoke of the Rome 'beheld with the eyes of my youthful imagination', the 'Rome of the future', 'the Rome that shipwrecked, dying, banished to the furthest depths of the American forests, I have never despaired of: the regenerating idea of a great nation, the dominant thought and inspiration of my whole life'.[25] Neither Mazzini nor Garibaldi ever ceased to stress the crucial nationalist task of reinvigorating the city. The expectation of and appeal for political and cultural revival were intense, leading to a heady brew of policy demands, exhortations to purity of spirit, and immediate material 'regeneration'.* It was a sacred struggle to

---

* Zola powerfully caught this sense of horror at the existing 'dirty' state of Rome and the nationalist desire for its regeneration: 'That all Italy, on the morrow of the occupation of Rome, should have been delirious with enthusiasm at the thought of at last possessing the ancient and glorious city, the eternal capital to which the empire of the world had been promised, was but natural. It was, so to say, a legitimate explosion of the delight and the hopes of a young nation anxious to show its power. The question was how to make Rome a modern capital worthy of a great kingdom, and before aught else there were sanitary requirements to be dealt with: the city needed to be cleansed of all the filth which disgraced it. One cannot nowadays imagine in what abominable putrescence the City of the Popes,

fight moral corruption and historical degeneration; Rome must be returned to health, for the sake of the Italians. In a letter of protest about the French 'invasion' of Rome in 1849, Mazzini had restated his view that the revolution required would be in the future, as it had always been in the past, 'holy in its right', free 'from all excess in its career'.[26] He claimed to speak on behalf of Italy and above all to identify the ideal future meaning of the Eternal City, true heir of its once glorious past: 'I come forward, therefore, to protest in the name of Rome'.[27]

Of course, Rome was not alone among the Italian cities in provoking a heady mix of adulation *and* dismay. Nowhere, after all, was more captivating and troubling than Venice, '*La Serenissima*'; nowhere more difficult and enticing to describe than this watery and sometimes deadly delight.[28] Many other cities have also been understood through specific personifications as well as airy abstractions; and, plainly, the metaphors of femininity, of corruption and of death that came to characterise the Eternal City had powerful associations in other environments too. Concern about the scourge of malaria in Italy itself was also not, of course, confined to Rome and its region. As we have seen, rates of illness and death in various areas of the state were being studied, charted and compared, in increasing detail, during the late nineteenth century.[29] Malaria and other

---

the *Roma sporca* which artists regret, was then steeped: the vast majority of the houses lacked even the most primitive arrangements, the public thoroughfares were used for all purposes, noble ruins served as storeplaces for sewage, the princely palaces were surrounded by filth, and the streets were perfect manure beds which fostered frequent epidemics. Thus vast municipal works were absolutely necessary, the question was one of health and life itself' (Zola 1896, pp. 248–9). For examples of such breathless expectations about the future role of Rome, among Italy's governing elite, see Vidotto 2002, ch. 3.

serious diseases shadowed social life and public discussion in Italy, and became powerfully linked to the fate of particular cities and to the perceived prospects of the nation at large – cholera in Venice and Naples, to take the most obvious examples.[30]

Yet, for a variety of reasons, Rome was seen by many to have a uniquely charged psychic, cultural *and* political significance for the Italians themselves and for the future direction of the nation. That first moment of entry into the city was a subject of great existential curiosity. Diagnoses of Rome's languorous effects and sickly moral atmosphere, explorations of its erotic and spiritual allure, and assessments of its power to promote or prevent nation-building were also given special emphasis by innumerable Victorian visitors. These often coalesced with discussions of the physical health and well-being of the population in and around Rome: the stakes of success or failure here were seen to be vital to the potential of the new state.[31] Fever, it was claimed, explained the decline of classical art in Greece and in Rome, the growing sentimentality of thought, the gathering pessimism of philosophy, the increasing numbness of feeling apparently evident in ancient societies at large, the decline of moral fibre, the depletion of racial endowment.[32] Of course, to note the questionable moral or biological conclusions drawn about 'Roman fever' by many writers in the past is not to doubt the all too real human cost of malaria.

Angelo Celli once declared provocatively, but perhaps rightly, that malaria had laid siege to Rome more insidiously than any human invader; it encroached gradually, working its way inside the boundaries of the Aurelian walls, compelling the city to shrink within ever narrower confines.[33] Malaria, he concluded, was 'the indomitable and implacable mistress of the destinies of this region'.[34] Garibaldi was by no means the only national figure in post-unification Italy to point out that sickness and social degeneration played into one another; the disease undermined the very possibility of a vigorous society or economy and, in his view, it prevented the emergence of strong families.

Thus the complexity of the city's religious, political, medical and cultural history converged; its health risks, its association with moral corruption and its reactionary diplomatic role in European and Italian affairs were often linked together. The vast shadow cast by its ancient history, culminating in the dissolution of an empire, the enduring visual spectacle of its ruins, the scientific enigmas of its rural hinterland and a certain mysterious quality of its light and atmosphere were endlessly discussed. The Eternal City was also to feature repeatedly as a way of describing mental states themselves: as though it not only induced an emotional reaction, but was itself a beguiling, betraying or bereaved person with whom the visitor interacted. Rome became the most remarkable symbol and personification of decadence and death, love and longing, misfortune and mourning. Seen in this context, is it any wonder that Garibaldi invested Rome with such intense human qualities? For the General,

Garibaldi pronunciava il solenne giuro di ROMA o MORTE....

With the words 'Rome or Death', Garibaldi
makes his fervent pledge to his supporters in 1862

the Eternal City was akin to a patient to be restored, a woman to be loved, a captive to be freed. His evocative mantra, 'Rome or death', had powerful resonances for him personally, but it also brilliantly stirred the imagination of Victorian society.

Even after unification, when in theory the Church had been severely contained (or in some eyes, humiliated), Garibaldi complained that a rotten religious establishment preyed upon and vitiated good government.[35] The Vatican was associated not simply with reaction, but with a history in which hopes of reform were first raised, and then crushed. As we have seen, the notorious shift in Pius IX's policy, from apparent support for nationalist sentiment, to opposition, was to loom very large in the grievances of both Mazzini and Garibaldi. Initially, after all, Mazzini had appealed to Pius, to lead the national revival.[36] Even when the republic was in operation, Mazzini and his colleagues had sought conciliation with Catholics. Certainly, there were swift moves to liberalise the economy, to foster free speech and an open press, and to promote a few ambitious programmes of urban reconstruction, including restoration of churches and improvements to public thoroughfares, such as the new road created by the Tiber.[37] But, no less notably, the republican constitution of 1849 declared Catholicism the official state religion and guaranteed the Pope's spiritual authority. In his brief tenure in Rome, Mazzini risked offending the more stridently anti-clerical Garibaldi by encouraging regular services and ceremonies.[38] With the Pope ignominiously departed from Rome and Mazzini (with two colleagues) in charge of the Eternal City, the Church made this kind of rapprochement impossible. It excommunicated members of the assembly and those who had voted for them. Meanwhile, tales of persecution against priests and vile acts of terror and cruelty spread. In the eyes of the religiously devout and politically affronted, what more striking instance of the dangers of social change in the Papal States than descriptions of the Tiber foaming with blood amid revolutionary terror? Historians have found relatively little evidence of such extreme, politically motivated violence in Rome in 1849. But at the time, vague rumours were recycled as fact and presented in horrific terms as innocent blood spilled into the indifferent currents of revolutionary history. Such modern 'barbarism' was seen as a return to the ferocity of the pillagers of Rome, the invaders who had destroyed ancient civilisation.[39] Reports of violent death on the Tiber continued, more or less implausibly, even after the papal restoration. There were a number of secret vendettas against the French troops, but fact and fiction were often to blur together. Lurid depictions did the rounds, featuring revolutionary and/or counter-revolutionary abominations committed in the quiet of the Roman night: 'Soldiers were inveigled into low drinking-booths in Trastevere at dusk, were intoxicated, and then dropped into the river.'[40]

The political machinations within republican Rome in 1849, the position of Mazzini and others in determining the complexion and policies of the new government, the saga of Garibaldi's arrival in the territory (where he was made first a colonel and then a general), and ensuing tensions with Mazzini as well as with a certain General Pietro Roselli may be consulted in any biography. They are not the central issue here. Garibaldi became the republic's last best hope, and yet finally he had to face the impossibility of the task assigned to him. His ultimately vain endeavour to save Rome from the French-led supporters of the Pope has generated much historical heat and become a cherished national narrative. While Garibaldi's failed defence, and specifically his exploits on the Gianicolo Hill in Rome against the French, made him internationally famous, his immediate circumstances were bleak, and he had to flee.

Garibaldi failed to hold Rome in 1849, but he returned

still more dramatically to the fray a decade later, sailing south from Liguria, with his thousand volunteers, swiftly capturing Sicily and the southern mainland. He wanted to march all the way to Rome, but the complex chess game of international politics, orchestrated by the great Piedmontese diplomat and statesman Cavour, was to thwart and divert him once more. As Garibaldi's army marched north from Calabria, the troops of the Piedmontese Army

Victor Emmanuel II, Cavour and Garibaldi

marched south. Finally, when he met Victor Emmanuel and his army, Garibaldi surprised everybody by the extreme modesty of his demands. He had achieved so much, against the odds, having become the ruler of Sicily and the dictator of Naples, semi-divine in the eyes of many. Yet in quintessentially Garibaldian fashion, with a gesture of astonishing humility, he then eschewed the Machiavellian game of politics and renounced power and worldly gain. Despite the grave alarm of Cavour about his future intentions as he stormed up through the peninsula in 1860, despite his reputation for arrogance and ruthlessness, Garibaldi meekly relinquished his conquests to Victor Emmanuel, at their renowned rendezvous at Teano in the conquered Neapolitan Kingdom. The victorious military commander had worn his poncho and 'under a little pork pie hat he had tied a handkerchief to protect his ears from the morning dew'. Garibaldi had a polite, if

Garibaldi's meeting with King
Victor Emmanuel II, Teano, 1860

awkward, conversation with the King, who made plain his wish to 'rest' the General and his volunteers, whereupon he hailed the monarch, 'raised his hat in farewell and trotted sadly away down a side road to Caserta'.[41]

Increasingly, Garibaldi's exploits were accompanied by a plethora of admiring historical chronicles, celebratory hymns and breathless celebrations of his life – a collective enthusiasm that reached fever pitch after his death.[42] Paeans were penned by three famous French writers, Sand, Dumas and Hugo, but there were also memorable orations later on by Giosuè Carducci as well as the homage of the poet and, later, Fascist supporter D'Annunzio. In short, there was a continuing tide of literary representation of the Italian hero.[43]

Garibaldi's insistent indifference to worldly gain in 1860 was to provide an unforgettable image, a kind of secularised and nationalised adaptation from the script of Christian asceticism. It was the noble making, rather than the worldly holding, of Italy which became the declared purpose of his life; it was a style and a theme taken up with alacrity by his biographers. While he was in favour of industry, trade and the harnessing of science, Garibaldi was also a romantic, who eschewed such values as utilitarianism or materialism. He was, in his personal life, impressively impervious to the seductions of money or the cruder gratifications of power. Offered an estate, a dukedom, honours in profusion, he took back to Caprera two horses, a portable bath, some bags of coffee, sugar and dried beans, a sack of dried fish and a case of macaroni.[44] He let it be known that the reclamation of the Roman Campagna would mean more to him than any personal honour. Reputation was all, and although he did not, in the end, repudiate completely the need for financial recompense and pension arrangements, for himself or, more importantly, his family, there was something about the idea of paid service that offended him mightily.

In his struggles to win Rome and revitalise Italy, Garibaldi had at times almost seemed to court death. In part, this expressed his view that personal sacrifice was essential to the cause; but it also seemed to reflect, as he made clear more than once in his memoirs, a kind of weariness with life, and all its painful compromises. Either way his courage in war was enormously impressive, and became central to his charismatic image. He evidently cared deeply about the example he provided and sought to influence the contemporary and retrospective meanings that would be given to his life. He always insisted to his followers that there was something higher – greater – than the individual life, objectives more important than personal survival itself. Given his reckless disregard for his safety, Garibaldi's own continued existence seemed little short of a miracle, awesome to his followers. If he compromised pragmatically, often enough, to avoid civil war in the course of Italian unification, he was bitter at the unworthy 'squalid' bargains of others, and made no small use of irony – as when he spoke of certain 'very honourable' members of parliament.[45] Asked who the people should vote for, he once remarked that they should place their trust in those who had no particular wish to be politicians.[46] No deal struck him as more unforgivably ignominious than Cavour's accord with Louis Napoleon, in which Garibaldi's birthplace once more reverted to the French. Henceforth Cavour became, for him, the 'salesman of Nice'.[47] Cavour, he complained in 1861, had made him feel like a stranger in his own country.[48]

In the 1860s, Garibaldi made two further attempts to capture Rome. In the deep south, at Aspromonte in 1862, as he prepared a new march on the great city, the General's will would once more be diverted. The underlying political situation was murky and confused, but in the end, Garibaldi was stopped by the new state – indeed, government troops had to be sent to prevent him upsetting the still delicate

Garibaldi during his slow convalescence from a bullet-wound in 1862

apple-cart of international diplomatic relationships regarding the papacy. To the consternation of his many admirers around the world, he personally was fired upon and wounded.★ Moreover, his wound (from a bullet that pierced his ankle during this skirmish) did not fully heal.[49] He endured

★ These plans for the seizure of Rome were rudely blocked by the 3,500 royal troops who lay in his path. In a skirmish, he was hit by two bullets. Menotti was also injured. The affair was soon over and Garibaldi found himself treated relatively harshly. He was held in custody, albeit with various doctors and his son in tow. He underwent an operation for his injuries during November 1862 in Pisa. Victor Emmanuel eventually offered an amnesty to the participants, but the General's tribulations were not over: he endured a long and excruciating period of convalescence. These setbacks prompted contemporary descriptions of Garibaldi's martyrdom, as the national saviour was placed once again in chains, or 'on the cross' (Scirocco 2001, p. 326).

Garibaldi 'on the cross'. In the aftermath of his retreat at Aspromonte, the General is shown crucified, as perfidious members of the government look on. The Pope and Napoleon III dance in the background

months of bedridden torment as a result. It was said to be but a physical token of the injured moral feeling of this relentless nationalist. The remarkable 'about-face', in which Garibaldi, Italy's most celebrated modern creator, would be physically attacked, imprisoned, put on trial by the new state, became the stuff of scandal and his suffering was represented in various drawings, paintings and descriptions. The lead itself, when extracted from his flesh, was to become coveted; large sums were offered to Menotti for this prized possession. Once again, the General's plans had been derailed, and public emotion ran high, in the face of this latest humiliating indignity and rebuff. As Christopher Hibbert writes:

Sympathy [for Garibaldi] had swept not only across Italy but across the whole world. Telegrams and letters, poems and presents, cigars, flowers and books were heaped beside his bed. Over twenty doctors from all over Europe came to his bedside to offer their advice as to how the ball in

101

his foot might best be extracted; a thousand guineas were raised in England towards the cost of two visits by an English surgeon; and Lady Palmerston, appalled by the Irish who ran through the streets of London shouting 'No Garibaldi! The Pope for ever!' sent him an invalid bed.[50]

Intrigue flourished through these interim years. The General apparently could not rest until Rome belonged to Italy, or he died in the attempt. Injury notwithstanding, he continued to hanker after the city. In 1866, he was again at work on a new scheme to take Rome, a plot that also ended in fiasco. Mazzini had opposed it, since he did not want the Eternal City 'liberated' for the monarchy. Garibaldi was also warned that the state would not support him, such was the delicacy of the international situation. He continued regardless. As in 1862, he appeared impervious to warnings. Those in whom he placed his trust were by no means always in good faith and he was on more than one occasion to be badly double-crossed. 'Garibaldi himself has proclaimed that he goes to Rome not hoping to conquer, but determined to die,' reported *The Times* in 1867: 'Italy, he thinks, can only be redeemed by sacrifice.'[51] As one of his biographers put it, the General's obstinacy, in many cases his greatest asset, became his ruin.[52] Many things went wrong with these latest military plans, including the failure of a scheme by some followers to sail quietly along the Tiber with a small cargo of arms. Facing fierce armed opposition, Garibaldi was heard to shout to his comrades, 'Come and die with me.' He did not die, but the rebellion was quickly quelled, this latest campaign lasting less than two weeks. His volunteers pulled back and eventually surrendered to the French at Mentana.

Garibaldi was, once more, briefly detained, but by the end of November he was back in Caprera. Soon after (in August 1868) he resigned his post as a deputy. The Polish writer Józef Ignacy, who visited him on the island in December 1869, described seeing a broken man, with a decrepit body, legs swollen, face pale. Before him, 'Garibaldi could see only a desert'.[53] Many of his supporters were surprised that he was alive at all and would reluctantly have agreed with the visitor's verdict that 'mere human heroism is not equal to sheer impossibilities'.[54] Yet once again the General had defied death (despite himself), and the legend lived on. In less forlorn times, it had been said that he was worth a hundred, a thousand, perhaps tens of thousands of soldiers in his own right.

Garibaldi's military exploits were astonishingly prolonged, full of unexpected 'encores'. Whenever they seemed to be over, circumstances or foreign admirers revived them. Abraham Lincoln had had the genial idea of procuring the Italian's services during the 1860s, in the American Civil War, an offer the General had declined. Even then, however, his military adventures were not quite at an end: in 1870, he found himself on the side of the French republicans who had taken over after Louis Napoleon's departure and were continuing to resist the invading Germans. The accomplishments and vicissitudes of Garibaldi's martial career help make sense of his formidable reputation and set the scene for the patriotic sentiment that surrounded his journey to Rome in 1875.

With Italy's capture of Rome in 1870, Garibaldi's earlier reverses in 1849 and the 1860s could finally be seen as but a temporary setback in an ultimately successful story of national integration centred upon the supreme prize of Rome. Late Victorian biographers, such as J.T. Bent, could thereby offer a happy ending to the story of Italian liberation. In the upbeat words of G.M. Trevelyan, author of a famous trilogy of books on Garibaldi, Italy had not yet been 'ripe for union' at the mid-century: it needed a few more years for the endeavour to mature and bring an unhappy despotic history to its final close.[55] The year 1870 was retrospectively cast as the very goal of the entire trajectory of the Risorgimento. Garibaldi may never have 'won' Rome in person, but the birth of the state and the capital were his achievement as much if not more than any other person's. Cavour, Mazzini,

Garibaldi: here was the (un)holy trinity that had 'made' Italy. In the clichéd formulation, they became, respectively, the statesman, visionary and warrior of the nation, her Brain, Soul and Sword.[56] Yet no sooner had Italy been created and Rome established as its capital than Garibaldi's final period of political mourning began.[57] The new state was but a pale shadow of his hopes and dreams, a symbol of inactivity and passivity.[58] And he in turn became a symbol of resistance to cynicism and intrigue. In 1872, Garibaldi characteristically declared, 'Today I complete my sixty-fifth year; and though for the greater part of my life a believer in the improvement of the race, I have been embittered by the sight of so much evil and corruption in this self-styled age of Civilization.'[59]

In the 1870s, enthusiasm and admiration for Garibaldi were still immense. But he was less intent on enjoying 'Italy' from semi-retirement than in contemplating the reforms necessary to transform the existing political order and to breathe some life into a government which seemed to him unimaginative, slothful and anaemic. It was not so much, or at least not only, the precise political complexion of the regime – right or left[*] – that preoccupied him, as the sense

---

[*] The right, heirs to Cavour, were in power from 1861 to 1876. The left, combining various attenuated currents of Mazzinian republicanism and some vestiges of Garibaldian radicalism, came to power in 1876, under Depretis, but it was in fact the latter's notorious policy of shifting alliances and deals, '*trasformismo*', that was seen to characterise this period of government, rather than its reformist intent. Depretis died in 1887, but *trasformismo* endured. The most prominent political figures thereafter were Crispi and Giolitti, who held sway from 1900 to 1914, and whose liberal regime was associated with further political and financial scandal. Giolitti was once memorably described as 'Minister of the Underworld'. Some have seen *trasformismo* as a useful term to characterise the entire political history of modern Italy. Mussolini, according to such an argument, serves as the classic example of the slippery political opportunist, a master of reversal, for whom even socialism could be given over to, or reworked into, the mystic delusions of Fascism. For a concise discussion of this theme, see the article, 'trasformismo', in Ginsborg 1994.

of structural impasse, the betrayal of the ideals of his own volunteers (their political welfare remained a personal passion throughout his later years), the built-in difficulty of securing clear principles and executing decisive actions. One way Garibaldi filled his time was in dreaming of Rome's material and moral reform, not least the conquest and trans-formation of the Tiber.

Both Mazzini and Garibaldi, observes the historian Denis Mack Smith, were perhaps more naturally religious and yet more anti-clerical than was Cavour.[60] If the General used to call priests 'wolves' and 'assassins', blaming national retar-dation on clerical domination, he also made his own private accommodations with religion. His acceptance of the legit-imacy of other religions in Italy was evidence of his resist-ance to Roman Catholicism – why should the priests have a monopoly? – but it also reflected his view that the spir-itual needs of the people should be met in whatever form was best suited; and even that he himself should become a sacred symbol for this purpose. In Naples during 1860, to the annoyance of some of his own followers, Garibaldi had permitted the importation of Bibles and the construction of evangelical churches. Throughout the south, Garibaldi's popular image had become fused with Christian iconog-raphy. Invitations to attend Mass (which on occasion he accepted) were part of this complex stance. It was the Church, not religion, which he rejected. 'I am as Christian as you are,' he told the nationalist stalwarts of the Hungarian delegation in 1860, 'it is the Pope who oppresses the people, blocks Italian independence and inverts the basis of religion . . . he denies the very principle of Christianity – he is the Anti-Christ.'[61] Was it any wonder that Garibaldi was horri-fied that 'grubby' politicians could now interfere with his plans for the purification of Rome, the Campagna and the Tiber?

6 Life and Times

'[Garibaldi] was a poet, in all save literary power.'
George Macaulay Trevelyan, *Garibaldi and the Making of Italy*

In the Tiber affair, the General was not a solitary campaigner; nonetheless, the saga was rightly identified at the time as his personal crusade, an obsession, a 'sacred mission'.[1] He had made a first journey on the Tiber, in the spring of 1825, alongside his father, with whom he had travelled by barge, carrying a cargo of wine to Rome. It proved difficult to get far inland by boat and they needed to procure buffalo to help drag the vessel upstream. This in turn led to a quarrel and legal difficulties, when Giuseppe's father, believing he was being grossly overcharged by the owner of the cattle, refused to pay the sum demanded. Father and son had to wait weeks in the city for the affair to be resolved. In this interim, the young man had time to take in something of the historical patrimony of Rome. A Church official eventually settled the dispute, concluding that the visiting mariner would indeed have to pay in full for the hire of the livestock. In the 1870s, Garibaldi confided to a friend that this first encounter with Rome and the Tiber was the original stimulus to his river-diversion project.[2]

If we are to make sense of Garibaldi's latter-day Roman mission, autobiography, evidently, must play its part. Or rather, we must take note of the General's recollections of and preoccupation with his own past, and consider the degree to which these weighed upon him, later in life. Thus, alongside certain material facts about malaria and flood, Garibaldi's story must be given its due. Equally relevant were the webs of cultural fantasy surrounding the General. How could his view of himself not be affected by the continual idealisations and massive projections to which he was subjected? There was a complex two-way traffic between this man and his public, involving conscious and unconscious investments of many kinds. Nobody was more powerfully mythologised than Garibaldi. Yet he was not merely a recipient of the dreams and dreads of others; he distributed his own very liberally indeed across the screen of contemporary affairs. He saw the external world as the playing out of an inexorable drama between good and evil, and likened Italy to a violated, languishing woman; he sought to resuscitate and protect the nation's deepest values: to make her whole and virtuous again. His views on the forces of life and death at work in his motherland were often merely vague reflections of Mazzini's sentiments, but in his supremely dramatic life and arresting image, Garibaldi also shaped the collective protests, romantic gestures, febrile writings, melodramatic speeches and political yearnings of his time.

In the reminiscences of an admirer who observed him on the warpath: 'I shall never forget that day when I first saw him on his beautiful white horse . . . He reminded me of nothing so much as of our Saviour's head in the galleries – everyone said the same. I could not resist him. I went after him; thousands did likewise. He only had to show himself. We all worshipped him. We could not help it.'[3] One of his soldiers captured the attitude of so many of his followers when he declared to the French traveller Louise Colet that one saw fire in Garibaldi's eyes. His gaze 'devoured' his enemies, consumed them and crushed them.

He was apparently quite overwhelmingly wonderful company; to be with him was likened to the deepest spiritual nourishment, as personally significant as a visit from an archangel.[4]

Many men and women, Italian and foreign, were only too happy to be enchanted. An Englishwoman, Harriet Meuricoffre, resident in Naples, described the iniquities inflicted upon the population by the Bourbon rulers of the Kingdom, before lauding the General as a veritable saviour: 'I cannot tell you how it makes one's heart go out to Garibaldi, no longer merely as an embodiment of one's political principles, but as a saving angel, as a man to whom we owe the lives of our children and all that is dearest to us.'[5] To see him in the flesh was an unforgettable experience:

> I have seen today the face of Garibaldi; and now all the devotion of his friends is made as clear as day to me. You have only to look into his face, and you feel that there is, perhaps, the one man in the world in whose service you would, taking your heart in your hand, follow blindfold to death. I never altogether understood that feeling until his presence made it clear to me. It is the individual man and his personal influence that are so strong, but then it is the man exalted and sanctified, as it were, by his own single-minded devotion to and faith in a holy cause; and it is that which you see in his face, as though written in letters of light, and which carries your thoughts from him as the man, to him as the type and representative of his cause.[6]

'It is nearly impossible to describe the almost electric enthusiasm which the very name of the Dictator inspires,' declared a journalist who watched the hero's entry into Naples in 1860.[7] An English admirer who witnessed the crowds that greeted the General in the south referred to the 'Garibaldian epidemic'.[8] As another contemporary observer noted, he approximated more to the head of a new religion followed by a crowd of fanatics than to a military leader: 'The women, no less enthusiastic than the men, even brought their babies to Garibaldi so that he could bless and baptise them.' It was recognised that something quite irrational was going on, and the man's power over the people was likened to a magnetic current, as well as to a collective delirium.[9] Given the opportunity, many people found themselves sidling up to the great man, seeking to meet his eye. It was said that he occasionally resorted to the use of a 'double' to sleep in his bed, so that he could find a little uninterrupted rest elsewhere. In his final years, assistants were required to draft responses to the entreaties contained in an ever more bulging postbag. Opening the mail may have been overwhelming – while in Rome he was receiving up to four hundred letters a day[10] – but it was surely not dull. Every crank seemed to know Garibaldi's address and to play upon his notoriously warm political and moral sentiments or his passionate interests in technology. Correspondence ranged from the plea of an unhinged priest that Garibaldi act now to drive Lucifer's representative, the Pope, from Rome, to the entreaties of an overexcited boffin, who claimed to have invented a war machine that could destroy thousands of men in one flash.[11]

The General's style was self-effacing, but he was widely known to be a modest man with nothing to be modest about. When he had swapped the dictatorship of Naples for a role as an MP, he had meekly accepted the ritual of form-filling (like everyone else). Once asked to spell out his profession in the parliamentary register, he cheekily declared himself to be merely a humble farmer.[12] His sense of theatre was unforgettable. Arriving in Turin in April 1861 to take up his seat, Garibaldi had worn a red shirt, grey poncho and a sort of sombrero (such sartorial details were always striking and figured large in the literature, becoming central to his public image).[13] Some colleagues stood up to applaud; others were appalled.[14] After 1860, he was elected to eight successive parliaments, but almost invariably stayed away.[15] For the sake of his dearest causes, including the Tiber, he threw such caution to the winds, promising to enter the political theatre of plots, trade-offs and half-baked compromises that he scorned. He may have declared himself a committed socialist late in life, but he was frequently to insist on the need for the dictatorship of a single strong ruler and the transcendence of the petty, procrastinating 'talking shop' that was parliament.[16] His modesty remained a talking point: when it was suggested, in 1875, that the new canal he proposed to dig around Rome be called 'the Garibaldi', he quickly responded that it had better be named after the King, Victor Emmanuel.[17]

Garibaldi was a nationalist fighter whose achievements and personality came to symbolise far more than any single political struggle. His character and exploits were to be immortalised in dozens of publications, cartoons and monuments; he was a living legend, a figure with astonishing international allure, the man who had liberated the Bourbon South.[18] This is how the great English statesman William Gladstone, fresh from his own tour of Italy, had previously described the horrifying *ancien régime* injustices that existed in Naples:

It is not mere imperfection, not corruption in low quarters, not occasional severity that I am about to describe, it is incessant, systematic, deliberate violation of the law by the Power appointed to watch over and maintain it. It is such violation of human and written law as this, carried on for the purpose of violating every other law unwritten and eternal, human and divine; it is the wholesale persecution of virtue when united with intelligence, operating upon such a scale that entire classes may be with truth said to be its object, so that the government is in bitter and cruel, as well as utterly illegal, hostility to whatever in the nation lives and moves, and forms the

mainspring of practical progress and improvement ...
The governing power, which teaches of itself that it is
the image of God upon earth, is clothed, in the view of
the overwhelming majority of the thinking public, with
all the vices for its attributes. I have seen and heard the
strong and too true expression used, '*È la negazione di
Dio eretta a sistema di governo*' – 'This is the negation of
God erected into a system of government'.

Gladstone's condemnation of the Neapolitan regime went
together with his own growing sympathy for the cause of
Italian liberation.[19] He viewed the venal states of pre-
unification Italy as having produced an absolute inversion
of the values that any moral system worthy of the name
would hold dear. The emancipation of Naples from such
monstrosity was music to such English ears.[20]

For many of Garibaldi's Victorian admirers, mere literature chronicling the iniquities of the past and the triumphs
of the present was not enough. The demands of sexual fetish,
religious token and commercial profit were soon combined
in the purchasable Garibaldian 'relics' of the day. On his visit
to England in 1864, stories of public infatuation abounded;
tales that soapsuds from his basin were treasured may have
been apocryphal, but red shirts did a roaring trade; visitors
rushed to performances of a Garibaldi musical show and
large numbers enjoyed the various goods, including the
eponymous biscuits, that have traded upon the reputation
of the inimitable Italian. The General was overwhelmed by
letters, from bishops, princes, politicians, working men and
women, requesting his company at social events or the
endorsement of their own pet projects and beliefs. He was
given banquets at livery companies, made a freeman of the
City of London, taken to see the Crystal Palace and shown
Eton College to great applause. There were invitations from
rifle clubs and working men's associations, from lords and
ladies, and northern industrialists. And, according to the

radical *Reynold's Newspaper*, Garibaldi was 'the greatest man by whom England has ever been visited'.[21]

Many people clearly fell deeply in love with the very idea of him. During this remarkable visit, as the personal guest of the Duke of Sutherland, he met the great and the good, but Garibaldi had a classless aura, an effortless confidence *and*

Garibaldi is greeted by massive crowds in London, 1864

humility that awed people of all ranks. He was the champion of the liberal world, the living emblem of the fight for freedom. When the General appeared in London, enthusiasm reached epidemic proportions. At the Floral Hall in Covent Garden, it was reported that feverish women flew upon him, seized his hands, touched his beard, his poncho, his trousers, any part of him that they could reach. The press ecstatically recorded how the people were overwhelmed with excitement at this hugely exotic visitor. Gladstone, Florence Nightingale and the Archbishop of Canterbury all made his acquaintance. Disraeli and Queen Victoria were among the few notables not drawn into the convivial atmosphere (although some other royals were smitten). For many, he was an irresistible attraction, and a fascinating outsider.

There was still a certain aura of danger around Garibaldi, however meek his manners.

Back in Italy, his every move was tracked with considerable suspicion by an Italian regime of the right that shared little of his home-spun moral sentiments or political ideals. Much to the General's disappointment, the governments that ruled the fledgling state of Italy owed far more to Cavour (who died in 1861) than they did to his own brand of romantic nationalism or the republican radicalism of Mazzini. Garibaldi was the proverbial 'loose cannon', whose explosive potential aroused political anxiety and pleasure in equal measure. Yet Garibaldi was also forgiven a great deal by his contemporaries, even those uncomfortable with the political choices he made. For whatever the deficiencies and excesses of his arguments and allegiances, he was the steely-eyed commander who had led his ragged forces to victory over the foreign and despotic powers that had ruled and divided Italy. Many foreigners also sought to identify with him (becoming honorary Italians), or to claim him as their own – Garibaldi as a world figure, rather than a national hero. Contemporary enthusiasts from the north who got busy with genealogies and sought to redescribe him as the descendant of German ancestors, gave expression, understandably, to their emotional bond with 'the hero of two worlds', but failed to convince his Italian supporters that they had a case. One biographer who looked into the claims noted tartly that there was a dearth of evidence to support them. On the contrary, Garibaldi was, by race and by temperament, the very embodiment of an *Italian* redeemer.[22] His body and soul were indeed something to contemplate; on the General's death, his one-time comrade-in-arms, the politician Francesco Crispi, extolled Garibaldi's perfect craniological proportions and the total harmony between his physical, spiritual and moral qualities.[23]

The General has always been a receptacle for the wishful thinking of his admirers; he has been deployed to illuminate many things about human nature, character, even the unconscious workings of the mind. He could be said to dramatise the idea, now elaborately theorised by psycho-analysts, that desire is inevitably in excess of what can be realised in the world, our unconscious longings never exhausted in the fulfilment of our conscious wishes and demands. Garibaldi drew attention to this breach between 'how things are' and 'how they might be'; his presence and personality seemed to remind others of the discrepancy. He would never let anyone forget the difference between his utopian dream and his day-by-day experience of Italy; his life could be interpreted as a tantalising endeavour to close the gap or, alternatively, as a graphic demonstration of the impossibility of so doing. He embodied, in that sense, the suffering of Italian citizens (or all citizens), faced with the inadequacy of the state into which they are born.

After unification, Garibaldi spoke with horror of the murky compromises forged by the nation's politicians, the shameful treatment of his volunteer forces by the government, the degradation of Risorgimento ideals, the sordid international bargains struck in the name of Italy. In his diagnosis of contemporary Rome and his acknowledgement of a personal sense of betrayal, Garibaldi shared in a widespread perception. He struck a chord that still finds an echo in modern political and cultural discourse.[24] As the General wrote:

> The men who presided so unworthily over the destinies of Italy, and those whom we see still on their knees at the feet of overbearing potentates or of false protectors, – these men, I say, are false representatives of the nation. Italy has not deserved to be dragged through the mud, to be ignominiously made the laughing stock of Europe. Her army is intact, her volunteers are intact, and if the men who stand at the helm of affairs, at the head of her army, have the fibres of sheep – if they tremble before usurpers – I do not fear to become the interpreter of the nation. Here we tremble not; here is the conscience that fears not.[25]

Even before the great victories of 1860, Garibaldi had fought many small skirmishes and minor battles, but always with a hazy appreciation that it was for large things, even if he could not pin down the programme absolutely precisely. By comparison, the national regime that had finally emerged to run the country seemed, to so many onlookers, pathetically inadequate to the scale of that demand: it represented the most bitter letdown. It was bathos incarnate. That particular posture of dismay and ridicule was mordantly captured in a satirical account of the political elite (those proverbial 'new brooms' to sweep out the old regime) penned by the eccentric Ferdinando Petruccelli della Gattina.[26] This southern deputy did little to endear himself to his colleagues when he pointed out that the social composition of the Italian ruling class suggested a striking persistence of the old regime. The parliament's anything but plebeian ranks included two princes, three dukes, twenty-nine counts, twenty-three marquises, twenty-six barons (he himself was one), 117 knights, and so on.

To fight for this? No sooner had the new Italy opened for business than a clutch of intellectuals, artists and journalists were smitten by a certain nostalgia, a mournful and obsessive preoccupation with a lost world of idealism, linked above all to Garibaldi and Mazzini, an Italy that had been fought for and yet left unrealised.[27] Perhaps that nostalgia was inscribed in the Risorgimento from the start, only too ready to be re-evoked after the limitations of the national project had been witnessed for real. 'Disappointment' was to provide an enduring political mood and motif. Numerous pronouncements at the time turned between jeremiads on contemporary inadequacy and paeans to the prospects of a moralised and sanitised tomorrow. The vision of Italy reborn, conjured up in the writings and speeches of Mazzini or the sentimental novels and memoirs of Garibaldi, set the course and inspired the political language of those who developed the idea of nationalism in the early twentieth century. Garibaldi was neither the first nor the last to picture Italy as a funeral pyre on which the vanishing ideals of the Risorgimento were burning.

Italy was seen as humiliated. Against the embarrassment, the shame of this supposed collective reduction to a 'laughing stock', Garibaldi offered the dream of restored honour, dignity and virtue. So much was obvious. But he also entered powerfully into the subterranean fantasies of his time. For many people, Garibaldi seemed to merge into the figure of a personal loved one. He was himself the stuff of dreams. It was not only Sigmund Freud, looking on from afar, who found that the late General had invaded his own nightlife, merged with a dream of the doctor's dying father. 'Those of us who were standing round had in fact remarked how like Garibaldi my father looked on his death-bed,' recalled the author of *The Interpretation of Dreams*.[28] Although Garibaldi confessed to his own imperfection, he also offered himself up as the exemplary, fearless redeemer, a rallying point for those intent on restoring the political virtue of 'Italy'; he invited others to treat him as the point of iden-tification, a heroic ideal for the new nation: here he was, the very personification of incorruptible commitment, no 'mud' stuck to him. He wrote that his conscience was clear, his attitude defiant, his martial skills and expressions of pure love for the nation always at the service of the cause; as he defiantly insisted, 'here is the conscience that fears not'.

The need for drastic surgery to transform the ossified culture and polity of this 'sick state' was to become a refrain of Italian futurism and nationalism. In this particular regard, if not in most others, the last two *fins de siècle* have shared a certain political despondency; each in its different way has homed in on the pathology of 'Rome'. If one listens in to political discourse in the peninsula today, one can still hear expressions of gloom, and nostalgia for a lost ideal, or simply for the creation of national 'normality' (the condition often associated with neighbouring states to the north), that echo, sometimes loudly, such old laments.

Garibaldi exemplified the desire for swift, decisive action and transparency; he frequently complained about the malignancy and opacity of the old order, and the sloth and corruption of the new system that replaced it. His experience came to resonate with many other stories of bureaucratic perversity in the modern state, whose mode of functioning still owed much to the pre-unification era, when the notorious Bourbon regime ruled the south, the Pope controlled central Italy and the Hapsburg Empire held sway in much of the north. The latter was sometimes applauded for being, relatively speaking, the more rational and efficient of these polities, but whatever the differences, the notion of a systemic disorder remained fundamental in and beyond the age of Garibaldi, and he expressed, for his generation and those beyond, the profound sense of consternation at the administrative shortcomings of 'Italy'.★

Nationalism has always required personification: not only myths of the past, invented traditions, grand manifestos for

---

★ In *The Italians*, Luigi Barzini nicely captured this malaise, describing 'the bureaucrats' thus:

> As a rule they are impatient, overbearing, hurried, ignorant, indifferent to other people's problems, insolent and sometimes corrupt. There are a few, however, without whom the State apparatus would stop functioning altogether, who are intelligent and efficient. They know no better than the others what the laws are, but devise short cuts through the tangle of red tape and obsolete regulations; they keep the masses of paper slowly moving; they manage to solve some problems. There are two or three in every large bureau, who cheerfully do everybody's work. The others place their hats on the hat-stand, to prove they have not left the building, and go for walks, go home, or to another better-paid job. The few good ones are obviously not enough. Things inevitably get delayed. Claims for damage done by Garibaldi and his Redshirts to property in Sicily in 1860, for instance, were still being paid in 1954, ninety-six years later, in lire which had lost all value and meaning, to heirs who barely remembered the reason why they were entitled to receive such pitifully small sums of money. (Barzini 1968, pp. 126–7)

the future, but also its exemplary theatrical figures and charismatic heroes. Garibaldi provided an embodiment of nationalist desire, but he was also the living incarnation of disappointment, that deep and inevitable dissatisfaction necessarily attendant upon nationalism's own utopian and impossible aspirations. His appeal lay both in his strength and power (even megalomania), and also in the impotent position into which he was cast. He represented a dogged insistence on the ideal, and the chronic mourning of its loss. The nation could grieve, with the General, over the impossibility of 'Italy', that ideal nation of political fantasy and dreams, never realisable 'on the ground'. His career exemplified resistance to so-called 'realism'; but his affect often seemed to be that of the mourner. He was the antithesis of that spirit of '*me ne freghismo*' (or 'don't give a damnism') that he abhorred, and yet in the end, he also became the dramatic exemplar of all frustrated, helpless individuals, unequal to the cynicism and intricacy of the 'system'.

Despite his military achievements, Rome was always to tantalise and frustrate the General. The city loomed large in his thoughts and wishes, a holy site, even for this most anticlerical of Italians. The circumstances of his brief victories and ensuing painful defeats in the Eternal City were widely discussed and quickly written up by followers, journalists and historians. Far more than just 'foreign news', the details of his military and political exploits were pored over by many avid sympathisers in Europe, the Americas and other parts of the world as a decisive moral drama of the age.

Much was written on Garibaldi's accomplishments, but also on his unforgettable sense of occasion, his idiosyncratic mode of dress and his instinct for the telling gesture – a politics of style that became inseparable from the central events of his career. In the purple prose that has proved irresistible to so many of his chroniclers, he was always 'larger-than-life', the mesmerising master of escape and derring-do. In a later memorable recollection in *The Times*, Garibaldi was remembered as the 'mysterious conqueror', the man of 'mythical prestige', whose deeds of arms were so remarkable as to disarm even the most doubtful critic. Garibaldi, it was declared, disproved once and for all 'the old taunt that "Italians don't fight"'. Where Cavour and Mazzini's contributions to the Italian cause might perhaps be judged realistically, Garibaldi's transcended any sober assessment, appealing 'to the imagination as something unauthenticated, like William Tell – a mere undemonstrable episode – a legend'.[29]

Even within his own lifetime, Garibaldi was to gain a status usually reserved for mythical ancient champions or semi-divine heroes. He acquired a long-term influence and popularity that transcended social barriers and crossed ideological divides. While nobody could call Garibaldi a chameleon, his views were often sufficiently misty, and sometimes contradictory, as to lend themselves to extremely diverse interpretations. Given the ambiguity of his political declarations, it is perhaps not surprising that, by the twentieth century, his moral mantle was claimed by all-comers, from exponents of communism to ideologues of Fascism.[30] Crucially, he was seen as an opponent of inaction, of lethargy or of moral compromise. He was the martial idol par excellence: as the bellicose nationalist Enrico Corradini put it, 'the sword of Garibaldi and the passion of Mazzini were extolled, inspirations for militaristic young people in the twentieth century'.[31] Overseas, Garibaldi also continued to be widely admired. His biographer Jasper Ridley observes that Garibaldi achieved the rare posthumous feat, at the height of the Cold War, of appearing on postage stamps in the USA and the USSR.[32]

Garibaldi's existence had taken the form of a serpentine journey, across continents, back and forth from Italy. The basic facts have often been told – the relatively humble family background in Nice, where he was born in 1807. At that time Nice was a French city and Garibaldi was born a subject of Napoleon.[33] In 1814, Napoleon was overthrown and Nice was returned to the Kingdom of Sardinia, only to be given up to the French later on by Cavour, much to Garibaldi's disgust. The eventual 'hero of two worlds' was the third child of Domenico Antonio and Rosa Raimondo: 'My father, a sailor's son, and himself a sailor from his earliest years.' Domenico Antonio had little education although he was a moderately successful trader and owned a substantial ship, the twenty-nine-ton *Santa Reparata*, on which he would often take his sons. Garibaldi received some schooling, privately; he was taught by two priests and one layman. His first tongue was a local dialect, and he acquired in due course Italian as well as French. Later, he learned Spanish and Portuguese, and gained a grasp of English. He also developed a passionate interest in Roman history.

Giuseppe evidently adored and idealised his mother, a devout Roman Catholic. 'Of my mother, I say with pride that she might have been a model to all mothers, and I can say no more.'[34] She died in 1852 and a solitary picture of her continued to adorn his bedroom to the end of his life. He spoke of her as the Catholic faithful might speak of the Madonna. On one occasion he wrote: 'Though far from being superstitious, yet repeatedly at the most critical moments of my stormy life – when I escaped unscathed from the wild Atlantic breakers, or from the leaden hail of the battle-field – it has seemed to me that I beheld my loving mother, on bended knees before the Infinite, a supplicant for the life of her son.'[35]

The General had three brothers; a sister, Teresa, had died before he was born after a hideous accident, in 1799, at the age of two, together with her nurse. The child's bed had burst into flames, thanks to a carelessly treated candle. Other children followed,* but Teresa's death was the first of many painful

---

* The next child was a boy, Angelo, born in 1804. Giuseppe was born three years later, followed by a fourth child, Michele, in 1810 and a fifth, Felice, in 1813.

losses to befall the family in years to come. It is surely a vital key to Garibaldi's character that, in the course of his life, he faced the loss of his parents, of siblings, of his adored first wife Anita, of many friends, of three of his daughters and several of his grandchildren. His first daughter Rosa (by Anita) died in South America in 1845. He was devastated. A second, also called Rosa (this time by Francesca, who later became his third wife), died as a toddler in 1871, while Garibaldi was fighting the Prussians in France; her death, he confided to his friends, hit him extremely hard. In years to come, his grief for this lost daughter remained intense; he often walked down to her grave, under a juniper tree, off the track which led to the house at Caprera. Death and illness chronically clouded life in Garibaldi's household. His daughter Teresita (by Anita), who would eventually give birth on nine occasions, was several times faced with the death of her babies. Clelia, another of Garibaldi's daughters (by Francesca), nearly died in 1872, of a fever (whether malarial or not is unclear). In 1873, Francesca gave birth to a third child, Manlio, about whose health there were also considerable concerns. A third daughter, of whom more later, also known as Anita, died in 1875.

From childhood, Giuseppe was strikingly energetic, warm-hearted and brave. An accomplished swimmer and sailor from his early youth, he caused his parents anxiety by heading off on reckless private trips far around the coast. By 1824, he had gone to sea for a living, travelling to Odessa and the Canary Islands, and soon found himself promoted to a mate. He spent much time away from Italy, and for several years, beginning in 1828, was based in Constantinople. Meanwhile, he had had his youthful romances, and took an early amorous betrayal phlegmatically. Italy was increasingly a love object in her own right. Before long he had seized on the ideas of Italy's most influential nationalist, Giuseppe Mazzini; these chimed in with his own homespun sentimentalism, rebelliousness and iconoclasm.

A couple of years older than Garibaldi, Mazzini came

from Genoa. The birthplaces of the two 'Giuseppes' were not far removed from one another, although they were only to link up much later, at the time of European revolution in 1848–9. Their careers were often to be connected during the struggle for unification, but they were of decidedly different temperaments. Mazzini was to become, in the period from 1830 to 1870, a hugely significant, but somewhat squeamish, revolutionary – not some simple firebrand. He was to be accused of extremism where compromise was required, and vice versa. It is true that many of Europe's political radicals came to dismiss Mazzini's assertions about the need for a revived moral 'spirit' in Italy as cant, the confused ravings of a closet reactionary, but in this regard Garibaldi saw eye to eye with him. In the anarchist Bakunin's judgement, Mazzini was the last great priest of religious idealism and metaphysics,[36] and it is true that his thought was laced with romantic assumptions and dreamy spiritual aspirations. Marx was also scathing in his view of the Italian, whom he dismissed as an 'ultra-reactionary'.[37] Hated and sometimes despised as he was by such critics, Mazzini remained nonetheless an indefatigable conspirator, always at work on plans for the republican overthrow of the old order.

The son of a professor of anatomy, Mazzini had been so shocked by the experience when he attended an operation that any further thoughts of a career in medicine had soon been put aside. A sense of religious vocation – even Messianic ambition – was apparently fostered by his mother.[38] Medicine abandoned, he switched to law and joined a secret society in 1827. This clandestine organisation, known as the Carbonari, has a complex history; its style drew on Masonic rituals; its aims included self-help, comradeship and resistance to foreign rule. In the early nineteenth century, it attracted astonishing numbers of members, especially in the south. For Mazzini, membership was but a prelude to the establishment in 1831 of his own more focused and overtly nationalistic 'Young Italy' movement ('young' meant no over-forties). This new group was founded in Marseilles, where Mazzini had recently been obliged to flee.

Mazzini acquired a reputation for vacillation and depression — sometimes visitors reported how he would fall into sobbing fits — and he had a strong preference for black clothes. His more energetic or extreme supporters were occasionally dismayed by his tendency to dither and backtrack, rather than implement decisive martial plans (hardly an accusation that could be made to stick against the strong-minded Garibaldi, although even he sometimes frustrated the hotheads in his ranks by biding his time). Yet many found Mazzini impressive both as a thinker and in person. In England, Jane Carlyle clearly fell heavily under his spell, while her husband, the social critic Thomas Carlyle, looked on, increasingly askance.* The Italian's very eye was said to compel. One admirer, Felix Moscheles, who met Mazzini in London, described him thus:

> His eyes sparkled as he spoke, and reflected the ever-glowing and illuminating fire within; he held you magnetically. He would penetrate into some innermost recess of your conscience and kindle a spark where all had been darkness. Whilst under the influence of that eye, that voice, you felt as if you could leave father and mother and follow him, the elective Providence, who had come to overthrow the whole wretched fabric of falsehoods holding mankind in bondage.[39]

There was a touch of extravagance, and a broody charisma, that some found winning. He had a penchant for canaries

---

* Mazzini was highly impressed by Carlyle; the latter expressed some praise of the former, although declared that 'we soon tired of one another, and he fell mainly to her [Jane's] share' (quoted in Ashton 2001, p. 211). Jane, as a friend put it, 'was stirred as if by an electric shock when she heard Mazzini's voice in the hall, and when he came in she caressed his beard, trembling and exclaiming with tears in her eyes how grey it had grown' (quoted in ibid., p. 309).

and allowed them to fly around his room in London (where he lived for many years in exile), to the amusement or consternation of his visitors. Yet he took himself very seriously indeed. When he was briefly in charge of the Roman Republic in 1849, after the Pope had fled, critics accused him of delusions of grandeur. 'He thinks he is [the] Pope and infallible,' wrote one. Or as another observer acerbically put it: 'He is pontiff, prince, apostle, Priest . . . He has the nature of a priest more than a statesman. He wants to tether the world to his own immutable idea.'[40]

The 'prophet of Italy' wrote prolifically, although it is unclear quite how much of this literature his more plain-spoken and practical brother-in-arms, Garibaldi, waded through directly. The central ideas, repeated again and again in published declarations, clearly reached him. It was a torture, Mazzini insisted, for any 'true', native-born Italian, to endure governance by 'the caprice of eight detested masters' – that is to say, the various rulers of the patch-work states of the peninsula.[41] The very principle of monarchy was anathema to Italy, Mazzini argued. It was a system imposed in the sixteenth century, under the domination of the foreigner.[42] Garibaldi's shift from republican to loyal servant of King Victor Emmanuel II grated on the more intransigently anti-monarchist Mazzini. Nonetheless, they shared the belief that a social, political and moral revolution was required, which would take up the word of Christ, but without the constraint of orthodox religion. It was a fight of and for the soul. Mazzini appealed to his toiling compatriots and to kindred spirits across the world:

Working men! We live in an epoch similar to that of Christ. We live in the midst of a society as corrupt as that of the Roman Empire, feeling in our inmost soul the need of reanimating and transforming it and of uniting all its various members in one sole faith, beneath one sole Law, in one sole Aim, the free and progressive development of all the faculties of which God has given the germ to his creatures. We seek the kingdom of God *on Earth* as it is in Heaven, or rather, that Earth may become a preparation for Heaven, and society an endeavour after the progressive realisation of the Divine Idea.[43]

If one were to identify a single, pivotal year in Garibaldi's political education, it would undoubtedly be 1833 when he first absorbed Mazzini's ideas about Italian freedom, unification and moral renewal, following an encounter with one of his followers during a voyage to the Black Sea. By the end of the year he had joined Mazzini's Young Italy movement. Shortly before this, Garibaldi had also learned about the far-reaching economic, social and political ideas of Henri de Saint-Simon. In their different ways, as we have already seen, both Mazzini and Saint-Simon offered beguilingly optimistic blueprints of the future, extolling the virtues of comradeship and sacrifice, and powerfully challenging the shibboleths of possessive individualism.

As mate of the brig *La Clorinda*, on which some of Saint-Simon's flamboyant followers sailed to Constantinople, Garibaldi had an opportunity to observe the group at close quarters and to discuss their philosophy at some length. The colourful rituals and dramatic songs of these outlandish radicals were matched by their vivid clothes and style: they wore black boots and gloves, loose white shirts and long red gowns, and their wild uncut hair and beards flowed over the dark scarves they wrapped around their necks. As they headed for the Bosporus, Garibaldi was introduced to Saint-Simon's beliefs, his criticism of the clergy, aristocracy and monarchies of Europe, and his praise for industrial and scientific entrepreneurs. Political and social parasitism was contrasted with the virtues of honest labour and technical expertise. He also had an affinity for the quasi-mystical Saint-Simonian appeal to the benefits of human association and cooperation – the brotherhood of man.*

Garibaldi's legendary first encounter with Mazzini in 1833, when he makes his pledge to the cause of 'Young Italy'

Fired up by intoxicating social and spiritual programmes for the future of Italy, Europe and the world, and above all inspired by Mazzini's visions of securing national liberation from detested foreign rulers, Garibaldi was drawn into various clandestine revolutionary activities. Adventures followed in dizzying succession, enough to rival the plot of the most improbable Victorian pot-boiler. His participation in a dramatic, ill-fated, revolutionary plan of 1834, nominally orchestrated by Mazzini, had huge personal consequences. Garibaldi had secured a post in the Piedmontese Navy and was supposed to foment mutiny in Genoa as part of a wider republican rebellion led by Young Italy.[44] He had managed to leave his ship and to obtain shore leave by claiming to be suffering from

* On Garibaldi's death, his book collection was found to include an old copy of Saint-Simon's *Le Nouveau Christianisme*, alongside Shakespeare and Byron, Plutarch, La Fontaine, Voltaire, Humboldt and various works on ancient history. He was known to have read the great Italian poet Foscolo and to have admired the ideas of Enlightenment sages such as Voltaire, Rousseau and Beccaria (Hibbert 1987, p. 324). For details of Garibaldi's first encounter with the Saint-Simonians, see Byrne 1988. For Garibaldi's reading, see also Scirocco 2001.

venereal disease, requiring urgent treatment.[45] But while the initial ruse succeeded, the plot as a whole ended in fiasco. Under threat of arrest and the prospect of capital punishment (a sentence was duly passed *in absentia*), Garibaldi had to flee. In what became his hallmark, the escape was to prove as memorable as the action which had preceded it. His many escapades on this latest dash for safety included a surreptitious crossing of a freezing swollen river, the Varo.[46] He found temporary refuge in France and then eventually, in 1836, arrived in Latin America, under the identity of a certain Joseph Pane. Other pseudonyms followed – his best-known cover in the world of Mazzinian intrigue became 'Borel'.

Few historical figures can have been more widely travelled or variously employed than Garibaldi. Often he was driven from place to place by necessity. He had to work in order to survive, and sometimes to take whatever employment came his way. On many occasions, he was liable to arrest or death should he have stayed too long in one place. Yet voyaging was also evidently his vocation. He was not able to remain immobile for long – the endless

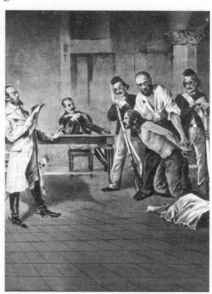

Tortured in 1837, by order of Leonardo Millán, military commander of Gualeguay, after Garibaldi refuses to name his associates

adventures, irregular occupations and shifting horizons gave expression to some deep-felt curiosity and restlessness. A sailor from his early youth, he went on to become a hospital attendant (during the Marseilles cholera outbreak of 1835), a tutor, trader, soldier, farmer, cattle drover, candlemaker, factory worker, writer, entrepreneur and politician. At one time he was based in Constantinople, at another, on the North African coast, and then for much longer in South America, where in 1837 his military career took off, the start of many adventures in the forests and waterways of Brazil, Uruguay and Argentina.[47] There were to be remarkable events on land and sea: long days of buccaneering and periods of extreme privation, the drama of a shipwreck, military and naval service for assorted political causes, half baked or not. He placed his fate 'on the line', staking everything on behalf of rebellious movements, in defiance of those giants, Brazil and Argentina, while images of the tyrannical forces that dominated and divided Italy were never far from his mind.[48] These were the years in which he fought and was captured, maltreated and tortured before being released, to fight again. In various Risorgimento images of

his early misfortunes, the Christ-like aura of his suffering at the hand of a morally inferior opponent was often emphasised.

In 1839 came the fateful meeting in Santa Caterina, Brazil, with Anita Ribeiro. Anita was to become his wife, and the mother of four of his children – one of whom died of fever at an early age.[49] She was, he declared, 'the companion of my soul'.[50] Anita had in fact already been married when Garibaldi

A portrait of Anita Garibaldi

first met her, but he was not one to be constrained by orthodox pieties. Four years earlier, Anita had wed a shoe-maker, Manuel Duarte, who turned out to be a violent and abusive drunk. In 1842, she married Garibaldi after being told that her husband had been killed (although there was, apparently, no proof of this).[51] After the loss of his first wife, he was to marry twice more, and would conduct other love affairs and liaisons,* but he revered Anita above all other partners. This woman, he later made abundantly clear, remained the great romantic love of his life. Various doting Victorian biographers implied clearly enough that a kind 'spirit' must have reigned over their stormy South American life. The intrepid young couple several times narrowly escaped death, as bullets flew past amid the Latin American bandit fights and internecine wars that contributed so much to Giuseppe's early military education.

Garibaldi brought back to Italy, from his long South American exile, the style of the gaucho. He had been away from Europe for the best part of fifteen years and had even come to describe himself as 'José Garibaldi'. He returned with extensive experience of skirmishes on land and sea,

---

* Garibaldi is known to have had several affairs in the 1850s and 60s. He did not lack for opportunity. In the autumn of 1854, for instance, a mature widow, Emma Roberts, fell in love with him. Like several other women, she became emotion-ally embroiled not only with Garibaldi but also with his children. Emma arranged education and medical advice for Garibaldi's son Ricciotti in England. In due course, Garibaldi cooled towards her and, not for the first or last time, prospec-tive marriage plans were abandoned. Garibaldi's reputation as something of a Don Juan has certainly also been embellished by legend. In the 1870s, a number of young people wrote to him, claiming him as their father. These letters became so numerous that they had to be administered by a trusted associate, Luigi Coltelletti. The correspondence remained in the possession of Coltelletti's family for half a century, before a decision was taken to destroy it. These letters were apparently burned by Coltelletti's son (who had been named, in homage to the hero, Giuseppe Garibaldi Coltelletti) and grandson (Ridley 1974, p. 598).

and a known ability to inspire his men and to improvise in the light of local circumstances. He was the very antithesis of the armchair general. As Jessie White Mario (a devoted friend) wrote some years later about the march of Garibaldi and his men through the countryside near Rome: 'He and his staff in red shirts and ponchos, with hats of every form and colour, no distinctions of rank or military accoutrements, rode on their American saddles, which when unrolled served each as a small tent.'[52] Yet tough and even ruthless as he was, Garibaldi exuded an air of puzzlement, as much the perplexed victim as the master of circumstance. In this regard, he has much in common with an earlier military man whom he admired, General Simón Bolívar. This South American soldier and statesman had spearheaded revolutions against Spanish rule, and had become the leader (in effect the dictator) of Colombia (1821–30) as well as Peru (1823–9). His vision of independence had apparently been inspired by his trip to Europe in 1804, when Napoleon dominated the Continent. Standing on Monte Sacro, contemplating Rome, and excited by the spirit of change in the Old World, he vowed to liberate his own land. Bolívar's extraordinary power and success, his restlessness and resilience in defeat, his bitterness at what he saw as betrayals by former colleagues and companions in war, his conquest of illness, love affairs and remarkable charisma bear comparison with Garibaldi's; so also do the enigmas of his private feelings, the sometimes ambiguous quality of his intentions, the mercurial aspect of his plans.[53] In each case, we encounter a man of war, who achieved remarkable, unexpected victories, but who also exuded a sense of bewilderment, always in movement, heading for an unpredictable terminus.[54]

For much of his life, Garibaldi appeared to be a man bravely committed to losing causes, the political margins and ultimate disappointment, but he was also a symbol of determination and hope, of victory 'against the odds'. With unification, the story of this long-time underdog would have to be rewritten: Garibaldi now transformed into the astonishingly successful war leader. Many came to worship him as the man of fortitude par excellence, the one who refused to take no for an answer, the dogged soldier for nationalism who could turn aspirations into events, words into deeds. He stood for the ideal of practical endeavour, moral principle in action, the will realised in worldly deed.[55] His fortitude in the face of physical and emotional assault became inseparable from the myth: the passion of a man true to himself, wounded, let down, but always indomitable. Nationalism, as we have seen, has required very specific, edifying incarnations, and Garibaldi supplied them in abundance. In his case, the heroic spirit of limitless possibility and achievement was tinged with a melancholic air, connoting a mood of disenchantment and a painful sense of incapacity that resonated with a wider cultural mood of let-down and political disappointment, after the making of 'Italy'. This double identity was to be symbolised, on the one side, by tales of his stupefying, near superhuman, escapes from death, and, on the other, by his chronic wounds and painful illnesses. He was a military giant, a man of remarkable stamina, but also a frail, struggling invalid, full of aches, pains and failing, creaky bones.

The catalogue of Garibaldi's physical suffering and injury was indeed remarkable, ranging from a wound to the neck following a skirmish with pirates, to torture at the hands of Leonard Millán, a Latin American military commander and foe; from a bullet in the thigh in the 1840s to a further serious gunshot injury in his effort to seize Rome in the 1860s. Garibaldi was struck down with malaria (probably not for the first time) during a visit to Panama in 1851. Back in Italy, he also required, in 1854, the healing properties of mud and water to deal with the recurrent excruciations of his arthritis and rheumatism.[56]

One has only to turn to his biographers to see how his character and ordeals have attracted such varied writers and compelled so many historians, long after his Victorian heyday. If he is always somewhat idealised, he also comes across, inevitably, as a puzzle, each new author embellishing as well as probing the sometimes two-dimensional figure of nineteenth-century legend.[57] When one also considers his dramatic defence of the Roman Republic in 1849, together with a succession of escapades around the globe in the long years of exile – itineraries of escape, trade or sheer adventure that took him to China, Peru and Australia – it is easy to see how overwhelmingly epic his life story had become, even before his decisive contribution to the creation of a unified Italy in 1860, when Garibaldi and 'the thousand' – his improbable volunteer army – seized the military and political initiative. Famously, he sailed for Sicily, overcame larger forces and took possession of the entire south. These events were to provide defining images and narratives in the story of Italian unification.

A round of battles in the north and the south brought the modern state into being between 1859 and 1861, but it was still devoid of certain key territories, most notably the cities of Rome and Venice. Garibaldi was not alone in believing their inclusion to be indispensable to the moral and political viability of any true Italian state. Venice, controlled by Austria, was captured in 1866; but Rome, still directly ruled by the Pope, remained the crucial object of desire not only for Garibaldi but for many fellow activists and writers. Rome was finally inaugurated as the new capital in July 1871. The King established court at the Quirinal – formerly the Pope's residence. In November, the first full Italian parliament began work in Rome.[58] The Vatican commanded the faithful to reject Italian elections and parties since this would effectively sanction the new, unacceptable political reality; in fact, the strictures of the high command were not always obeyed. Even within the ranks of the cardinals there were many shades of opinion on the question of whether it would be best to negotiate seriously with the

new authorities.[59] Although a law of guarantees to assure
the Pope's role as reigning monarch in the Vatican was established, it was not until 1929 and the Lateran Pacts that the
relationship between Church and state was really clarified,
and the papacy made its peace with Italy.

General Garibaldi's struggle to capture and transform the
Eternal City was cast as a struggle of good against evil. His
descriptions of the city's importance drew heavily on religious imagery, despite his anti-clerical intentions. In the
script of this supposedly secular drama, the prelates were
presented as akin to workers of the Devil. In this heated
atmosphere, the politics of land reform, urban regeneration
and malariology were to become remarkably fused with the
lofty ideals, spiritual yearnings and demonology that ran
through the General's own political and social thought. But
in venturing to move the Tiber in 1875, Garibaldi may also
have been mindful of a more personal disaster. In seeking
new legislation for Rome's regeneration, he was, very likely,
seeking not only to repair the national past, but also to
retrace, redeem and perhaps recover from a traumatic
moment in his own history – namely, the harsh, fever-ridden
march through the Campagna, into which he had been
forced in 1849. It was an experience more often recounted
by the General and his followers in biblical terms than as a
piece of national history. It became, in Garibaldian legend,
a defining journey of the soul. And at the centre of this
personal trial lay the drawn-out suffering of Anita Garibaldi.

7 Via Crucis

> 'What street in Rome, what ancient ruin, what one place where
> man had standing-room, what fallen stone was there, unstained
> with one or another kind of guilt!'
>
> Nathaniel Hawthorne, *The Marble Faun*

Having fled the Eternal City in 1849, amid revolutionary turmoil, the Pope had taken temporary refuge in the south, at Gaeta. He then called on loyal Catholic powers to come to his aid and restore his temporal authority in Rome. This appeal did not go unheeded, and several foreign contingents were sent to topple the regime led by Mazzini and his allies, that had been set up in place of the papacy. Despite Mazzini and Garibaldi's best endeavours, the republic's days were to prove strictly numbered. In the course of the battle to hold Rome, Garibaldi saw some of his men die, including close companions. It proved a decidedly unequal struggle. Among those who fell was Garibaldi's black attendant, Andrea Jaguyar, who had travelled back from South America with him, and of whom he had been very fond. French troops came ever closer to overwhelming his battered and exhausted stalwarts, making their last stand on the Gianicolo. With the end in sight, the General rushed dramatically to the assembly, advised his dismayed colleagues that military retreat was the only viable option and was given permission to pursue the struggle from the provinces. He rejected an offer from the American ambassador of safe passage into exile by ship. Mazzini, on the other hand, did escape by this means, slipping away in July, with a false passport, under the name of George Moore, eventually reaching England, via Marseilles. Garibaldi and his wife Anita, by then perhaps six months pregnant, chose to flee under their own auspices, by land, accompanied by the remnants of the republic's volunteer army.

The General gathered his ragtag supporters in front of St Peter's, in preparation for this exodus. Estimates of number have varied; some spoke of two, others of five or even ten thousand men preparing to leave with him.[1] One day, Garibaldi insisted, they would return in triumph, but for now the only choice was to run. The Eternal City, he insisted again, would always be engraved in patriot hearts – no matter how long they waited, nor how far they travelled, Rome would arouse their deepest love.[2] With such sentiments, Garibaldi sought to console his disappointed followers. They left the city in the evening by the Porta San Giovanni and took the Via Tiburtina. Garibaldi was on horseback, at the head of thirty cavalry men. Behind them a column of soldiers on foot stretched back several kilometres. The General may have thought to carry on the battle from the countryside near Rome, regrouping his forces and then reigniting the dying embers of revolution in a guerrilla campaign. But the state of his troops and the power of his opponents made it increasingly obvious that this was not possible and gradually, as the arduous march continued, the numbers of men with him declined. Soldiers broke off from the main party in small groups, making their own way home, if they were able to evade the extensive network of hunters who were now prowling after them.

The pace that Garibaldi set was ferocious and his course, characteristically, was a confusing zigzag, designed to put his pursuers off the scent. The ultimate destination was to be the Adriatic coast, although this was by no means clear at the start. The General often worked around two sides of a triangle. For some time, he travelled up the Tiber valley, negotiating some grim marshlands. He was tracked by forces that were far superior in number: at the height of the chase, many thousands of soldiers, from the French, Neapolitan, Austrian and Spanish armies were involved. A couple of thousand more, provided by the Duke of Tuscany, added to the pressure.[3]

At times attacked, at others aided by local people, they could not afford to stop for long as they moved across the inhospitable terrain. After the apparent wavering of their course, and in the face of sometimes hostile peasants, they had set a route towards the Adriatic. Near Orvieto they had to thread their way through a particularly nasty maze of dykes, bogs and canals. A modern enthusiast who has followed the itinerary on foot, from Tivoli through Terni, Todi, Orvieto, Montepulciano and Arezzo to San Marino, testifies to the extraordinary speed of that fraught retreat, and the remarkable physical stamina that must have been involved.[4] In the later stages of the journey, Garibaldi indicated that he wanted to join Daniel Manin, leader of the Venetian Republic, who was now engaged in his own desperate rearguard action against the resurgent Austrians. Repeatedly, the General was to discover that there was no way through, by land or sea. Venice finally fell on 22 August 1849.

It seemed as though Garibaldi relished the extremity of the choice that had been forced upon his supporters. From the outset, he had promised them much hardship ahead, a vale of tears. Those who accompanied him on the march were offered no pay, no provisions and little rest. He had openly warned his men that they faced hunger, heat and cold, battles, perhaps even death. The warning was not unrealistic. Later, he spoke scornfully of those who would prove unequal to the task, and with bitterness harked back to the lack of enthusiasm among the general population and the sometimes blind opposition of the peasants. Words such as 'hermaphrodites', 'effeminates' and 'degenerates' occasionally seasoned his speeches and reminiscences, and were used to characterise those who had not been willing to make the necessary sacrifices for the greater good.[5] A few deserters from the column, who were caught before making their escape, were shot apparently by direct order of Garibaldi.

That Anita was with him at all during this painful journey was not of the General's making. He had tried to dissuade her from coming to Rome in the first place. Now in retreat, he urged her not to accompany him further but somehow to make her own way back to Nice, where their children had been left with Garibaldi's family. Anita was a seasoned campaigner, fiercely anti-clerical in sentiment, and no stranger to wartime privation and danger; her insistence on staying with her husband and the republican army carried the day. She had asked a woman to cut back her hair, before putting on men's clothes and climbing into the saddle.[6] Dramatic illustrations of the Garibaldis' hard ride, their winding route along the remote tracks of central Italy, with the General on his white horse, Anita on a light bay, would soon proliferate.

Anita was faced not only with an advanced state of pregnancy, and the harsh conditions of the trek, but also with fever, almost certainly malaria.[7] She was not the only one – troops on both sides of the Roman conflict had been much afflicted (as they would be again at the time of Garibaldi's victorious march from Sicily to Naples in the summer of 1860). Growing weaker and more depleted by the day, defiant of danger, but broken by illness, Anita's situation became critical. A house in the main square of one of the settlements that they passed through bears a plaque; here, it says, Anita rested on 6 July 1849: 'together with the throb of maternity there beat the heroic heart, the dream of Rome and perhaps like a sunset light there came to her the Annunciation of Death.'[8] One of the General's followers and biographers, Enrico Emilio Ximenes, described the couple's flight from Rome as their Via Crucis. Their searing course would indeed involve the most terrible sufferings; there was to be desperate thirst, fever, hunger, danger and death. A number of men, split off from Garibaldi's party, were caught by the Austrians and shot, among them an important follower, Ugo Bassi, who was cruelly imprisoned before being executed, a new martyr to the cause, whose tale would later loom large in the culture of the Risorgimento.[9] Another supporter, Colonel Forbes, who had a separate substantial group of soldiers under his own command, marched north with the General only to be captured at the eleventh hour of the adventure, subsequently to be released after discreet negotiations with the British authorities.[10] Forbes was an outlandish old Etonian, ex-Coldstream Guards officer, who had a predilection for thin cotton suits and who wore a 'white chimney-pot hat'.[11] He and his Italian wife had settled in Tuscany where he had become an increasingly passionate advocate of the Risorgimento. Forbes had fought in both the north and south of Italy on behalf of the nationalist cause before coming to the aid of the Roman Republic and then taking flight with the General.

The exhausted fugitives had used obscure paths to evade the Austrians in a final covert push to the coast. The men had tried to help Anita as best they could, but it had proved impossible to make her comfortable. At Cesenatico, a small port on the Adriatic, Garibaldi attacked and rounded up a group of Austrian soldiers. In the hope of reaching Venice, he then succeeded in taking command of some boats belonging to local fishermen. Storms gathered, and it proved unrealistic at first to reach the open sea. Drinking water was by now in very short supply and all were stricken with appalling thirst. When they could, they sailed for hours on end, tracking along the coast. On the first night, the sky was clear and they discovered that they were close up against a group of Austrian ships. By this point they were only some eighty kilometres from Venice but, faced once again with the enemy, they had no choice but to head back for the shore. Many were captured as they tried to reach the sand-banks and eight of their boats fell into Austrian hands. The sailors of three other vessels (including one boat containing Garibaldi and his wife) did manage to disembark their crew on the shore of a lagoon island, Comacchio. The unwilling fishermen, whose boats had been commandeered, were only too keen to be rid of their highly risky human cargo. The General (with Anita prostrate in his arms) was forced to wade through the shallow waters. All plans of sailing to Venice were now abandoned. Lightly disguised as peasants and with a donkey somehow procured to carry Anita, they made their way through a field of maize and succeeded in reaching a house, where sympathisers were able to offer the desperate patient a bed. She was carried into a farmhouse, but nothing could be done, despite the arrival of a local doctor.

Garibaldi and a companion carry the ailing Anita ashore

In his *Autobiography*, Garibaldi describes the frantic march across country and the horrific sea journey — a deadly cat-and-mouse saga — with which generations of Italian school-children have been made familiar.[12] In fact, he owed his survival as much to the generosity of local sympathisers, and a fortuitous meeting with some followers of Mazzini, whose secret organisation was able, finally, to help spirit him away, as to his own remarkable fortitude and will. At several times during the chase that preceded his eventual escape, the Austrians had come very close to taking him prisoner. At San Marino, for instance, he had been temporarily encircled but still managed to slip away from his pursuers at night, with a company by then reduced to perhaps just two hundred men. Anita had fiercely defended her right to continue the ordeal alongside him, and dismissed – as did he – suggestions from his allies in those final days that she stay behind: either way her fate became perilous in the extreme. She was desperate not to be abandoned as they were temporarily trapped in San Marino in the farmhouse, suspecting that this was exactly what was being planned: '*tu vuoi lasciarmi*' ('you want to leave me'), she is reported to have said to her husband as hope faded, although how far this was directly intended as a cutting reproach, we do not know.[13] Garibaldi himself later recalled the words, and the extreme painfulness of the occasion, but confined his interpretations to his own anguished state of mind, and not his wife's despairing thoughts.

By the last excruciating days of their journey, nobody, except perhaps Garibaldi, held out any real hope of her survival. Anita's decline had been evident enough for all to see. She had become increasingly weak and pale, racked with fever and pain. As she sank ever further, she poignantly anticipated her own death, asking her husband to remember her kindly to their children. As the end came, Garibaldi sat in silence, his eyes hidden by his hands. When he finally stirred it was to mutter, 'What will I say to my children when they ask for their mother?'[14]

When Garibaldi laid her on the bed and looked into her face, he knew that she was dead. He felt her pulse but the veins in her wrist were still. He knelt down and suddenly burst into tears.

For a long time he knelt by her body, unable to control his sobbing, close to hysteria. 'No! No! She isn't dead,' he protested, 'it is just another fit. She has suffered so much, but she will recover. She isn't dead. Anita! Anita! It is impossible. Look at me, Anita! Look at me! Speak to me! Oh, Anita, what have I lost!'[15]

Later, in the company of his admirer and editor Alexandre Dumas, he would recall these last desperate moments with his wife: 'I drew in with my lips her trembling sigh, I kissed alas! Dying lips; alas! I strained a corpse to my breast, and I wept the tears of despair.'[16] Even after the doctor had pronounced her dead, he was to be seen frenziedly kissing her, leaving the room to escape, but then returning, distraught, unable to accept her parting.[17] Finally he went away, utterly bereft.

After Garibaldi's departure, Anita's body was superficially and hastily buried in the dunes by friends. They were fearful for their lives and had little time for ceremony. The corpse

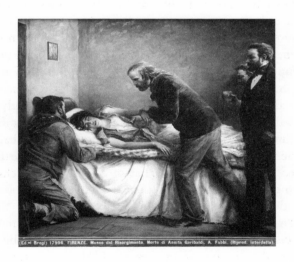

The death of Anita Garibaldi, by Fabio Fabbi

141

was soon discovered by children playing on the coast; apparently they saw a hand poking through the sand. These unusual events were drily reported back to police headquarters in Ravenna on 12 August 1849.

There was trouble over offering Anita a Christian burial; variants on the story later circulated among the *garibaldini*, and their opponents. Not only was Anita politically suspect, but gossip had it she might be Jewish.[18] Other rumours cast her as a whore (although among the General's supporters she was soon described as an angel).[19] Before long, the cadaver was disinterred from the sand, and burial finally agreed, after a bishop quashed the hesitations of more lowly priests and allowed that she be accepted at a local cemetery.[20] Suspicions and apocryphal stories abounded. Some figures in authority apparently suspected the woman had been suffocated, perhaps even by Garibaldi himself.[21] But the General's followers and biographers knew this was quite inconceivable, and spoke to one another of his anguish, before and after her death.

Be that as it may, Garibaldi was not prostrated for long. Had he been, he could not have survived at all. To avoid certain capture, he had no choice but to leave in a hurry, for the Pope's proxies were still in pursuit. There had been nothing he could do to save her, nor to spare himself, after her final departure, from the guilt of his own inevitable 'desertion'.[22] Keeping a very low profile, the fugitive trekked on, fording rivers, climbing mountains, hiding out in the hills and backwoods of Italy,* before reaching France, from where he travelled to Tunis and, eventually, in 1850, to New York, the start of a new period of exile.

Four years later – after further extensive journeys, including to Panama, Peru and China – he was able to return to Italy where he engaged in new rounds of political discussion with leading figures in the nation-building endeavour (not least with Cavour, whom he met on more than one occasion) as well as in subterranean plotting. In

September 1859, he went back to the church cemetery near the Adriatic Coast where his wife was buried, accompanied by his teenage daughter and son, Teresita and Menotti, and some close friends and supporters, intent on moving her remains closer to home. Garibaldi spoke briefly to an awed local audience, before leading a procession to the little church where his wife's black and gold coffin had been placed on the altar, surrounded by candles. When the priest referred to Garibaldi as 'Your Excellency', the General cut him off severely. Otherwise he stood dead still, lost in his own thoughts, oblivious to the watching crowd. Understandably, people were moved by his dignity and quiet emotion; for a time, he rested his head on the coffin. On leaving, he obliged the anxious priest to take some money for the poor. The coffin was then laboriously transported to Nice, where it would stay until 1932, when Mussolini arranged for the remains to be brought back to Rome.[†]

How precisely those memories of his men's suffering on this long cross-country march, and in particular his wife's torments and death, came back to haunt Garibaldi in the Eternal City in the 1870s, we cannot be sure. But no doubt the intensity of his commitment to Rome in later life, and,

---

[*] His route took him via Prato to Colli Val D'Elsa, through the Maremma, to the coast. From there, he managed to reach the island of Elba, and eventually gained safe passage to Nice. Here he would meet his elderly mother for the last time. All of this was unknown to the public. Rumours still circulated that he had managed to reach Venice with Anita. Garibaldi had the greatest difficulty in confronting his children with the sad truth of their mother's death. The meeting was all too brief, and he had to flee again.

[†] In a piece of spectacular, funeral theatre, directed by Mussolini, and aimed at reviving the cult of Garibaldi, Anita's remains were removed from their resting place and reburied on the Gianicolo. The ceremony was designed by Il Duce to coincide with the fiftieth anniversary of Garibaldi's death (Valerio 2001).

in particular, his last-ditch stand to divert the flood-prone and fever-inducing river once and for all, regardless of cost or difficulty, bore some relationship to his enduringly painful feelings about the entire, cruel retreat that had culminated in Anita's untimely death.

Garibaldi during a banquet at the Mausoleum of Augustus, Rome, 1875

At a public ceremony in Rome in the Mausoleum of Augustus, on 15 February 1875, Garibaldi was reminded of this most painful episode, but his reaction is unknown. He was handed a battered old felt hat retrieved by a loyal follower – a sculptor called Luini – many years earlier. Luini had apparently preserved it, aware that it was the very same one that the General had lost in the Campagna's swamps in 1849. The presentation of the hat occurred at a banquet prepared in Garibaldi's honour by the Society of Couriers, Cooks and Waiters, of which he was honorary president. In a speech delivered after the feast, he attacked the papacy, declaring that it had once been a great agent of civilisation but was now a force for death. On this occasion he urged Italian working men to emulate English steadiness of purpose. *The Times* reported his remarks warmly, noting particularly his comparison of ancient Romans with modern Victorians.[23]

To be incapable of saving Anita, despite his indomitable will and formidable energies, was never an easy thought for the General to bear. Of his love and grief at that time, and of his suffering thereafter, there can be no doubt. The death of his wife struck him a terrible blow. Indeed, her loss was always cast by Garibaldi and his biographers as the most devastating personal misfortune he endured, even as the defining tragedy of his life. Some said that he was never the same again.

At points, Garibaldi appeared intent on disavowing any guilt and projected all of his attacks upon those 'villains' he could fight in war or denounce in print; at others, he seemed racked by remorse and appeared desperate to put his own past wrongs to right. He more than once hinted that his 'character' was not a happy one, even drawing attention to a depressive aspect of his own personality.[24] Throughout his life, he celebrated the virtues of heroism and the noble aspirations of political liberation, and yet he also presented himself on some occasions as personally inconsolable, as though he had never found or at least had lost irretrievably some vital 'good'. One way to explore such a question is to focus upon the 'trauma' of experience; another is to ask how far such experience is itself coloured by and complicated by our psychological attitude. How far, in other words, might we differentiate here a work of mourning from the intractable complaints of melancholia?[25]

The fluctuations of emotional attitude described in Garibaldi's writings and expressed in his actions invite our psychological speculation, just as they aroused intense interest, curiosity and sympathy among his contemporaries. The picture of Garibaldi's deep and enduring struggles with loss and misfortune became central to his own self-depiction, to later political legend and to the cultural legacy of the Risorgimento. That the General found so little solace or contentment in old age, despite his weighty achievements, has become a crucial aspect of his public story. One of Garibaldi's early biographers, Giuseppe Guerzoni, remarked how sad it was to have to chronicle his final ten or fifteen years of life, in which he was so diminished in power and so haunted by regrets and self-reproaches. In 1875, Guerzoni adds, Garibaldi 'was almost crucified' by the thought of not having done enough for his cause, and particularly for Rome.[26]

We could speculate further, no doubt, about his wish to revisit, evade or overcome the cruelty and violence of the past. What was the nature of this deeper remorse and rage that shadowed him, as a leader in war and in peace? How far did he chronically suffer the pain of the survivor, with all of its potential, attendant guilt? Did he perhaps hope somehow – miraculously – to obliterate his own self-recriminations, or, in the face of the impossibility of a perfect 'reparation', did he feel an unconscious need, masochistically, to re-enact various components of these earlier setbacks and mortifications already endured? Was there not, at least, striking evidence of an obsession with the redemption of the 'holy city' that led him to make the most dubious military and political decisions? Some people were indeed puzzled by his indifferent refusal to heed his own tactical acumen, the storehouse of his prior experience, and wondered how he became embroiled, before and after 1870, in a self-defeating pursuit of an impossibly elusive 'Rome'.

To be sure, he was egged on to action, during the 1860s, in pursuit of the capture of this prized possession, by the new Italian government, and by his own cronies, only to see political support melt away when the going got rough. But that is not all. It seemed that however 'down to earth' Garibaldi sought to be, an obsessional factor continually interfered with his judgement, and partially fashioned his actions. Running through his speeches, writings and gestures was evidence of intense political and moral commitment, but also of more mysterious, undisclosed passions and nostalgia – a chronic yearning for another more innocent time. Set against such an imagined place or moment, in the past or future, lay the unhappy experience of the present, full of discontent and frustration. Garibaldi radiated sadness and anger about the real Italy that fell so far short of the ideal. He occasionally confided to others the thought that he would have to resign himself for ever to a certain level of gloom and dissatisfaction. Explaining to the father of his lover Countess Raimondi, in 1859, why marriage would be difficult for him, he made reference to his advancing years, but also to his 'natural' tendency to melancholia.★[27] 'I become daily more sceptical and misanthropic,' he observed of himself in 1873.[28]

Historical evidence of the government's failings and incapacities, or scrutiny of the appalling state of health and hygiene in the Eternal City and the Campagna, or, again, explorations of cultural representations at the time, in part explains the reason for Garibaldi's mission to regenerate the capital in 1875. But such forms of evidence cannot provide a full answer to the question posed at the start of this book: what prompted Garibaldi to take the extraordinary action that he did? Again and again, something in his 'story' defies obvious logic, drawing us back to the enigma of his private emotions.

In speeches and novels, Garibaldi provided ferociously moralistic images of good and evil: pure 'red shirts' on the one side, black cockroaches (priests) on the other. His popular yarns and considered historical accounts divide Italy

---

★ Unfortunately, as it turned out, that disastrous second marriage went ahead anyway for reasons nobody has ever quite understood. He spent years seeking a divorce. Could it be, perhaps, that the very name of this unlikely second spouse whose charms briefly enthralled Garibaldi, and whose sexual adventures with other men so appalled him, contributed to the difficulty? The Countess had shared, almost to the letter, his mother's maiden name.

into the pure and the impure; good men and women on one side, sullied whores, pimps and lackeys on the other. There seemed little room for the ordinary muddle, for recognition of the mixture of good and bad elements that might exist in the same person, institution or system of belief. In part this no doubt also reflected the genre in which he was, knowingly, writing or speaking – his speeches were designed to stir his followers; his novels provided required 'Gothic' elements of sensationalism, mystery and melodrama. Yet the overwrought depictions articulated more than just convention. On every occasion, he sharply contrasted his perfectly righteous fighters with morally 'stunted' enemies; he idealised the patriot, while denouncing the ineptitude and cowardice of those who set their faces against his missions. The corruption of Rome and Italy was presented as akin to a noxious swamp to be drained away: metaphors of unspeakable putrescence, sexual depravity, feverish illnesses and fetid marshes made their appearance.

For the historian to pursue such lines of thought through the hinterland of Garibaldi's obsession cannot but lead into a thicket of uncertainties. To be sure, the various published commentaries offer evidence enough of the conflicting attitudes that Rome provoked in him. His preoccupation with moral and physical purification is clear from the record. As chroniclers, we may well take note of the excesses of his behaviour, ponder the secret passions of his ardent speeches and track his actions and utterances, to see how they sometimes contradicted themselves, on occasion running *against* the grain of the ideology and cultural beliefs he overtly espoused. His concern with Rome, the Tiber and the Campagna expressed social and political concerns, but also exceeded any realistic 'agenda' for material change. To note the urgency, instability and personal idiosyncrasy of his 'project' is not to have plumbed its full depth.

Alongside the personal story of the General and his desperate quest, we must consider the biography of Rome. Thus, the widely remarked charismatic power of the city and the complex psychology and mythology of its would-be liberator require close scrutiny. Neither set of questions can be left out of consideration in explaining why Garibaldi sought to move the Tiber and regenerate Rome. Cultural history often risks bypassing, unsatisfactorily, such 'interior' biographical questions altogether, while psychoanalytical approaches to history have often been accused, rightly, of sounding too sure about the unconscious motivations of the dead, sometimes telling us more about the interpreter's beliefs, or imagination, than about plausible worlds in the past.[29] Alert, if possible, to these twin risks, we need to see how far the explanatory force of 'culture' and 'depth psychology' may take us, while also noting the difficulty, in the present case, of separating out the two.

Garibaldi's aims and actions must be placed in social, political and cultural context before we can begin to ask what enigma of the individual remains to be explained, or to be accepted as inexplicable. How far were Garibaldi's infatuations also commonplace attitudes and feelings of his time? Two other illustrious visitors to Rome, Goethe and Henry James, both famously observed that the Eternal City could never be seen or experienced entirely afresh, not even by the greatest writers, the most individualistic travellers. They spoke, with a hint of regret, about this uncanny cultural familiarity of the city, even on first viewing. However far the newcomer strained to avoid received opinion and cliché, it was never entirely a personal encounter. Even upon first arrival, the city was always already 'there', half 'known' beforehand, shaping a pattern of response. The desire to be original was itself driven by an 'anxiety of influence'. For each new 'take' on Rome could not but be mediated, in one way or another, by the weight of familiar evocations. In evidence everywhere were images and narratives of this classical site; a web of writings and pictures, constituting as well as reflecting the significance of this extraordinary place, and sealing its very particular associations with death and desire.

8 Rome Desired

'Now let us, by a flight of imagination, suppose that Rome is not a human habitation but a psychical entity with a similarly long and copious past – an entity, that is to say, in which nothing that has once come into existence will have passed away and all the earlier phases of development continue to exist alongside the latest one.'

Sigmund Freud, *Civilization and its Discontents*

For Garibaldi, 'Accursed is the Roman who does not feel the degradation of his country, and who is not willing to bathe his sword in the blood of these monsters, who humiliate it, and turn its very soil into a sink.'[1] In his moral world, heroes vied with villains, liberators with despots, free spirits with self-imprisoned subjects, and he considered his own life and the fate of his associates in these terms. While acknowledging that in his history 'good and evil have been mixed, as I suppose they have been in the lives of most men', he often contradicted precisely this 'warts and all' view of himself and of Italy. Instead, he was drawn to endorse an extremely split representation of the world and a partial picture of himself: no bad thought, it seemed, belonged to him, no good thought to his enemies. He introduced his *Autobiography* thus:

I can conscientiously say that I have always sought to act

rightly, both in fulfilling my own personal duty and in seeking the good of others. Any wrong I may have done has most certainly been unintentional. I have ever been the sworn foe of tyranny and falsehood, being firmly persuaded that these are the source of all human misery and corruption.[2]

He was frequently dismayed by the lack of national sentiment that he detected in his compatriots, and sought to kindle in others the same passion that burned in him. He hoped to find a love of Italy lying, as it were, dormant in the souls of the inhabitants of the peninsula, and merely requiring to be awoken. Garibaldi energetically sought such an awakening, through his actions, declarations and stories. He presented contemporary degradation against the stark backdrop of grander, nobler times in the past. He reminded Italians that their true destiny was to liberate their motherland. On the one side, he depicted a disgustingly craven present-day reality, an Italy marred by sleaze, and on the other, the purified nation that would be created by heroes and martyrs. Physical and moral decline become inextricably linked in his writing and systematically contrasted with the potential purity of the future nation. He protested against the cynicism that infected the politicians, Cavour foremost among them, and against the corruption that ran through the Roman Church.

Garibaldi conceived his actions and beliefs as motivated above all by the moral imperative to reverse the dissoluteness and decay for which he held the papacy deeply responsible. Italy was imagined as the violated 'good' body and personified as a woman betrayed.[3] In the sexualised imagery so often found in Garibaldi's own novels, and more widely in the writing of the Risorgimento, Rome was likened to a female victim of a cruel tyrant. Garibaldi even declared the Church to be worse than a pimp: it spoke of moral purity but conducted abominable orgies. He used images of priestly carnality and violence to bring home to the reader the Church's fundamental moral hypocrisy. There are many instances of such sexual–political depictions in his work. Take his novel *Cantoni il volontario*, in which the heroine Ida is captured and her body threatened by vile priestly assault. The 'cannibalistic' priest prepares to rape her, but she is saved, just in time, with the aid of a dagger hidden in her clothes and the ministrations of some true Italian heroes. This story resonated with other more illustrious tales of his time, and of the imminent *fin de siècle*. Recall here the sexual '*prezzo*' demanded by the villainous police chief Scarpia in Puccini's opera *Tosca* (itself modelled on the popular drama set in the Eternal City by Sardou) and the heroine's dramatic and finally suicidal resistance.★

Rome's supposed femininity was itself seen in various ways, for instance as alluringly warm, provocative or deadly. Could her original virtue and sanctity be restored? Nobody was sure, but the image of Rome as a body and the idea that the city had undergone a profound moral fall were widely explored; the fervour of the wish to restore 'her' was not in question. This perception is nicely captured in a story by Matilde Serao, *The Conquest of Rome*, published in 1885. Serao conveys, through the eyes of a first-time visitor, an inexperienced

★ Victorien Sardou's five-act play, *La Tosca*, was first performed in 1887. Sarah Bernhardt played the part of the eponymous heroine, who was presented as something of a royalist, but regarded as scarcely better than a Jacobin by the ultra-conservative Church authorities in Rome. The action was set in Rome in 1800; French Enlightenment and Italian religious obscurantism were placed in dramatic conflict. Tosca's beloved, Cavaradossi, was linked to Parisian thought and art, and described as an ex-pupil of the French painter David. His father was said to have kept company with the *encyclopédistes*, while his mother was related to Helvétius. Angelotti was described as having languished for three years in prison in Naples for the crime of possessing a book by Voltaire. Scarpia, the evil tormentor of Tosca, was portrayed as a pitiless Sicilian, prone to hypocrisy and a frequent debaucher of women.

southern Italian politician, Francesco Sangiorgio, Rome's rich promises. She records his voluptuous anticipation of entry into the Eternal City and the ensuing disappointment. First, the optimistic young man must cross the Campagna. Despite passing through that 'imperial desert ungraced by any tree, undarkened by any shadow of man, untraversed by any flight of bird', the name of Rome still sounds intimate and sensual, beckoning him from the distance: 'The name was short and sweet, like one of those flexible names of women which are one of the secrets of their seductions, and he twisted it about in his mind in queer patterns, in contorted curves.'[4]

Sangiorgio has not yet known Rome; he arrives with a powerful abstract conception, the city 'as a huge, strange vision, as a great fluctuating thing, as a fine thought, as an ideal apparition, as a vast shape with shadowy outlines'. He is overcome by 'a tumult of fantasies, a crowded jumble of imaginations and conceits'.[5] Desirous of Rome, casting it in a series of alluring feminine forms, '[h]e seemed to hear, through the night, a woman's voice uttering his name with irresistible tenderness, and a voluptuous shudder ran over him'. The man feels he is hastening to Rome, 'like a lover to his lady'.[6] He sees the city in his mind's eye, 'stretching out maternal arms to clasp him in a strenuous embrace'. The capital demands his obedience, compels his purity and purpose. 'Sacred as a priestess, mother, bride, Rome must have expiations and sacrifices, must have a heart unalloyed and a will of iron!'[7] The story shows it to be otherwise. Purity is in singularly short supply. Rome is marked by 'the fever-tainted breath which seems to be emitted by the houses'.[8] Instead of the city of the man's dreamy hopes, the novel explores a stifling and morbid reality. This is the 'sentimental education' that Rome appears to offer up: 'a heavy oppression sank down upon his breast, upon his soul; he must have taken a fever in the bogs of the Coliseum and the Baths, in the tepid humidity of the Churches'.[9]

It should be no surprise perhaps that the language of the

body and the image of its martyrdom played so prominent a part in such representations of the new Rome. The endeavour to transform the material environment coalesced with ideas about the secular salvation of 'the people', their moral emancipation from the Church, vice and illness. Souls and bodies were at stake. An array of nineteenth-century ideas about 'the social organism' and various fashionable analogies between physiology and society within the 'body politic' lurked in the background, but neither Mazzini nor Garibaldi troubled themselves much with the details of the latest European scientific theories of progress, evolution and degeneration. They spoke at an altogether more elevated patriotic and spiritual level. Nonetheless, images of individual health and collective hygiene were drawn into these soaring flights of rhetoric and ambition for 'Italy' that such nationalists provided. The moral and physical restoration of Rome became the central reference point of their political endeavour. To salvage the city was, apparently, to reclaim, personally and poignantly, the most vital love object, to see her 'unsullied' once again. 'I worshipped, with all the fervour of a lover,' was how Garibaldi summarised his relationship to the 'mistress' that was Rome.

These Italian nationalists were not, of course, alone in their adoration of Rome and their detestation of its current, degraded reality. The 'Mediterranean passions' of many nineteenth-century writers found their most acute expression in the Eternal City. This location was indeed said to be uniquely desirable, overwhelmingly seductive. While the appearance and the political circumstances of the city changed very markedly between 1800 and 1900, certain utterances and reactions remained strikingly consistent: expressions of rapture – and consternation – at the twinned vitality and morbidity of Rome echoed down the years. Romantics were entranced: for Shelley, arriving in 1818, the impression of Rome 'exceeded anything I have ever experienced in my travels'.[10] Death was part of the lure: it is a city, he wrote, 'as it were, of the dead, or rather of those who cannot die, and who survive the puny generations which inhabit and pass over the spot which they have made sacred to eternity'.[11] As for the deadly environs of Rome, Shelley made no bones about the fact that he loved them, confessing to his friend Peacock that 'the much belied Campagna di Roma [is] infinitely to my taste'.[12] Words would not suffice to capture the intensity of his experience: he urged his friends to join him at the feast and savour the city and the countryside for themselves: 'Come to Rome. It is a scene by which expression is overpowered; which words cannot convey.'[13]

Rome had always stimulated and challenged the eloquence and lyricism of poets, and for any but the most blithely ignorant modern visitors, tempted to put pen to paper, or brush to canvas, there was indeed a daunting sense of tradition to struggle with, often an acute uncertainty about how to know that one really encountered the city *personally*, and how to render its experience afresh. The image of Rome was not built in a day, and those with any sense could not be sure that they were ever representing the emotions it induced, truly 'for the first time'.

Rome, it was said, revealed our passions, but also made us strangers to ourselves. It could alienate and invigorate in equal measure. The city was, apparently, a great aphrodisiac, offering up its sensuality to the visitor, but all this was titillatingly disguised under a mock-pious façade: no wonder Dr Johnson's confidant, James Boswell, on a sightseeing tour of Rome, took the opportunity to 'indulge in sensual relaxations'. He told Rousseau about his adventures:

I sallied forth of an evening like an imperious lion, and I had a little French painter, a young academician, always vain, always alert, always gay, who served as my jackal. I remembered the rakish deeds of Horace and other amorous Roman poets, and I thought that one might well allow one's self a little indulgence in a city where there are prostitutes licensed by the Cardinal Vicar.[14]

No less a visitor than Goethe also explored Rome's arousing effects, casting the city as the natural site for aesthetic and artistic joy, and also for the renaissance of his own sexual pleasure. His 'Roman Elegies' have lost nothing of their freshness and exuberance; their playful tone is commensurate with the pleasure he re-found, with his mistress, in the Eternal City. For Goethe, arrival here in 1786 meant that '[a]ll the dreams of my youth I now behold realised before me', and he relished the strange familiarity of the place. Rome uncannily revealed qualities and feelings half known and appreciated before: 'all that I had long been acquainted with through paintings or drawings, engravings or woodcuts, plaster casts and cork models are here collectively presented to my eye.' '[I]t is all just as I had thought it, and yet all is new.'[15] He expressed delight at living among a sensual people, referred to the mixed pleasures and pains of encountering the city's historical riches, and noted a certain melancholy effect, despite the intense joy that the city yielded. Rome was the centre to which he had been attracted by an 'irresistible impulse'; 'indeed for the last few years it had become with me a kind of disease, which could only be cured by the sight and presence of the absent object'.[16] It was as though the wishes stirred up by 'absent' Rome were akin to an illness; conversely, the city's presence was required to affect a 'cure'. Rome appeared here as a kind of addiction, offering a vital infusion of feeling and joy.

The specific provenance of such literary and amorous encounters *with* Rome – or *in* Rome – matters less here than the cumulative impression they provide of the city's bewilderingly compulsive pull on the outsider. Rome was regarded as disgusting, or fascinating, in contrast with other great cities, other states (especially states of the north). The figure of the foreigner 'at home' in Rome, but not quite of it, became, increasingly, a trope. Innumerable pages on the curiosities of the Eternal City would be read, or penned, from this outsider vantage point, as late-nineteenth-century visitors sipped their tea, in suitably commodious establishments around the Piazza di Spagna, while thumbing through the exquisite descriptions and tempting itineraries in Hare's *Walks in Rome*. Foreign literati often sought immersion in 'Italy', even if they maintained a decidedly 'outsider' subculture (American, German, French and English enclaves all existed). Some very eminent Victorians, of course, were attracted back to 'Rome' in the religious sense, their faith restored by the 'mother Church'. Such at least was the hope. But even for those quite impervious to such attractions, Rome was widely seen to be uniquely bewitching, despite the negative qualities that have, as far back as anyone can remember, infuriated resident and visitor alike. What is so striking, again and again, is the depth of the sensual and emotional effect simply of being there.★

Alongside the famous rhapsodies of the literati, nineteenth-century conversation was seasoned with expressions of pity and horror at the state and fate of this city: Rome and its environs were pictured by many reformers as the site, par excellence, of oppression, corruption, cruelty, ineptitude, avarice, tyranny, poverty and disease. Charles Dickens had a thing or two to say about macabre and grotesque displays,

---

★ The English historian Thomas Babington Macaulay recorded incredulously: 'I had no idea that an excitement so powerful and agreeable still untried by me was to be found in the world.' The French writer, Alfred de Musset, spoke of the city's 'enchanted sky, so pure that a sigh rises to God more freely than in any other place on earth'. The American Henry Adams remembered Italy as 'mostly an emotion' – an emotion that was naturally centred in Rome. The city, before 1870, was seductive beyond resistance. 'The month of May 1860 was divine . . . The shadows breathed and glowed, full of soft forms felt by lost senses.' 'Rome is beautiful, wonderful, magical,' the playwright Ibsen wrote in 1866. (Quoted in Barzini 1968, pp. 54, 55, 73.)

in his *Pictures from Italy*, as he joined the ranks of those who sought to get to the Roman essentials. In his novels, Dickens often sought to shake middle-class readers, to force their squeamish gaze upon certain unwelcome sights. Mazzini made much the same point about the political responsibility of the tourist. Turning a blind eye to injustice, while enjoying artistic treasures, was unacceptable: one of Mazzini's bitterest complaints against the art- or nature-loving visitors was their frequent refusal to take full note of the misery of the native people, held captive under tyrannical political regimes across the peninsula.

Like his contemporaries and fellow residents in London, Carlyle and Dickens, Mazzini insisted that the privileged onlooker should face full on the unjust social reality of present-day political arrangements; he demanded that foreign visitors no less than bourgeois Italians cease to avert their attention from the unpleasant face of Italy. Nobody should be allowed to close their ears to the stifled, but agonised, cries of protest and pain.★ If he attacked the foppish tourist,

---

★ Here is a characteristic passage from Mazzini, excoriating the complacency of the aesthete or self-absorbed convalescent, blind to the cries of 'Italy':

> In Italy nothing speaks: silence is the common law. The people are silent by reason of terror, the masters are silent from policy. Conspiracies, strife, persecution, vengeance, all exist, but make no noise: they excite neither applause nor complaint . . . The stranger in search of health, or the pleasures of arts passes throu' this fairy land on which God has lavished without measure all the gifts which he has divided among the other lands of Europe; – he comes upon a spot where the soil has been recently stirred, and he does not suspect that he is treading on the grave of a martyr. The earth is covered with flowers, the Heaven above smiles with its divine aspect: the cry of misery which from time to time convulses his native country, is rarely heard here . . . what cares he for the *Present*? He says to himself: there is here abundance of food, there is sunshine, there is music in the air; what more can this indolent race desire? (Mazzini 1845, pp. 9–10)

he also criticised the hard-headed utilitarian reformer who might be tempted to see Italy merely in economic and political terms.[17] Italy, Mazzini said, was more akin to an enslaved family; liberty was an absolute value, not to be subordinated to any material considerations. Cost-conscious Cavour and his followers were to become an obvious target for this form of moral attack in and beyond the 1850s.[18] The country could not be reduced to so many beautiful sites, nor to so many thousand square miles peopled by so many millions of bodies, declared 'the prophet of Italy', to his audience of Italian and foreign nationalist sympathisers.

Aesthetic enthusiasm and moral or political disgust blurred in what Mazzini ironically called this 'fairy land' of Italy. The disgust was to be closely associated, in Rome, with extreme forms of religious enthusiasm. Many Protestant visitors considered these monstrous. Mazzini and Garibaldi were both well acquainted with Victorian England. In many respects they both admired the country. Perhaps they drew more than they consciously acknowledged on the frequent anti-Roman speeches that enlivened various forms of Victorian religious discussion. Often, Protestantism was viewed as an essential *English* virtue, with 'Romanism' as its pathological antithesis.[19] The denunciation became extremely shrill. Take the case of the Reverend John Cumming, a popular preacher, who spoke to packed congregations in Covent Garden on Sundays from the 1830s to the 1870s, and who regularly thundered out the message, as George Eliot complained, that 'Romanism is the master-piece of Satan [with] Anti-Christ enthroned in the Vatican'.[20] (Some Englishmen hailed Garibaldi in the 1860s specifically as the scourge of 'Popery'.)[21]

England had no shortage of Protestant groupings, publications and speakers who stoked up the fires of anti-papal sentiment. Such arguments and expressions increasingly ran together with support for the Italian 'liberators'. Admittedly, in the case of the family of John Ruskin, distaste for Catholic excess did nothing to produce enthusiasm for revolutionary disruption. But it is noteworthy that the young critic, intent as he was on studying art and architecture, found himself overwhelmed by a sense of sickness and malaise in the Eternal City: something here repelled him and his father deeply. The sense of disturbance was generated above all else by that religious extravagance to be witnessed in the people and the built environment of Rome. 'I have today witnessed one of the grandest Church Ceremonies to be seen in the world – with the Pope in St. Peters,' John James Ruskin wrote home to a friend. 'How infinitely I would prefer a sermon from Dr Croly.'[22] Or as his son, with less restraint, wrote at the same time: 'St Peter's I expected to be *disappointed* in. I was *disgusted*.'[23]

Such squeamish Protestant tourists depicted Catholic religious devotion as close to madness. Signs of such 'religious mania' were, after all, plentiful in Rome and in some sceptical northerners' eyes, one detects, at times, a quasi-anthropological fascination with the bizarre and exotic practices of another, more primitive, or perhaps more decadent, society. For sensitive souls such as Ruskin it clearly went even beyond that. Rome affected him more powerfully than he could explain. Here in 1840, convalescing from a mystery illness that had interrupted his undergraduate career at Oxford, he wrote of his terrible sense of foreboding and aversion, a sickness in and of Rome that was particularly difficult to pin down and name:

[T]here is a strange horror lying over the whole city, which I can neither describe nor account for; it is a shadow of death, possessing and penetrating all things. The sunlight is lurid and ghastly . . . the shadows are cold and sepulchral; you feel like an artist in a fever, haunted by every dream of beauty that his imagination ever dwelt upon, but all mixed with the fever fear. I am sure this is not imagination, for I am not given to such nonsense.

And, even in illness, never remember feeling anything approaching to the horror with which some objects here can affect me.[24]

Dreams and fevers are run together in this passage. Rome produces a terrible sense of malaise. Ruskin spoke of a 'diseased and dying population', of the sickly earth and air, the accumulated human corruption, the idleness and cheating that characterised life in the city. He languished in Rome and found that he was suffering from a slight fever himself. There were evidently many causes of his hostile and troubled perception. Not the least of them was his sympathy for John Keats, whose burial site, in the Protestant Cemetery of Rome, he had visited, not so long after he himself had been coughing up blood. The sadness of the past and the anxieties of the present came together, reinforcing Ruskin's association of Rome with sickness and excess, rather than recuperation and cure. Despite all this, reassurance came fairly quickly that he was not going to die on that particular occasion. He found that his own frightening symptoms were not a sign of tuberculosis, and an early consignment to the grave, in the manner of Keats, was by no means his own inevitable fate.[25] In any event, the Romans and the Italians at large affected Ruskin in intense but contradictory ways. A lifelong Italophile, always returning for more (especially more of Venice), Ruskin nonetheless often made the connection between Italy, decadence and death. Despite his relentless fascination with the artistic patrimony of the peninsula, he could also speak with passion of his loathing of the art and architecture he encountered in the south. As Ruskin's biographer Tim Hilton observes: 'Neither Rome nor Naples, at this date or any later date, were to win one word of approval from Ruskin.'[26] This wretched land got him in the guts and he left his correspondents in no doubt about the intensity of his Mediterranean experience, for good or ill. 'Take them all in all,' Ruskin wrote to his father in 1845, 'I detest the Italians beyond measure . . . They are Yorick's skull with the worms in it, nothing of humanity left but the smell.'[27]

Others with less quick-fire opinions than these felt that fair judgement of Rome, Italy or its people was difficult if not impossible. It was precisely because the city and perhaps the entire peninsula were felt to be so lethally seductive that assessment could never be quite rational nor properly historical. A sense of consternation was widely remarked about an Italy that left its visitor quite unable to gauge consciously its full effect. 'The charm of Italy,' Stendhal had earlier declared, 'is akin to that of being in love.'[28] Italy was frequently likened to a dreamland. Bulwer Lytton wrote: 'Clime that yet enervates with a soft Circean spell, that moulds us insensibly, mysteriously, into harmony with itself . . . Whoever visits . . . seems to leave earth and its harsh cares behind – to enter the Ivory Gate into the Land of Dreams.'[29] Something in the atmosphere erotically possessed the city's guests. Rome was the supreme diversion. It aroused and inspired, but it also led to states of abandonment, inducing profound deviations, the undermining of conscious will and intent.

Rome's impact upon each visitor's mind, upon the very fabric of the internal world, owed much to its cultural sites, but there was something else here – a surplus of emotion stirred up, a psychic effect that could not quite be accounted for simply by way of the history book or the tourist guide. In the end its transformative impact – turning a feeling of life into death, death into life – was mysterious. The Russian émigré socialist Alexander Herzen tried to capture these contradictions of experience on a visit in 1847. The trouble was, he suggested, that the life forces of the sixteenth and seventeenth centuries had not really replenished Rome. He hated the empty pomp, the trouping of unhappy cardinals, the hypocrisy of that clerical life 'led in duplicity and solicitation'; he identified it with lack of freedom, love of power, envy, readiness for revenge, the absence of everything human and warm.[30] It was as though '[a] vampire lay on weak and backward Rome and sucked its blood'.[31] Yet, for all its pathology, its unproductivity, its deadness, the longer you live in Rome, Herzen confessed, the more its dark and petty sides disappear, and the more your attention comes to be concentrated on objects of infinite graciousness. The dirty passageways, absence of modern conveniences, narrow streets, empty shops and absurd apartments, of which he complained, gradually ceased to matter, and the melancholy greatness of it all took over. Before long, Herzen was admiring the ruins and the sunsets, undone by the majesty of the city and the Campagna alike; he fell prey, like many others, to the vampire's attraction.

There was a puzzle of fascination and repulsion in Rome, as the American writer Nathaniel Hawthorne acknowledged in *The Marble Faun*. Some of the sentiments expressed were in similar vein to Herzen's, but drawn out into a remarkable, extended meditation on the visitor's longing for and uncomfortable captivation by this lethal city. Those who have once known, and then departed, the Eternal City, he wrote, have left behind the image of a 'long decaying corpse'. We love it and hate it in equal measure, never quite able to extricate the one attitude from the other. The city retains, in the mind's eye, a trace of its noble shape, 'but with accumulated dust and fungus growth overspreading all its most admirable features'. What remains, in memory, includes much ugliness; Hawthorne refers to narrow, squalid streets, alleys and hovels, chill winds and deadly air, confusion and cheerlessness, sickness and trickery, bad food, nastiness, the whole 'pretence' at holiness, 'myriads of slaughters', desolation and ruin, the hopelessness of her future, the horrors of her past, and more. And yet, despite it all, having left Rome 'in such a mood as this we are astonished by the discovery, by and by, that our heart strings have mysteriously attached themselves to the Eternal City and are drawing us thitherward again, as if it were more familiar, more intimately our home, than even the spot where we were born'.[32] If the ruins themselves suggested loss, they were also troublingly enjoyable. In Henry James's words: 'To delight in the aspects of sentient ruin might appear a heartless pastime, and the pleasure, I confess, shows a note of perversity.'[33]

These diverse 'pictures of Italy' to be found in reports, novels, poems and travel writing frequently shared, at least, the conclusion that Rome was psychologically and emotionally baffling. It was, apparently, not just a city, but a symbol of the passage of time, a metaphor of mind, a psychic place, an origin. Rome transcended comparison with other locations on the Grand Tour; it was the basis from which all comparisons might then be made. Rome's 'infinite superpositions of history' (as James put it in his novel, *Roderick Hudson*) were shown to inspire *and* to disillusion like nowhere else.

Rome's great writers endlessly played around with its contradictions and complications, and were often to be found reminiscing about the unique pleasures and pains of the city. Rome made many tourists feel strangely sad. One found oneself in a state of mourning or melancholia, shadowed by an ineffable 'something'. You needed a long time to get to know the Eternal City, Stendhal observed. A young man who has never met with '*le malheur*', he acutely noted in the *Promenades*, cannot comprehend the sensations that Rome has to offer.[34] Years later, James also described the delicious '*malheur*' of Rome. His wistful regard and nostalgic delight were themselves exquisitely and self-consciously mannered. A not-untypical Jamesian day here was 'to be enjoyed with a substrain of sadness'.[35] Although markedly different in style, Zola's perception of the city and the Campagna was in fact no less melancholic; he too recorded a 'frightful sadness that one felt' and how this 'arose from the fact that so creative and great a past had culminated in such present-day impotency – Rome, that once covered the world with indestructible monuments, now so reduced that she could only generate ruins, priests, aesthetes'.[36]

Did anywhere else induce quite so intense a mixture of pain and pleasure, languor, desire and frustration? To many distinguished nineteenth-century visitors the answer was clearly no. Exultation and debasement, euphoria and sadness vied for supremacy in many of the classic renderings of the city. Hawthorne again:

> The result of all is a scene, pensive, lovely, dream-like, enjoyable and sad, such as is to be found nowhere save in these princely villa-residences in the neighborhood of Rome; a scene that must have required generations and ages, during which growth, decay, and man's intelligence wrought kindly together, to render it so gently wild as we behold it now.[37]

Here it is easy to feel the most severe sense of personal insignificance, amid 'the myriads of dead hopes that lie crushed into the soil of Rome'.[38] In Hawthorne's account, Rome brings out the visitor's own latent psychic state. 'The happy may well enough continue to be such, beneath the brilliant sky of Rome. But, if you go thither in melancholy mood, – if you go with a ruin in your heart, or with a vacant site there, where once stood the airy fabric of happiness, now vanished, – all the ponderous gloom of the Roman Past will pile itself upon that spot, and crush you down as with the heaped-up marble and granite, the earth-mounds, and multitudinous bricks of its material decay.'[39]

First contact with Rome was sometimes said to be made through a veil or as though in a reverie. On the other hand, the city was likened to the most materially solid of all places, making everywhere else seem insubstantial by comparison. James insisted not only that the real Rome he saw far outstripped the city he had preconceived, but also that '[i]t beats everything: it leaves the Rome of your fancy – your education – nowhere. It makes Venice – Florence – Oxford – London – seem like little cities of pasteboard.'[40]

Nineteenth-century fiction is littered with references to the city's subliminal effects, the unconscious cause and consequences of entering – or avoiding – Rome. Thus Freud spoke to a well-known theme when, at the close of the nineteenth century, he referred to his 'tormenting wish' to visit Rome.[41] When he got there, he named his arrival one of the high points of his life, despite the slight diminution in enjoyment caused by too long postponement.* He drew attention to the unconscious psychic significance of the Eternal City and also to the unconscious aspects of the 'Roman passion' in himself. He saw how the city and its history became woven into the very fabric of his neuroses. The risk of contracting malaria (to which he made passing reference) was, of course, only part of the reason for his fabled inability to reach the Rome he longed to see. Freud had some notable Italian examples to offer in *The Interpretation of Dreams*; indeed, he refers to a 'series of dreams which are based upon a longing to visit Rome'.[42] He added this footnote in 1909: 'I discovered long since that it only needs a little courage to fulfill wishes which till then have been regarded as unattainable', and inserted the following in 1925, 'and thereafter became a constant pilgrim to Rome'.[43]

In a letter to his friend Wilhelm Fliess, Freud had referred to a dream set in Rome, where he found himself in the

---

* Letter of 19 September 1901, in Freud 1985, p. 449. He was totally absorbed by ancient Rome but could not freely enjoy Christian Rome; its atmosphere troubled him. He felt it difficult to tolerate 'the lie' concerning man's redemption. 'Italian Rome', by contrast, he found likeable and 'full of promise'. The weather was hot but tolerable until the sirocco blew up and he found himself feeling 'knocked out'. On the day of his departure, he fell ill with gastroenteritis, which continued to trouble him back in Vienna.

Italian city, walking about streets that had curiously acquired German signs and shop names.[44] He linked this with his wish to meet Fliess in Rome rather than Prague (as planned). He went on to suggest that he had a special identification with Rome's enemy, Hannibal: 'My longing for Rome is, by the way, deeply neurotic. It is connected with my high school hero worship of the Semitic Hannibal, and this year in fact I did not reach Rome any more than he did from Lake Trasimeno. Since I have been studying the unconscious, I have become so interesting to myself. A pity that one always keeps one's mouth shut about the most intimate things.'[45] There was, no doubt, more to tell, but Freud refrained. On less personal ground, he would later link the mind itself with the manifold layers of the Eternal City in an extended analogy that he pursued and then abandoned in *Civilization and its Discontents*.

Psychoanalysis has opened up, among much else, quite new possibilities for understanding our deeper attachments to particular places; our preoccupations with idealised 'geographical' spaces or with golden 'historical' times; our nostalgic or phobic obsessions with 'other countries', past and present; and our ambivalent fascination with history itself as a chronicle of the life and death of forebears. And what site could be more symbolically 'invested' than Rome? Long before Freud, of course, literature had repeatedly explored, as it were, the visitor's ambivalent emotional projections on to Italy, past and present, the cultural and personal baggage that accompany us, wittingly and unwittingly, upon our first encounter with its principal cities. In many representations of Italy, images of degeneration and death seem to intrude quickly into each 'picturesque' vignette, troubling the most blissful of images, the liveliest of accounts, the most simple of enjoyments. Rome's very beauty and richness, it has often been argued, point up painful contrasts between the past and the present, evoking a sense of dismay and heartsickness, or at least bringing a stark awareness of mortality and loss. The experience of treading the ground of Rome produced in many writers a visceral feeling of engagement with the past, and a near supernatural sense of connection with the dead, as though muffled cries and whispers could be heard rising out of the earth. 'Rome' never let go, holding each new visitor in thrall. It was, indeed, enthralling. Here you could turn a corner, from one world to another, imagining the sedimentation of the ages, the crossroads of civilisation, in which the city's ancient defenders and attackers, masters and slaves, pagans and Christians came back to life, demanding recognition. It is a place, as Dorothea discovers in George Eliot's *Middlemarch*, 'where the past of a whole hemisphere seems moving in funeral procession with strange ancestral images and trophies gathered from afar'. Or as Hawthorne conceived the city in *The Marble Faun*:

> You look through a vista of century beyond century, through much shadow, and a little sunshine, – through barbarism and civilisation, alternating with one another like actors that have prearranged their parts, – through a broad pathway of progressive generations bordered by palaces and temples, and bestridden by old, triumphal arches, until, in the distance, you behold the obelisks, with their unintelligible inscriptions, hinting at a past infinitely more remote than history can define. Your own life is as nothing, when compared with that immeasurable distance; but still you demand, none the less earnestly, a gleam of sunshine, instead of a speck of shadow, on the step or two that will bring you to your quiet rest.[46]

Behind such meditations on the suggestive ruins and echoes of the ancient world lay a range of Enlightenment enquiries into the rise and fall of the empire that had transformed the understanding of the city's fabric and fate. Gibbon's great study of Roman decadence exerted a powerful influence on nineteenth-century thought.[47] But this and other important accounts of that history, produced by various hands in the late eighteenth and first half of the nineteenth century, were increasingly to be joined, after 1850, not only by exquisite, avowedly subjective 'travelogues', but also by new environmental, medical and scientific theories of Rome and the Campagna's profound incapacity and degeneracy.

Evidently there was nothing new about the coupling of Rome and death; visitors had, for many centuries, observed and marvelled at the sense of decay, and, in their wanderings among the ruins, had allowed themselves to hear the ghosts of empire. But gradually a new attitude emerged in which elements of political utopianism, medical diagnosis and moral anxiety about the national population blurred together. Images of corruption and dissolution, or, conversely, ecstatic descriptions of recovery, purity and integration, frequently seasoned the language of nationalism. Garibaldi's rhetoric was often spiced with references to the Italian perverts, degenerates and living 'abortions', who failed to support the holy cause of 'Italy'. It seemed that there might be special scientific reasons why Rome was so decrepit, so morally wasted. While the fascination with the ruin — and ruins — of Rome was evidently enduring, it acquired different inflections. In the eighteenth century, Piranesi had drawn extraordinary images of its relics and ruins, just as Gibbon had chronicled them, but thereafter the particular cluster of swamp-filled associations, the metaphors of rank decay, the scientific anxiety about malaria and the moral concern with the racial aspects of the city's supposedly exceptional depravity were increasingly to converge.

Specialist medical studies emerged in the Victorian period, examining the consequences of fever upon the bodies and minds of the inhabitants of Rome and the Campagna, and plotting the supposed racial, political and cultural consequences. Commentators emphasised the pernicious material properties and physically corrupting environment; they highlighted the debilitating impact of the terrain upon the morals and health of the population, from ancient times to the present. Italian and foreign onlookers repeatedly conceived the Campagna as the quintessential land of fever and feverish desire, picturing it as a place that epitomised physical, psychological and political oppression, and the hitherto hopeless endeavour to resist the ravages of nature.

In the second half of the nineteenth century, two influential French enthusiasts for science, and stern critics of Church 'superstition', Ernest Renan and Hippolyte Taine, also reflected on the fatal aspect of Rome's stagnation, analysing the pernicious effect of the city and of the religious system it enshrined. They joined a prolific debate raging in France during Louis Napoleon's Second Empire, regarding the future of the papacy and the appropriate diplomatic stance that foreign powers should take towards it.[48] How, wondered Renan, could Rome's degradation ever be reversed? The city had been such a hotbed of murder, intrigue and deception; it was characterised by infinite misery and sadness, surrounded by fever and a 'desert'. How could a banal modernity ever really 'pierce this compact mass of sacred ruins'?[49] In 1868, Renan wrote that it was difficult to imagine a historical force better designed than the Italian Counter-Reformation to stifle the spirit of liberty.[50] Renan's view about the dead hand of the Church was only confirmed by the Vatican Council's reassertion, on 18 July 1870, of the infallibility of the Pope. Critical outsiders they may have been, but Renan and Taine (both of whom had some influence on Zola, as he wrote his extraordinary anti-clerical finale *Rome*) were interested in the re-emergence of powerful religious beliefs, illusions and delusions in the modern age. Taine compared the Italian past with the present, and doubted the inevitability of progress. Indeed, he saw signs of regress rather than advance. Even with the various civic reforms achieved during the reign of Pius IX, he sniffed contemptuously, the city was still stuck in the Middle Ages with regard to science. Taine suggested that in Rome one understood more deeply than anywhere else what resistance to modernity really looked like. And the sickness could not be confined; he declared the city to be 'an abscess affecting the entire body' of Italy.[51]

But was the deadliness and the desirability of this landscape somehow connected? In some eyes, there was clearly a link, a kind of voluptuous enjoyment of the ruin and decay. Hawthorne suggested that, perversely, it was the very morbidity of the Campagna that enhanced its captivating effect; to enjoy it to its full meant risking death. Hawthorne described the paradoxical attraction of the malaria-ridden terrain. Here was a very particular twist on the familiar Victorian aestheticisation of illness:

> The final charm is bestowed by the malaria. There is a piercing, thrilling, delicious kind of regret in the idea of so much beauty thrown away or only enjoyable at its half-development, in winter and early spring, and never to be dwelt amongst, as the home-scenery of any human being. For if you come hither in summer, and stray through these glades in the golden sunset, fever walks arm in arm with you, and death awaits you at the end of the dim vista. Thus the scene is like Eden in its loveliness; like Eden, too, in the fatal spell that removes it beyond the scope of man's actual possessions.[52]

Nobody captured better than Hawthorne this sense of Rome and the Campagna's insidious pull. In pursuit of some mysterious essence of the Roman experience the visitor was dragged into drowsy, dangerous states of enchantment, even a love affair with self-abandonment and death itself. It was only too easy to overstay, to wander into harm's way, to ignore the firm advice of the guidebooks as to safe times and zones.

Twilight, as everyone knew, was not a time to be caught in the Campagna, or in the city's low-lying ruins. Rome's sense of menace (fever, crime, depravity) also became part of its temptation. Here, apparently, boundaries were constantly transgressed and the city provided a constant, seductive invitation to self-destruction. Rome was 'the native soil of ruin!'.[53]

In this period, you could find the image of that tainted, enervating air of Rome in the most erudite historical discussion or the columns of the papers.

No surprise that Henry James's Daisy Miller should catch her death by the Coliseum. In the *Illustrated London News*, Rome was declared a 'moral plague spot, at once contagious and infectious'.[54] The Italian writer D'Annunzio went on to describe this in poetry, sometimes suggesting an alluring quality to the Roman disease, as when he wrote of malaria's beguiling power. At the same time, he applauded efforts to reclaim the capital from such torpor and sickness. In his homage to Garibaldi, D'Annunzio spoke of the 'sacred fever of Rome' while extolling the Eternal City that rose up inexorably, finally triumphing over death.[55]

Visitors to Rome in the 1860s had sometimes spoken of living in frozen time or the 'lull before a storm'; those who described the city in the 1870s, after the city's integration into Italy, were struck by a sense of embryonic awakening, confused signs of urban metamorphosis. In Rome, one could witness an old provincial papal world in collision with the new juggernaut of Italy. 'I thought again of the poor disinherited Pope,' wrote James, on a visit in the 1870s, 'wondering whether, when such venerable frippery will no longer bear the carpenter's nails, any more will be provided. It was hard to fancy anything but shreds and patches in that musty tabernacle. Wherever you go in Italy you receive some such intimation as this of the shrunken proportion of Catholicism, and every church I have glanced into on my walks hereabout has given me an almost pitying sense of it.'[56]

James caught beautifully this curious historical moment, with Rome on the cusp between two worlds. The new capital depicted in James's *Italian Hours* was seen with some regret, yet he also showed the city's capacity to disrupt any predictable emotion and reverse it. The Eternal City, he wrote, makes us sad, gloomy, ecstatic, moment by moment: 'Rome, which in some moods, especially to new-comers, seems a place of almost sinister gloom, has an occasional art, as one knows her better, of brushing away care by the grand gesture with which some splendid impatient mourning matron – just as the Niobe of Nations, surviving, emerging and looking about her again – might pull off and cast aside an oppression of muffling crape.'[57] *Italian Hours* was concerned precisely with the cliché of Rome, the received images and commonplaces, as well as the unforgettably acute literary or visual accounts of illustrious predecessors, which one could avoid wanly repeating only with the greatest difficulty. James sought to absorb, without parroting, such renditions. The views of Claude, the writings of Goethe, Stendhal, Keats, Shelley, Browning or George Eliot, all inform James's Rome. Indeed, he insisted that the environment that we perceive is never simply before us, here and now, but is always already constructed from past thoughts and images:

> In the foreground a contadino in his cloak and peaked hat jogged solitary on his ass; and here and there in the distance, among blue undulations, some white village, some grey tower helped deliciously to make the picture the typical 'Italian landscape' of old-fashioned art. It was so bright and yet so sad, so still and yet so charged, to the supersensed ear, with the murmur of an extinguished life, that you could only say it was intensely and adorably strange, could only impute to the whole overarched scene an unsurpassed secret for bringing tears of appreciation to no matter how ignorant – archeologically ignorant – eyes.[58]

Rome Desired

Back in Rome, the moral complications of attitude, emotion and judgement chronically exceeded expectations. The city was again and again conceived as the *mise-en-scène* of primary loves and hates, pains and pleasures, excitement and confusions, hope and gloom; above all the site for disillusionment, in all its many guises. Rome invited depressive acceptance of what could not be restored, what could not be brought back, or made new and pure. James's expression, 'substrain of sadness', defines something essential to the Victorian rendition of Rome. Here was the city of pained enlightenment, the place par excellence where the naive or gauche suffer an unexpected truth, forced to wake up to the intricate moral complications and painful lessons of the 'old world'.★ Was this not the script – Rome as the melancholic place in which innocent hope was first prolonged,

★ As Hilda finds in Hawthorne's *Marble Faun*, the city confronts its visitor with new troubling knowledge, 'heretofore unknown to her vivacious though quiet temperament':

> Hilda all along intended to pass the summer in Rome . . . Nor did she dread the summer atmosphere, although generally held to be so pestilential. She had already made trial of it, two years before, and found no worse effect than a kind of dreamy languor, which was dissipated by the first cool breezes that came with autumn. The thickly populated centre of the city, indeed, is never affected by the feverish influence that lies in wait in the Campagna, like a besieging foe, and nightly haunts those beautiful lawns and woodlands, around the suburban villas, just at the season when they most resemble Paradise.

But before long, Rome produces a more acute disturbance, 'like a half-dead serpent knotting its cold, inextricable wreaths about her limbs. It was that peculiar despair, that chill and heavy misery, which only the innocent can experience, although it possesses many of the gloomy characteristics that mark a sense of guilt' (Hawthorne 1860, p. 779). The novel itself, as a reviewer observed in 1860, was 'rimmed with an impalpable fringe of melancholy moss' (James Russell Lowe, in *The Atlantic Monthly*, April 1860, in Kesterson 1971, p. 4).

then postponed, and finally extinguished – to which Garibaldi also played?

This is not to say that the General's attitude to Rome was directly influenced by any single novel or piece of travel writing, but it is to ask how far a common stock of images, stories and complaints echoed diffusely through the public conversation and expectation of the age. We do know that Garibaldi's fictions, and his actions, above all in the 1860s and 70s, suggested a continuing obsession with the morass of Rome, and with its political, moral and physical rescue.

Evidently, visitors of different nationality in different decades expressed their own predilections and tastes in Rome, and yet running through so many of the examples discussed here are similar themes and concerns; not least, an assumption that Rome was *bound* to be massively affecting and troubling, for *any* imaginable newcomer. Moreover, it was widely taken for granted that Rome would affect us in ways that could not be easily controlled, that exceeded reason and moderation, and that left us longing for more. For so many visitors, the city was like a drug, fostering the most intense affects, swinging us from fascination to frustration, euphoria to violent and vicious despair. Roman encounters were, if nothing else, the source of endless psychological speculation. As a final literary example, consider Zola's 1890s murder mystery *Rome*, where the city's pathology and power were set out in remarkable fashion.

The old French novelist and accomplished scandal-monger offered a sustained post-mortem on the Eternal City, and the contradictory emotions that it aroused. He provided a plethora of received views as well as a particularly mordant analysis of Rome's vices. The twists and turns of Zola's plot are less important here than the story's mood and its extraordinary inventory of Roman images. The book is also relevant to the interpretation of Garibaldi himself. Zola knew of his reputation, of course, and had seen him in the flesh in Bordeaux in 1871;[59] the noble fighter and visionary, Orlando, that he created in *Rome*, was loosely based on the General. At the centre of the saga, however, is another character, a hapless young idealistic priest, Pierre, whose sorry adventures illuminated the wider predicament of the bamboozled 'truth seeker'. Zola's account of Pierre's naive quest for enlightenment brilliantly captures that wider feeling of disillusionment and bewilderment in the hothouse of Rome.

Zola shows how Pierre enters a baffling network of institutional and social relationships. Against the backdrop of the Eternal City and the Vatican, the novel encourages us to think about the fate of good intentions and the nature of obsessive quests. Here, stated aims are remorselessly diverted. Pierre's plans are undermined and brought to nought. He wishes to visit the Pope, in order to gain a fair hearing from the highest authorities, after a book he has written on the regeneration of Catholicism is unexpectedly condemned and placed on the Index. Despite espousing moral renewal for the Church, Pierre finds his convictions regarded as improper by the very spiritual authorities he is supposed to obey. *Rome* traces Pierre's dawning realisation that his desire to affect change in the mother church cannot be fulfilled; reform is impossible within its moribund fold. Pierre is constantly blocked and thwarted. The reader must share in the frustration of the hero as he vainly awaits a satisfactory resolution. Held captive in the corridors of power, stymied at every turn, Pierre finally meets the Pope, but to no avail. It is a futile pursuit of reason and illumination; to the bitter end he encounters only mystification and absurdity. One of Zola's biographers has rightly drawn attention to the way the novel not only provided a blast of invective against Catholicism but also anticipated the 'involute perplexities' of Kafka.[60]

Zola himself had sought – and been refused – a meeting with the Pope at the Vatican. He also found his fiction sternly attacked and his work placed on the Index. In the weeks he spent in the city, researching his book, he had immersed himself in studies of religious obscurantism, had explored modern, medieval and ancient Rome, and uncovered dark secrets of the past as a means to understand the lethargy and deadliness of the city's current state. He mined literature for instances of baseness and folly, the accretions of evil and stupidity that had blocked so many luminaries and reformers in earlier centuries. There was, apparently, a terrible and undrainable swamp here, a festering mass of deceit and superstition that generated disease and despair, a decidedly unromantic agony.

And yet Zola was also alert to the city's attraction. Indeed, that was part of the problem. The Eternal City could not conceivably be left out of the political or emotional calculation; nowhere else would do, despite the fact that there were fatal obstacles to the successful creation of a modern metropolis on this site. If Italy was not to succumb to the corrupt embrace of Rome, some vast and decisive transformation in the very culture, environment and political direction of the city would be required. Rome was indispensable, but also an unbearable drag on the new state. There is a memorable passage in the book, in which Rome is compared to other Italian cities, all of whom are 'jealous of her', but none of whom can substitute her binding function, her emotional grip on Italians at large.★

★ First Florence, so 'indifferent and so sceptical, impregnated with a happy heedlessness which seems inexplicable when one remembers the frantic passions, and the torrents of blood rolling through her history'. Next Naples, 'which yet remains content with her bright sun, and whose childish people enjoy their ignorance and wretchedness so indolently that one knows not whether one ought to pity them'. Then Venice, 'which has resigned herself to remaining a marvel of ancient art', and Genoa, 'absorbed in trade, still active and bustling'. The future seems to lie with the cities of Turin and Milan, those 'industrial and commercial centres, which are so full of life and so modernised that tourists disdain them as not being "Italian" cities, both of them having saved themselves

This assessment of the compelling need for Italians to destroy as well as regenerate an old order, so as to create a new, more salubrious and efficient modern world, pulled together earlier diagnoses and laments, albeit in a powerful and sensational new form. The Campagna loomed large, a startling image of the potential of a land to deteriorate over the years.

Zola was fascinated by the racial composition of the Italians, and also by the indissoluble material debris strewn across the city, lying as heavy on the ground as the stench of (moral) corruption sat heavy upon the air. Such pollution, it was feared, could never be cleared away. There were ruins upon ruins; so vast a system of decay and decomposition that it was impossible to excavate it fully, still less to draw a line between past and present, or between the warring forces that lent themselves to sickness and to health. There was a veritable 'indigestion of ruins' here, as he had put it in his notebook.[61] This is a good metaphor not only for the complex composition of Rome, but for its over-determined meanings in modern culture. Something was perceived to be profoundly rotten in the state of Rome, and it was as much to be seen in the present-day explosion

---

from ruin by entering into that Western evolution which is preparing the next century'. In theory, they could provide a beacon, illuminating the path to a modernised Italy, but in so doing there must also be some violent destruction of Italian presuppositions, not least, a wholesale assault on the old dusty Museum version of Italy, that has been preserved, in its crumbled state, 'for the pleasure of artistic souls'. 'At all events there must either be death, death soon and inevitable, or else the pick of the demolisher, the tottering walls thrown to the ground, and cities of labour, science and health created on all sides; in one word, a new Italy really rising from the ashes of the old one, and adapted to the new civilisation into which humanity is entering. Here the death of one "Italy" is seen as the necessary precondition for the birth of another' (Zola 1896, pp. 551–2).

of buildings that was disfiguring areas of the city, for instance surrounding the central railway station, as it was to be glimpsed in the historical record, where violence, debauchery and venality were rife. Rome could not be ignored, but nor could her 'illness' be cured. Zola's novel moves from grand laments and metaphysical abstractions to the specificity of contemporary political and economic fiascos. Thus he savages the incompetent financiers and politicians who lay behind contemporary banking scandals, and the myopic architects of the building boom of the 1880s that was widely felt to be so damaging to the Roman environment.[62] *Rome* offered a compelling account of gruesome urban transformation, where so many houses and offices had arisen from the rubble, turned into blemishes or unwanted ruins before they were ever finished. It was driven by a form of megalomania:

> After the Caesars and the Popes had come the Italian Government, which was no sooner master of the city than it wished to reconstruct it, make it more splendid, more huge than it had ever been before. It was the fatal suggestion of the soil itself – the blood of Augustus rushing to the brain of these last-comers and urging them to a mad desire to make the third Rome the queen of the earth.[63]

Rome portrays the old order at its 'final gasp', and leaves its hero and its reader with little confidence about the shape of things to come.[64] To convey the city's hothouse atmosphere of intrigue and double-dealing, of political and moral frustration, the writing becomes ever more extravagant and arcane. There are many extraordinary passages in the novel, detailing in the very rhythm of the sentences, in phrase after phrase of opulent descriptive flourishes, the painful drawn-out postponement of enlightenment, as Pierre passes through an endless sequence of advisers and flunkeys, down seemingly interminable corridors, in pursuit of his elusive audience with the Pope.[65]

Pierre longs for the creation of a quieter, truer faith, and to find a modicum of reason in Rome, but detects precious little of either. What dominates is a kind of religious and political mania.* Fanaticism vies with greed. Pierre witnesses with horror the blind mass enthusiasm for the Pope, while behind the scenes the Vatican turns out to be a vast counting house, with His Holiness shut up, as another of Pierre's acquaintances, Narcisse, puts it, 'counting and recounting his treasures with cheerful care, arranging the rolls of gold in good order, slipping the bank notes into envelopes in equal quantities, and then putting everything away in hiding-places which are only known to himself'.[66]

This may be overblown rhetoric, but Garibaldi would no doubt have agreed with much of Zola's diagnosis of the Italian capital and of the papacy had he lived to read it in the 1890s. Zola's stories had never been shy to court controversy. His uncompromising diagnosis of the pathology of Rome's old and new guard emerged loud and clear from under the baroque extravagance of this latest novel. It is not difficult to see how one could move from either Garibaldi's or Zola's fictions to the demand for radical destruction and reconstruction, even to the iconoclastic manifestos of the futurists, who shockingly demanded the erasure of museums and all other petrified sites of the past, seeking to shake off this phenomenal weight of 'Italy', the crushing and stultifying force of all those prevailing images, conventions and assumptions that interposed themselves between thought

---

* 'But the crowds rushing on the grotto [at Lourdes], the sick dying of divine love before the Virgin's statue, the multitudes delirious with the contagion of the miraculous – nothing of all that gave an idea of the blast of madness which suddenly inflamed the pilgrims at the feet of the Pope' (Zola 1896, p. 217).

and action.★ Tradition here was seen as dead weight, a dead past that was haunting the present and the future; history not as the soil from which further progress could grow, but rather as a massive, inert obstacle, blocking the path of necessary change.

★ As Susan Sontag (Colombo and Sontag, 1998) put it, in a suggestive essay on old photographs of Italy: 'All of Europe is in mourning for its past. Bookstores are stocked with albums of photographs offering up the vanished past for our delectation and reflected nostalgia. But the past has deeper roots in Italy than anywhere else in Europe, which makes its destruction more defining. And the elegiac note was sounded earlier and more plangently in Italy, as was the note of rancor – think of the Futurist tantrums about the past: the calls to burn the museums, fill in the Grand Canal and make it a highway etc . . . The depth possessed by these images of an older Italy is not just the depth of the past. It is the depth of a whole culture, a culture of incomparable dignity and flavor and bulk . . . that has been thinned out, effaced, confiscated. To be replaced by a culture in which the notion of depth is meaningless.'

9 An Unconscious Contradiction

'The history of the Victorian Age will never be written: we know too much about it. For ignorance is the first requisite of the historian – ignorance, which simplifies and clarifies, which selects and omits, with a placid perfection unattainable by the highest art . . . It is not by the direct method of a scrupulous narration that the explorer of the past can hope to depict that singular epoch. If he is wise, he will adopt a subtler strategy. He will attack his subject in unexpected places; he will fall upon the flank, or the rear; he will shoot a sudden, revealing searchlight into obscure recesses, hitherto undivined. He will row out over that great ocean of material, and lower down into it, here and there, a little bucket, which will bring up to the light of day some characteristic specimen, from those far depths, to be examined with a careful curiosity.'

Lytton Strachey, *Eminent Victorians*

What really possessed General Garibaldi to battle so stubbornly with the Tiber, Rome and its hinterland? Contemporary ideas about the transmission of malaria played their part. The wish to promote social, economic and medical progress was a further, significant factor – Rome was to be rescued from flood, disease, indolence and corruption. Garibaldi made clear that he aspired to place Rome at the centre of the new nation and the modern world. To understand his urban and rural endeavour to achieve regeneration in the 1870s requires that we grasp the wider anxieties and ambitions of his age. But running through this book has also been the question of Garibaldi's personal predicament, idiosyncratic motives and contradictory behaviour. In transforming the environment that had dealt so cruel a personal blow to so many comrades-in-arms, and above all to his beloved wife Anita, the personal and the political merged.

The aim here has been to consider such public and private pressures; to trace Garibaldi's story and history of love and loss; to map the network of ideas, images and myths in which his plans and his own sense of self were caught up, and to offer a range of possible sources for his infatuation with Rome. To ponder these underlying purposes is to contemplate the problem of historical biography itself, and to note the limits and constraints upon what can be known for sure. Historians can reconstruct the broad political and medical context in which this curious affair with Rome took place, but it is by no means obvious that we can fully discover his deeper motives, or even how far we can truly differentiate the private from the public sources of his actions.

The General's Victorian admirers perceived his life as a marvellous story of heroism, redemption and climactic political achievement. Increasingly, each of his actions, in the course of his drawn-out political and military struggles, would be construed as uniquely pregnant with meaning for 'Italy'. Thus he heard about, and even read news of, his own imminent adventures, even as his plots were being brewed. His forthcoming exploits would be anticipated as the latest chapter in an extraordinary life, awaited by an expectant world. He was watched and studied like some theatrical star, whose play was unfolding before the public gaze. He lived the second half of his adult life amid a babble of speculations about what he would do next. He is known to have kept abreast of public events through the newspapers, and must often have read accounts of himself as seen from afar.

Garibaldi attracted colourful headlines and was likened

to a mythological figure. If he was not Adam, Abel or Moses, he was a latter-day Achilles emerging from his tent; Ulysses in search of his long-lost home; a latter-day David in conflict with the foreign Goliath; Christ on horseback; a male Joan of Arc; Robin Hood; Martin Luther; or George Washington.[1] For jaundiced observers of his frequent mishaps and debacles, Garibaldi was more like a dreamy Quixote who did not have a clue what he was actually doing.[2] He took on this burden of legend and in many ways became public property, the repository for the hopes and dreams of his nation. At the same time, he was hostile to empty epithets, priding himself on being, above all, his own person, a man of action rather than abstraction. Few could doubt his enduring practical and immediate commitment to Rome in the 1870s, as he put guns aside, studied blueprints for sewers and promoted designs for grand new docks at Fiumicino.[3] He expressed his wish to do more for Rome, saying that he had not yet done enough. No doubt the fact of his failure to hold the city in the past, or to seize it definitively for 'Italy' in 1870, strengthened his resolve to spearhead this new civic campaign. He seemed to believe that if he could quell the elements, liberate the people's health, and raise their morale, this would offer an important compensation for his earlier defeats, and for political marginalisation he had endured in the aftermath of national unification.

Pondering the Tiber's history of flood, after the disaster of 1870, Garibaldi became ever more impressed by the idea that modern engineering and science could transfigure the Eternal City. He had discussed Rome's requirements with a number of people, including Paolo Molini, a Tuscan journalist with some knowledge of geological matters, and Alessandro Castellani, a Roman follower of the General who had an amateur interest in archaeology. Both suggested that the deviation of the entire course of the Tiber from the capital would be worth considering. When he heard the full details, Garibaldi declared to Castellani that this plan would give Rome back its proper place in world affairs and strengthen its association with modern science and engineering. Such an initiative, he enthused, would also hold back all those countless, fleeing, famished Italians, giving them an incentive to stay. 'To think of the colossal advantages of your scheme,' he confided, is enough 'to drive one mad'.[4] The excitement at the opportunity and the frustration of its non-realisation did indeed take him over. Garibaldi was soon inviting a wider public to share his thinking and encouraging another member of his circle, Colonel Luigi Amadei, to sketch out plans on paper. Amadei, from a noble family in Rome, was an old follower; he had been with Garibaldi in the republican drama of 1849 and now threw himself wholeheartedly into the new campaign, much to the satisfaction of his mentor. Such action to deal with the Tiber, Garibaldi declared to various newspaper editors, should be a national priority. He insisted that this venture would be of benefit not only to Rome but to the whole of humanity.[5] The General's approach to the flood problem was nothing if not ambitious; it provided the spectacular scale that his supporters had come to expect from this most romantic of romantic war leaders. He had grown increasingly enthusiastic as the discussions and outlines developed, and envisaged a Rome worthy of its place in modern Europe, a fitting city for all of its returning exiles.

With various possibilities for such urban and rural regeneration percolating, the General decided to bring the good tidings to Rome and introduce the necessary laws to achieve wholesale reclamation. But as he prepared himself in late 1874, the government became uneasy at the scale of his initiative. As news filtered through of his intentions, the Minister of Public Works, Silvio Spaventa, was anxious to know exactly what Garibaldi had in mind and how much it would cost.[6]

Once installed in Rome in 1875, Garibaldi spoke loftily of the task ahead, but also directly appealed for funds and technical assistance. Thus he wrote to the readers of English newspapers to express his hope that well-wishers abroad would offer material support for the Tiber project – through their wallets.[7] Soon after the General's arrival in the capital he had been granted an audience with the King, at the Quirinal.* They discussed the Tiber as well as swapping recollections of past glory. During the following weeks and months, Garibaldi was to be guest of honour at various dinners and prominent public events.[8] He took a boat trip along the river, in the direction of Fiumicino, in order to study more closely the practical problems that lay ahead.[9] Advice and examples from Europe and the United States flowed in. He scanned maps and drawings, compared the Tiber with the Thames, the Seine, the Mississippi and the Nile. The details of canal projects and the design of great dams became his meat and drink. Some entrepreneurs were willing to offer their services free of charge or on the basis of future state funding. An English firm was ready to assist and offer credit to this

GARIBALDI NELLA SALA DI VILLA CASALINI ESAMINA I PROGETTI PER LA COSTRUZIONE DI UN GRANDE CANALE CHE UNISSE ROMA AL MARE

Garibaldi at Villa Casalini, Rome, studying a blueprint for the diversion of the Tiber

---

* Victor Emmanuel had gradually overcome his phobia about sleeping in Rome and was now installed in the Pope's former palace. He had taken some convincing, due to a prediction that he would meet his death, at the hands of God, on the first night spent in the conquered city. On his first visit to Rome after its unification with Italy, the King had not slept in the city at all; on his second visit he rejected the Quirinal in favour of the shelter and hospitality of a friendly aristocrat; third time around, he was willing to inhabit the great palace (D'Ideville 1878, pp. 25–7).

most fêted of adventurers and soon commissioned a boat on which to carry out surveys. An engineer, a certain Mr Wilkinson (from the firm of Wilkinson & Smith, Westminster, London), came out to help the General, happy to associate his name with the soldier who had so excited and delighted Victorian society. But later, when Garibaldi's project ran into difficulty, and payment signally failed to materialise, the firm (vainly) threatened to sue, complaining about costs incurred in covering these exploratory boating trips and all the work that had been undertaken planning canals and a harbour.

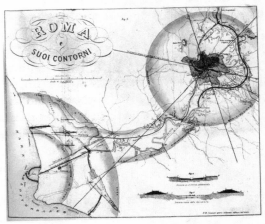

Map showing Garibaldi's first Tiber diversion scheme. This plan, developed by Quirico Filopanti, involved re-routing the river to the east of Rome

The General had sent word of his plans to experts and financiers at home and abroad; advisers from Austria, France, England and America were drawn into consultations and contact was made with the Rothschilds and Barings.[10] Meanwhile, a sympathetic aristocrat, Prince Torlonia, helped him plan the reconstruction of the Campagna and the straightening of various sharp bends in the Tiber. They considered the conversion of stagnant water pools into usable land and pondered the best way to create useful large ponds teeming with edible fish.[11] The details of various water-transportation systems were explored, as the General hoped to emulate the hydraulic feats of the ancients, and for that matter the engineers of Victorian England who were busy with their own plans to pipe water from one part of Britain to another. In one particular scheme, water from Tivoli was to be moved all the way around the Alban hills, to irrigate arid zones of the Campagna. Garibaldi hobnobbed with men of influence, plotting and networking with whichever opinion formers he could find. Not by chance did he promise to attend the opening, fixed for 4 February 1875, of a Masonic temple in Rome.[12]

In the early spring of 1875, Garibaldi appeared to be making progress. He held a meeting with the Prime Minister, Marco Minghetti, and decided the appropriate location of the port − it was to be close to Fiumicino, in preference to other sites, such as Ostia. He elaborated plans for breakwater constructions into the sea, for locks and canals, and for the creation of a new railway that would run from the site of the port to the capital. *The Times* assiduously reported these developments for the benefit of English readers.[13]

At least three distinct designs were associated with Garibaldi; they appeared between February 1875 and the end of the year. His overall project subsumed (or, to put it less kindly, vacillated between) these variants. First was that associated with his old colleague 'Quirico Filopanti' (pseudonym of Giuseppe Barilli), a professor of hydraulic engineering from Bologna University and another veteran of the Roman Republic of 1849. Filopanti offered a design based on the creation of a seventeen-kilometre canal and a vast lock above Rome.[14] He proposed that the waters be diverted to the east of the city to join the new canal. This proposal was on the table between February and March 1875. The second variant was similar; it was the brainchild of Colonel Amadei, and in this scheme the waters would again be diverted, while some of the Tiber's course through Rome would be completely filled over and new sewers would be constructed. Instead of

an unruly river, Rome would see the creation of a marvellous modern avenue. This blueprint was based on an earlier
proposal by a Frenchman, Rullier, in 1872, but it was now
further enlarged by Amadei. Soon, however, there was a third
plan, this time associated with one of the government's own
advisers, Alfredo Baccarini, who had gained the General's ear.
Baccarini had powerfully called into question the initial no-
nonsense premise that the Tiber be removed altogether from
the city and sought a more pragmatic and modest 'compromise' solution. Nonetheless, for a while, the prospect of the
Tiber's effective elimination from Rome had particularly
attracted the General: the plan had simplicity and boldness,
and, he hoped, would place the scale of Rome's urban reconstruction on a par with Paris.[15] How better to herald Rome's
arrival in the age of nationalism and mark its pre-eminence
among European cities than to replace these deeply sordid
and troublesome flows with a grand new thoroughfare? That
really would put Rome on the modern map: after all, not
even the formidable Baron Haussmann, who transformed
the appearance of the French capital in the period of the
Second Empire, had built over the Seine!★ But as the months
went by, all these schemes ran into the sand. His opponents
were relieved that he had not succeeded in overturning the
decision-making process in Rome with the same speed that
he had sometimes captured territory; if his '*idée fixe*' was
revealed for what it was, so much the better.[16]

★ An anecdote in which the English utilitarian and public health champion Edwin
Chadwick, on a visit to Paris in 1864, challenged Napoleon III to deal with the
sewers and the Seine, is worth recalling here. This was during the period in which
Haussmann was masterminding major works to transform the layout of Paris.
Chadwick noted serious problems in the Parisian drainage system and apparently
said to the Emperor, 'Sire, they say that Augustus found Rome a city of brick and
left it a city of marble. If your majesty, finding Paris stinking, will leave it sweet,
you will more than rival the first emperor of Rome.' Louis Napoleon's reaction
is not known (Halliday 1999, p. 38).

Whatever else afflicted and preoccupied Garibaldi in these years, the Tiber remained a consistent concern and source of vexation. Administrators and politicians had quickly sought to rein in his plans, flanking his heady group of advocates with more down-to-earth cost-conscious experts. An important politician of the political left, Agostino Depretis, a former ally of Garibaldi, but now a source of considerable disappointment, had been placed in charge of a special committee in 1875, which included engineers unimpressed by Garibaldi's approach to the technical questions.[17]

In Garibaldi's correspondence on the Tiber affair, one detects his personal frustration and even bitterness at the pace of change. He felt the opposition to be unhelpful and the speed of proceedings glacially slow. In the documents he wrote on the Tiber, lie the buried traces of recriminations, half-suppressed angry exchanges between the parties in Rome – some of whom were old friends and companions in war – records of small-scale manoeuvrings, the petty shufflings of blame and responsibility from individual to individual, amid a welter of hurt feelings and rivalries. The General was driven further and further towards distraction.

The officially sanctioned choreography of delay and diversion was soon in evidence. Surely the General cannot really have been surprised at some of these reservations. The government was seriously disquieted by the likely cost and scope of the plan he presented to parliament, and indeed by the whole tenor of the General's visit – why, it had been asked at the start of the year, when he first arrived, was he *really* there? Some observers wondered if there was more to this sudden burst of activity in Rome than met the eye; perhaps he was organising secret plots, preparing further military campaigns, raising the mob. Others wondered whether his domestic exasperation – the not inconsiderable matter of a blocked divorce with Countess Raimondi – might also be interfering with his judgement.

Garibaldi had fallen for the seventeen-year-old, when he

was introduced to her, near Como, during a brief respite from fighting the Austrians in 1859. He was impressed by her bravery and was clearly attracted. They slept together before marrying in January 1860. The marriage was short-lived and disastrous. Garibaldi heard reports that the Countess had been no virgin at the time he met her, indeed she had had a sexual liaison with one of his own followers, and had delivered a stillborn child a few months before encountering the General. Apparently he called her a whore and immediately broke off all contact. They were never to meet again. Garibaldi referred at one point to his marriage as 'unconsummated' in any real sense; he said that it had merely involved 'some copulations'. His long-running campaign to nullify this marriage was to prove deeply frustrating. The King, buttonholed by the General on the subject, is reported to have muttered something to the effect that if divorce could be felicitously arranged, he would be inclined to avail himself of the facility, but alas it could not be done.

Garibaldi and his third wife
Francesca Armosino

Despite appeals to the politicians and the court, it took twenty years for Garibaldi's unfortunate marriage to the Countess to be legally revoked. In the end, however, it was done. After various thwarted initiatives, a legal pretext was finally found to get Garibaldi out of his difficulties and to enable him to marry Francesca Armosino in 1880.[18]

Countess Raimondi also remarried and survived on until 1918.

He had been living with Francesca since the 1870s. A socially far more humble woman, she had come to work in his family as nurse and governess. When he eventually married Francesca, their daughter Clelia was nearly thirteen. His marriages and domestic goings-on became talking points in their own right. *The Times* sniffed, after the General's death, that 'It [was] painful, but just, to record how his facile credulity entrapped him into a mock marriage with the Countess Raimondi, a young lady of rank, at Como'. It was, apparently, no less 'melancholy, but instructive' to recollect the spectacle he exhibited with Francesca and his young children, 'the results of his domestication with the nurse'.[19]

This 'domestication' was to divide Garibaldi's own family. Francesca had originally come into his life by way of his daughter Teresita, who had married an Italian radical, Stefano Canzio, at the age of sixteen, and went on to have a large family. She employed Francesca while living with her father at Caprera in 1867. Jasper Ridley cites the following story about ructions in the household; this may be apocryphal in its detail but captures well enough the strained atmosphere that prevailed. Apparently, Teresita wished to engage a wet nurse for her baby. Garibaldi, like many other nineteenth-century radicals, took exception to wet-nursing, viewing it as an example of the oppression of the poor by the rich. Teresita was extremely distressed by Garibaldi's opposition and became increasingly frosty and difficult. As a result, she complained that she was disturbed by the noise of Garibaldi's four guinea fowls, to which he was greatly attached. Without informing her father, she arranged for the fowls to be killed and then served them up for dinner; but Garibaldi was so upset by the death of the birds that neither he nor anyone else would eat them. Eventually Garibaldi gave way on the question of the wet nurse. Later, Francesca was to be accused by Teresita of stealing items from the house at Caprera. What she really 'stole', Ridley suggests, was Garibaldi.[20]

The General was discouraged by impediments to settling his domestic affairs during the 1870s and also frustrated by the difficulty of realising his plans to save Rome, growing increasingly disheartened by the obstruction of his Tiber scheme. In October 1875, Garibaldi was unwell and returned for a time to Caprera. In letters to his Roman electors, he wearily confessed the scale of the administrative and bureaucratic obstacles he was facing. His supporters shared in the sense of dismay and joined in the recriminations.[21] They had been outmanoeuvred, and their leader was seen to be fighting a losing cause. On a variety of other issues through the 1860s and 70s, Garibaldi had already expressed his open dismay at the government's shoddy treatment of himself and his volunteers.[22] As impediments and barriers multiplied, he conveyed to his friend Jessie White Mario his deepening disappointment with 'Rome', not least with the strength of opposition to his Tiber plans: 'What do they want?' he asked incredulously; only to conclude: 'They've tricked me.'[23] With the establishment of commissions and inquiries, he could see that the politicians and administrators were going to ensure that the plan resulted in nothing, or at least nothing the General considered worthy of the capital. He sought to muster his old defiance, but with evident difficulty. In a forlorn echo of the great battle cry 'Rome or Death', he promised his old military comrade Amadei that 'here we will make the deviation canal or we shall die trying'.[24]

Garibaldi fumed and fretted, wrote letters, consulted and reconsulted his entourage, and revised the scheme as best he could. Yet he also conveyed a weary sense of disappointment and dismay, as though in this latest mishap, yet again, could be seen the saga of the good reformer lost in the hopeless labyrinth of the capital. Garibaldi's grumbling discontent, as he moved through the political system, vainly seeking to promote the renaissance of the city, did not pass unnoticed. Here, it was felt, could be glimpsed the predicament of the plain-spoken hero, tricked by the politicians, paralysed by the

Garibaldi as Gulliver, tied down in Rome, 1875

morass of the state. The agony was long-drawn-out. Amadei laboured at a revised scheme but, in November, rumour again had it that the government intended to kill off any hopes for Garibaldi's initiative. The General struggled finally to accept the writing on the wall – at one point petulantly telling the minister to go ahead with whatever half-baked engineering measure the government chose, but to count him out from all further deliberations.[25] That, no doubt, was precisely the aim of his opponents.

A picture that circulated around this time, of Garibaldi as Gulliver bound down by the Lilliputians, captured well his sense of bureaucratic imprisonment. The word often used by the General and his circle to refer to adversaries in government was 'pygmies'.[26] The flavour of his attack can be seen in the tone of one caustic letter, in which he described the government doing nothing because it was incapable of doing anything, other than wasting resources, cheating, deceiving, pulling the wool. He had long spoken of the scale of political corruption, and his disillusionment with the authorities echoed a far more extensive popular mood of dissatisfaction which was soon to be expressed in a voter revolt against the

195

right that led to the fall of the government. The *coup de grâce* for Garibaldi's project had taken place in a meeting at the Ministry of Public Works on 27 November 1875, with the General himself in attendance. He was decisively outmanoeuvred, and his scheme voted out. Anodyne reassurance and praise that he had done well to concentrate the minds of government on the problem – even if his particular proposals had been ill-starred – provided scant consolation. Various letters, complaining of this outcome, were aired in the press.

The schemes advanced by Garibaldi's protégés, Filopanti and Amadei, had both been regarded by government critics as profligate and scientifically inadequate. Since Garibaldi had given an ear to both men, historians have had a difficult task in establishing precisely which was the 'original' Garibaldi scheme of early 1875 and which the successor. The General had sought to reassure both of his advisers, causing much muddle as he flitted from drawing to drawing. At one time he had referred to Filopanti's project as 'sublime', only to revert to Amadei's sketches when the first scheme foundered.[27] Garibaldi had angrily rejected the financial and technical calculations of his opponents. He was sure that major savings could be made elsewhere in government, creating funds which could then be redirected to provide for river and port developments, railways, industry and any number of other enterprises. Amadei continued to complain to Garibaldi that the government's engineers had unfairly rubbished his design, and then undermined its prospects by exaggerating its cost.* The Colonel

---

* Garibaldi was also annoyed by the conclusions reached by an eminent engineer, Giovanni Amenduni, who had been commissioned by the government to attach some realistic prices to the General's rapidly evolving plans. Not surprisingly, he had found these unacceptably high and was unimpressed by protests from the General and his entourage that the costings were wrong. Garibaldi was not on strong ground here since he had always made clear that cost was a secondary consideration and that accountancy must not curtail ambition. Others took a different view, since the Italian state was in a dire financial position, having begun

referred bitterly to obscure government manoeuvres aimed at engineering his personal defeat. The tone of his letters, some of which were printed in newspapers, became increasingly carping. Garibaldi's adviser had evidently also fallen foul of another engineer, the aforementioned Baccarini, who had a senior position at the Ministry of Public Works.[28] Amadei sought to defend his reputation and insisted on his technical competence.[29] He accused Baccarini of belittling him, and in letters to government officials grumbled about the personal sacrifices he had made for the project, and the unrecompensed expenses he had been asked to bear. Amadei was at pains to exonerate the General himself from the charge of double-dealing; he attributed the relegation of his own scheme to the machinations of the surrounding entourage or the government.[30]

When the left came to power in March 1876, it brought Depretis to the head of government, and led to the appointment of a new Minister of Public Works, Giuseppe Zanardelli. Hope was briefly revived among Garibaldi's supporters. Previous decisions about the Tiber were once more frozen and the General's schemes were put back on the table. But the change of fortune was short-lived and the hopes ill-founded. Committees once again rejected his radical 'external' solution and reverted to the original wall-building measures within the river course in Rome. This time Garibaldi felt betrayed by his former allies on the left. Filopanti predicted that he was going to retreat to Caprera

---

life with huge costs, not least those entailed by its military campaigns and continuing post-unification struggle to deal with brigandage in the south. By the time Depretis and others had worked over the scheme, via committees and reports of various descriptions, the General's vision was shown to be ill-conceived, his blueprints left in tatters. The government thus derailed Garibaldi's plans, while appearing to support his broad aims, by providing advisers and facilities, offering careful budgetary exercises and furnishing 'helpful' engineering advice.

again, refusing to do any more horse-trading. He hoped that the General would not sulk in his tent like Achilles.[31] In fact, Garibaldi was subjected to various further manoeuvres and humiliations as he went helplessly around the bureaucratic loop. Filopanti likened him to the ghost of a giant.[32]

The General's note of bitterness over the Tiber scheme was in tune with his broad dissatisfaction over the whole direction of political events in post-unification Italy. He complained about the miserable state of national finances, the legacy of servility, the stranglehold exerted by feeble, incompetent ministers. The long-term material and spiritual property of the nation had been surrendered, he complained, to the false god of money. He yearned for the rekindling of the Risorgimento spirit, a moral force that would revitalise the nation's energy and thereby revive its health and economy. Sacrifice and service were his watchwords. Garibaldi pointed out how much morale could be improved and how much money could be saved by basing national defence on a citizens' volunteer force – a popular militia to be called upon as needed – rather than on a permanent army of 200,000 soldiers, unnaturally segregated from the rest of society.

Having initially sided with those who sought to divert the Tiber away from Rome, Garibaldi later accepted that the water course must be tamed, not eliminated from the landscape – such was the attachment of Rome's citizens to their river.* Whatever the precise scheme, the crucial point

* Around this time, a great deal of new civic interest was being shown in the Tiber. For example, an association was formed, to some international fanfare, for the exploration of Roman treasures thought to be buried in great quantities in the river bed (*The Times*, 21 August 1871, p. 6). As *The Times*'s Italian correspondent enthused (while reporting the progress of this archaeological initiative): 'The Tiber received all that Rome could not keep from it, and whatever went into it was never afterwards disturbed. The Romans look on their stream as the safe receptacle of all lost things. Search, they say, and you will find. Probe the shattered piers of the Sublician Bridge, they tell you, and you must reach the helmets

for Garibaldi was to keep in mind the big picture: the revi-
talisation of Rome and the Campagna, their reclamation
from the forces of death. But nothing was to save his river
designs. They were found wanting by engineers, accountants and many politicians; they were even criticised by
conservationists, for lack of sensitivity to Rome's architecture and beauty.[33] He could accept that point, but the spirit
of opposition to his grand endeavour depressed him; the
unhappy fate of his scheme seemed to Garibaldi evidence
of a deeper national malaise: 'old' Rome was still fatally
undermining 'new' Rome. He suspected that the continuing 'infestation of priests' in the Eternal City played its part
in this obstruction, as in so many others. A withering analysis
of craven Catholic rituals went together with a critique of
the administrative failings of the post-unification state, which
had, as it were, inherited and further perpetuated the profli-
gacy, waste and decadence of the Vatican. Italy, he insisted,
remained in a spiral of decline. The General spoke of the
historical deterioration which had taken place in the bodies
of the people – the beautiful Italian race impoverished
because the very soul of Rome was tainted.[34] Instead of
witnessing the accomplishment of great projects to tame

---

and cuirasses of those Etruscan warriors whose bodies have been rotting there
ever since the victorious townsmen of Horatius Cocles hurled them in, 2367 years
ago' (*The Times*, 21 August 1875, p. 9). Here, beneath the currents, 'lay the sink of
Rome, which was the world's sink'; 'while everything around decayed and perished,
and the world passed away, leaving the site of Rome a dreary solitude, the ancient
stream flowed on, sweeping away the debris of Rome's wreck, and awaiting the
day in which it should be called upon to give up its memories' (ibid.). A different
kind of enthusiasm for the Tiber was expressed by muscular Roman youths, who,
in September 1874, had participated for the first time in a splendid and well-
attended regatta. Rowing contests through central Rome were held, in imitation
of English boat races. Intrepid competitors negotiated the 'treacherous' waterway,
with its rapid vortices and strong currents (*The Times*, 4 September 1874, p. 9).

rivers and develop better docks for Genoa, Naples, Palermo, Rome and Venice, Garibaldi saw an Italy burdened by the enormous salaries and pensions of its parasitic political class. Thus Italy's ancient mariner confronted his countrymen.

The scheme was, in all likelihood, technically feasible at the time, had sufficient funds been devoted to it.[35] It was perhaps no more challenging, in principle, than some of the other remarkable design and building feats that were accomplished in that period. However, given the parlous state of national finances, it was not surprising that the government blanched at the cost and sought cheaper alternatives. The obstructionism of the civil service and the misgivings of the government may be explained in the normal way, in terms of realistic financial constraints, sceptical engineering advice and cautious officialdom, as well as the customary 'horse-trading', interpersonal 'politicking', jockeying for influence, committee compromises and so forth that govern public business. But the nature of Garibaldi's personal investment merits close investigation. Although we cannot know whether, in his heart of hearts, he really expected to succeed with his full-blown plans, his earnest commitment to the endeavour cannot be doubted.

It is a mistake to conceive the issue simply in terms of who won or lost the parliamentary debate, what legislation was passed and which scheme foundered. Style, performance and theatre had always been vital aspects of Garibaldi's approach. He offered himself as an example, a living principle, and regarded tenacity and commitment, even if leading to melancholy defeat, as superior to sullied compromise. These qualities of doggedness and implacability were central to his self-fashioned legend. Historians and biographers have, of course, long noticed this performance-conscious aspect of his behaviour. Remarking on Garibaldi's distinctive clothes, white horse and aloof manners, a recent commentator observes that '[i]n such careful flamboyance, and setting-apart of himself, it is impossible not to see –

whatever its practical justification – the reflection of some need of his nature'.[36]

The endeavour to interpret Garibaldi's 'nature' has a long history. Nobody in the period was more closely dissected and wildly analysed. He was cast as an angel of divine justice, a child, a fool, even a madman.[37] His every action or expression was examined for hidden symptoms and meanings. Many people have evidently been interested not only in how Garibaldi performed publicly, how he 'did things with words'[38] or communicated thoughts through practical actions, but also what went on in the privacy of his own mind. Were his actions really as unpredictable as they looked, or was the General following a logic he kept to himself (or indeed from himself)? In the 1850s and 60s, fellow campaigners, as well as statesmen, ambassadors, foreign secretaries across Europe, had become deeply absorbed by the enigma of his plans, second-guessing his underlying purposes, diagnosing his personality, trying to resolve once and for all the question 'What does he really want?' Nobody had been more exercised by this conundrum than Count Cavour in the late 1850s, as he watched and sought to control the energies of that tumultuous 'hero of two worlds', who was so intent on uniting Italy, regardless of diplomatic complexities. (Admittedly, grasping the Count's deeper purposes sometimes proved no easier than diagnosing the General's.)

Of all his relationships, Garibaldi's difficult, antagonistic interaction with Cavour, on the eve of national unification, has been the most widely explored. The manoeuvres and mutual perceptions (or misperceptions) of the two men in the single crucial year of 1860 have been carefully dissected.[39] It is difficult, at times, to disentangle what view really belonged to whom, as wager, feint and bluff followed in dizzying succession, each leader and his entourage warily assessing the hidden meanings encapsulated in the declarations and actions of the other. If Cavour is generally cast as the consummately knowing manipulator, the shrewd card player who never revealed his hand, Garibaldi often was (or played) the ingénu. For some he was honest to a fault; his one real weakness, observed a passionate English admirer in 1860, was being 'too guileless for this world'.[40] His 'loving eyes', lack of affectation and apparent indifference to diplomacy were fondly described by numerous observers. His biographers rightly draw attention to Garibaldi's extraordinary gullibility over money, and his occasional miscalculations about the bona fides of associates, sometimes with disastrous consequences, as in the planning of the various Rome offensives of the 1860s.[41] His reputation hinged on this quality of innocence and a certain rather endearing ignorance of (or at least wilful blindness towards) 'the ways of the world'.

Perhaps neither Cavour nor Garibaldi fully understood what he or what either was up to, as each monitored the other, impelled into actions or declarations whose function was not always entirely clear at the time, even if they could be rationalised after the event. Some historians emphasised Cavour's diplomatic acumen and contrasted it with Garibaldi's blunt approach and modest intelligence. Yet it has also been widely observed that when the General's rivals and enemies underestimated him, they tended to rue their mistake.[42] At times he played up his simplicity and lack of guile to good effect, in order to disguise his deeper purposes. Garibaldi's image was manipulated by others but also by himself – his memoirs, novels, letters and speeches helped fashion his heroic status and his reputation for humility. The process of 'monumentalisation' continued after his death – most directly embodied in innumerable statues, images and place names (still to be seen in towns and cities throughout the peninsula).[43]

In a long obituary in *The Times*, it was observed that Garibaldi rushed to conclusions without troubling his head about arguments. He was seen to have crude notions of democracy, of communism, of cosmopolitanism and of positivism, all of which 'were jumbled together in his brain' where they 'jostled one another in hopeless confusion, involving him in unconscious contradiction notwithstanding all his efforts to maintain a character for consistency'. Garibaldi's mercurial quality made it difficult to find an adequate yardstick to assess his actions. The General was judged no idiot, but nor was he exactly wise:

> In sober moments he seemed to acknowledge his intellectual deficiencies, his imperfect education, the facility with which he allowed his own fancy or the advice of dangerous friends to run away with his better judgement; but presently he would lay aside all diffidence [and] harangue ... [He would] preside at meetings, address multitudes, talk with the greatest boldness about what he least understood, and put his friends to the blush by his emphatic, trenchant, absolute tone, by his wild theories and sweeping assertions, as he did at Geneva at one of the Peace Society Congresses, when, before a bigoted Calvinistic audience, he settled the question whether St Peter ever had or had not been in Rome – 'a futile question', he said, 'for I can tell you no such person as Peter has ever existed.'

Garibaldi was to be forgiven such a claim, insisted *The Times*, for 'with a heart like [his] a man may well afford to allow his brain to go a wool gathering'. Any errors of judgement he made were as nothing compared with his achievements and the remarkable magnanimity of his character: 'Let even his worst enemy write Garibaldi's biography and he will always appear the most single-minded and disinterested, the least self-conscious of all men.' The obituarist pointed out that for many years, 'with unshaken consistency', Garibaldi refused all rewards, shunned popular acclaim and revolted against the 'abject worship' of the crowd. He appeared stern and incorruptible, as women, men, and even priests in Calabria hailed him as 'Our Messiah! Our Redeemer!'; as mothers from Lombardy held up their newborn infants to

be christened by him, 'no other hand being so sure to bring
God's blessing with it'. In London, in 1864, he 'fairly ran
away from the fine ladies who seemed at a loss to know
how a true lion should be lionized'.[44] If *The Times*, among
others, found his family arrangements and sometimes his
political views rather preposterous, these were increasingly
taken as signs of his simplicity and trustfulness rather than
his dangerousness: 'He was the most loving, the least hating
of men.' Whatever follies or even crimes may have been
committed in his name, 'one may freely defy the world to
trace an act of meanness or a deed of cruelty, or even a
deliberately unkind word, to the man himself'. 'However
madly he dabbled in republicanism, his devotion to Victor
Emmanuel was proof against all slight or ill-treatment on
the part of the King's government. Whatever progress he
made in the modern school of philosophers, his faith in
God was unshaken. Unfortunately, his trust in men – and
women – transcended all discretion.'[45]

In death, as in life, Garibaldi was to make the most
profound impression on his contemporaries. Copious illustrations of him circulated at each crucial stage of his life,
and, finally prostrate, on his deathbed. But even when he
had been presented as very much alive, full of vigour and
energy, he was thought to possess a quality of stillness, a
presence 'beyond words', mute and serene that fascinated
his public. People were gripped by his silences as much as
by his utterances. Some commentators believe this
compelling quality to derive from a peculiar blankness
whereby '[e]veryone can find in him something of themselves'.[46] The landscape of his mind and motivation has been
much discussed. And yet, perhaps surprisingly, he has never
received the full psychobiographical treatment in the twentieth century to which a number of other internationally
important historical figures, from Luther to Louis XIV,
Woodrow Wilson to Gandhi, have been subjected.

Can one go further than a character sketch and interpret

Garibaldi's unconscious motives, the hidden knot of his Roman passion? Can one, for instance, get behind the loose notion of 'martyrdom' and consider what sacrifice or regeneration meant to him, within what *The Times* calls 'the unconscious contradiction' of his mind? His specific ambitions for the revival of the Eternal City reflected contemporary political thought as well as medical explanations of flood and fever. This book has sought to ponder collective cultural fantasies about the General; but also to wonder what Garibaldi himself may wittingly *and* unwittingly have been *doing*, or what he was publicly and privately *enacting*, as he took up opportunities, bridled against constraints, and navigated his way through the debates, drama and crises of his time.

Garibaldi's speeches and letters about Rome and the Tiber oscillated between grandiosity and humility. As he swept into the city with his dramatic 'solution' to its ills, he seemed utterly persuaded of his own case. In temporarily blinding himself to the practical and political shortcomings of his Tiber plans, he appeared to be driven on by an obsession. Was he not seeking magically to put the world – or rather his world – 'to rights'? He spoke of having failed to do enough for Rome in the past, but perhaps unconsciously the city also symbolised a still deeper, more personal, damaged 'place' that he longed to repair. As a war hero, his career was inextricably associated with idealised violence, blood and death. His later life was punctuated by successive attempts to turn his back on war, to bring peace and harmony to the world, through international congresses and grand schemes for civic and moral 'recovery'. Yet there was also, as some contemporaries noted, an omnipotent quality here too. They remarked on his continuing 'illusions' and the pathos of his diminished power: an old man still seeking to shake the elements. At times, he seemed persuaded by his own invincible rhetoric – as though anything was possible if only *he* insisted upon it long and hard enough. But for all his eloquence and energy, the dream was gradually punctured.

When in a state of mania, we tend to deny guilt and responsibility, blithely claiming that the damage we have done to ourselves or our loved ones can all be put to rights – internal conflicts and external obstacles are conjured away with jubilant confidence and abandon.[47] Was there not something of this evident in Garibaldi's blueprint for Rome? On the one hand, he promised dramatic action to redeem the failings and deficiencies of the past, brushing aside all opposition or criticism. On the other, he seemed intuitively to expect and to prepare for defeat, to mourn the impossibility of the all-powerful solutions he promoted. Garibaldi was public-spirited in his tireless quest to redeem Rome, but perhaps he was also seeking to resolve 'unfinished business' of a more personal kind. There were logical – and impressively altruistic – reasons for his endeavour, but it would not have carried the force it did for him were it not for the way it re-enacted deeper conflicts and dramas.

The information we have suggests that over and above the cultural, social, political or medical significance which Rome held for Garibaldi and his associates, as a prized object to be conquered, redeemed and purified, his view of a 'dying' city was coloured by particular unconscious preoccupations. He appeared increasingly transfixed by the idea that he should devote everything to the rescue and restoration of this tantalising city that he often directly likened to a loved woman. His wish was to repair the damage, heal the sickness and bring a new radiance to this revered but sullied site. He appeared to be prevented from doing so, however, by hostile and, in his view, vainglorious personalities, intent on keeping Rome ill. At the historical level, we can point to the real forces, in the world, that were indeed intent on thwarting him, and all he stood for. But had he not also displaced on to the salvation of the Eternal City malevolent, dying or dead figures buried in his own history – or thought – which appeared either beyond repair or who were committed to sabotaging his own good work? He seemed to be faced, interminably, by the failure of the quest fully to save and purify the object of his desire. He spoke at times as though an instant, quasi-magical moral (or medicinal) solution was possible. Of course he could not 'repair' the numerous real deaths with which he was confronted, but nor it seemed could he quite acknowledge his complicity with, even culpability for, the neglect of some of these important lost ideals, ambitions and people. At times, he claimed a monopoly of pure motives and would attack others who were vain and narcissistic, more concerned for glory, money or comfort than for taking care of the mother city or for nurturing the priceless newborn nation that had emerged from such historical pain and grief.

Under pressure, Garibaldi did compromise and adapt his Tiber plans, but he also spoke as though any compromise was death. There is much that is ambiguous in his 'failure'. Did he foster, somewhat masochistically, a further inevitable defeat? Or did his initiative really seek to demonstrate that only a dictatorship could work? To fail in so noble an aim as the regeneration of Rome was to dramatise his long-standing complaint about his own political marginalisation and the moral impotence of the new state. Was this the potent narrative of unrequited ambition that he sought to bequeath to the future?

Whether Garibaldi deliberately sought this or not, turn-of-the-century nationalists and, later on, Fascists, including Mussolini himself, clearly picked up that 'lesson', when they made use of the story of Garibaldi's defeats, and his unfinished political and social projects. The precise balance between Garibaldi's fantasies, and the broader cultural representations that were projected upon him, is a moot point: his actions and thoughts were themselves inevitably inflected by the pressure of collective expectations and the scale of public adoration and investment. We cannot claim to have grasped the precise configurations of Garibaldi's desire and anxiety, and yet it would be wilfully myopic were we to study the past as though such historical figures have no internal world.

Rome or Death

To ponder Garibaldi's public performance in Rome, during the later 1870s, as a performance of failure is not entirely to leave cultural history for the wilder shores of psychohistory. As discussed in Chapter 8, the story of the ingénu who comes to Rome, only to discover him or herself caught in the painful labyrinth of the Old World, was itself already extensively culturally encoded. Many writers shared with Garibaldi this sense of Rome as the site of disillusionment and despair, the city in which weary cynicism outwitted the naive outsider. Rome was to be presented in a large mass of writings as the site of mystique, and of the pained knowledge of human incapacity. It was also perceived as a hotbed of guile and corruption. And in twentieth-century politics too, of course, the need to reclaim and purify 'Rome' continued to inform the rhetoric, and sometimes the policies, of reforming politicians, even to feature notably in various forms of Fascist moral supremacism.*

---

* Close analysis of the idea of Rome in political and cultural thought in the twentieth century is beyond the scope of the present inquiry. Suffice to say here that in the final decades of the nineteenth century, commentators had a field day in deriding the shady practices that took place in Italy's new capital (Dickie 1993 and 1999). As the Italian political scientist Emilio Gentile (1996) has convincingly shown, a quasi-mystical appeal to collective 'regeneration' ran through the Risorgimento and was bequeathed to later thought. A curious hybrid 'secular religious' perspective emerged. This was passed from the age of Mazzini and Garibaldi to modern art and political movements. The idea of modern Italy as a giant betrayal of the Risorgimento's ideals, an ignominious flop, presided over by sleazy incompetents and cynics, was itself gaining ground at the time that Garibaldi's Roman reforms foundered. The shadowy ideal of 'Romanità' was also frequently used by politicians in search of 'vision'. This rhetorical identification of the present with an illustrious past served to underwrite particular legislative proposals or to associate an individual orator with the moral high ground. Depending on circumstances, one might deploy 'Rome' to signify corruption and decline, or grand historical power and ambition: thus Prime Minister Crispi appealed to the imperial past to justify the Italian war against Ethiopia as did Giolitti when, as head of government, he promoted further adventurist campaigns (Bondanella 1987; cf. Moe 2002).

An Unconscious Contradiction

During the Fascist period, and even through the 1950s, the moral reclamation of the Eternal City, from corruption, was to be a central political concern (Agnew 1995). In very different historical circumstances, in the late twentieth century, 'Rome' also loomed large in political rhetoric, notably in the stream of invective that emerged from the Northern League (see Mazzoni, 'Una problema capitale', in Ginsborg 1994, pp. 108–14). The disclosure of a massive system of political bribery, that came to be called '*tangentopoli*' (bribe city), a scandal that of course did not originate in and that was by no means ever to be confined to Rome, led to extraordinary political and institutional ferment. (This and the judicial campaigns and investigations that were named '*mani pulite*', clean hands, are particularly well charted and shrewdly analysed in Ginsborg 2001.) For the Northern League's leader, Umberto Bossi, Rome's disorder was sometimes attributed simply to the historical pathology of the south. In his view, it even appeared that 'Garibaldi should never have left for Marsala in 1860' (Ginsborg 2001, pp. 175–6; cf. Savelli 1992; Bull and Gilbert 2001). Political subterfuge, massive bribery, and worse, are certainly not mere fanciful inventions, but needless to say, 'Rome' merely serves as shorthand for practices now exposed across and beyond the peninsula. Denunciation of 'thieving Rome' has also featured notably in the discourse of Gianfranco Fini, the 'post-Fascist' leader of the far right party that he renamed the Alleanza Nazionale (Francia 1994). Recognition of the reality of direct and indirect corruption, conflicts of interest and the deep-rooted obstacles to progressive change has often given way to catch-all diagnoses, to ominous narratives and political solutions.

As an English journalist has recently noted, discussions of politics in Italy are frequently conducted in terms of illusion, conjuring and manipulation. The exposure of hidden political plots and secret 'Masonic' alliances (which have of course been shown to exist) easily mutates into a more lurid and paranoiac vision of impenetrable, secret and omniscient powers, running the entire system, often from the shadows of the capital. Although the phenomenon and perception of such forces are obviously not unique to Italy, the Italian language has a remarkably rich repertoire of words to describe the techniques of string-pulling, miscommunication and diversion:

There are some frequently used Italian words that may be useful here . . . *polverone* (a great cloud of dust) describes the confusion generated by extrava-

Perhaps Garibaldi was more comfortable as a loser than a winner. Despite all his achievements, he appeared to be haunted by his own sense of sadness and betrayal. He saw the political settlement that had emerged in the new nation as a terrible broken promise. He declared that Rome *was* the very essence of Italy and that future progress depended absolutely upon the repair and integration of the state's mutilated parts.[48] Increasingly, he railed against the degeneration of 'Italy', the fatal corruption of the ideals of the Risorgimento.

In the 1870s, family illness and death were much in his thoughts. After his young daughter Rosa died, while Garibaldi was fighting in France, he wrote: 'it seems to me that such beings are exotic plants, who willingly leave this vale of tears for happier regions'.[49] We cannot be sure how far he truly believed that. And even if he did, one might doubt how much consolation it really offered him. The following year, he was in agony about the illness of another daughter, Clelia, who was laid up with a fever for forty days, till she looked, he declared, almost like a skeleton. 'Is not this life of ours a valley of tears through which Time stalks, respecting neither the tomb nor the works of men, nor their relics, material or mental?' he wrote, in a pained letter to his friend and former mistress Baroness von Schwartz. He dreaded that he might outlive a daughter, for the third time.[50] Much to his relief, Clelia recovered.

In 1875, a further tragedy befell him, and one, perhaps,

---

and hotly contested versions of the same ambiguous incident; *fantapolitica* refers to fantastic, scandalous, usually paranoid accounts of what is going on in political life; *dietrologia* (behind-the-scenes-ology) is the obsessive study or invention of *fantologia* and in particular of the way life is *pilotata*, secretly and illegally manipulated (by one's enemies); *insabbiare* (to sink something in the sand) describes the process by which an overwhelming quantity of red herrings (often provided by mafia *pentiti*) and/or red tape can lead to a criminal investigations being *archiviato*, filed away and forgotten. (Parks 2001) which left him with a feeling of guilt or responsibility, after the death of his deeply unhappy and much neglected daughter, Anna Maria Imeni, who had soon come to be called by the name of his long-dead first wife Anita.[51] Her name and sudden death must have reminded him of the painful illness and loss of his much loved partner in the desperate retreat from Rome in 1849. His daughter Anita was born in May 1859, the unwanted outcome of his affair with a poor, young peasant woman, Battistina Ravello. Much embarrassment and mystery surrounds his dealings both with Battistina and their daughter. A half-hearted plan to marry his lover seems to have been quickly abandoned; certainly Garibaldi's extended family were appalled at the idea that he would commit himself to so rough and low a woman (although this did not stop him from marrying 'beneath him' later on, of course, when he formalised his long-standing relationship with Francesca Armosino). Quite what impelled him towards and then away from the affair with Battistina is not entirely clear. For a time Battistina and their daughter had lived in reach of Garibaldi in Sardinia, but when he got word that this woman, 'his woman', was intimately involved with a young local man, he angrily packed her (and Anita) off to Nice.★ Perhaps the daughter was seen as tainted too. He provided some financial assistance to the unhappy pair, but from a discreet distance. Eventually, using some guile, he managed to prise Anita away from her mother, and entrusted her care to Baroness von Schwartz.

By all accounts, his daughter Anita had already had an unhappy childhood when this painful separation occurred; certainly she had rarely seen her father, and her reaction to this surprise visit to Caprera, when she was nine, did little to improve things. The aim was to remove her, summarily,

★ As we have seen, there had been at least one important earlier occasion when Garibaldi's knowledge of a woman's sexual liaisons caused him to turn away in disgust and hatred, namely that of his marriage to his second wife, Countess Raimondi.

from her mother. Battistina herself appears to have gone along with the plan, half reluctantly. On learning of her prospective fate the child ended up sobbing, kicking and screaming, rolling around on the earth, and the mother had second thoughts. Anita was forced to leave with the Baroness, but back on the mainland, struck her a blow, thereby confirming the new guardian's view that what was required was the discipline of a strict school. The experience of an institution for genteel young ladies in Switzerland was not to prove a success, and after further difficulties and considerable heartache, Anita became, in effect, an unpaid servant in the Baroness's house in Crete, where she seems to have been a virtual prisoner. Initially, Garibaldi tended to side with the guardian and to view Anita's not infrequent complaints about her education and general treatment as a product of her bad character, and of her inappropriate airs and graces.* Eventually, however, even he became suspicious about the conduct of the Baroness, and after receiving a desperate plea from the long-estranged Anita, he finally sent Menotti to fetch her from Crete.[†] She spent six weeks with her family, most of the time on Caprera, but during the summer of 1875 this sixteen-year-old long-suffering

---

* 'He turned strongly against Anita. He endorsed all [the Baroness's] complaints against his daughter, refused to read Anita's letters, and stated that if he could use Anita as a crutch with which to walk, with his rheumatism, she might be of some use in the world. He eventually agreed to Speranza's suggestion that she should take Anita to her house in Crete; and Anita, having been forcibly removed from her protesting mother on the grounds that she would thereby receive a good education, seems to have ended up as Speranza's unpaid servant in Crete' (Ridley 1974, p. 598).

[†] Anita had apparently got news of Garibaldi's visit to Rome from reports in the press. She managed, secretly, to throw a letter, addressed to her father, from a window, thereby evading the watchful and suspicious gaze of the Baroness. It was received by a neighbour who forwarded it. She was taken to Frascati, close to Rome, and was reunited with Garibaldi and his new family. Her hair was found to be crawling with lice (Ridley 1974, p. 628).

daughter was seized by a serious illness, perhaps an attack of malaria (although some have suggested it was food poisoning or meningitis), which led abruptly to her death.

The ignominy of her treatment and the ambiguities of Garibaldi's earlier attitude to this apparently unwanted child and her mother produced no clear expression of guilt. What seems more apparent than a prolonged, conscious mourning for this particular daughter was an ever greater weariness and pessimism in general, an acceptance of, even a wish for, his own death, which reinforced a tendency already apparent much earlier. So often Garibaldi had presented himself as indomitable; but he also sometimes declared his wish for his life to draw to a close. He had spoken publicly many times of his willingness, even eagerness, to die for Rome; more quietly, he confessed to the unbearable pain of outliving so many loved ones.

10 Death

'Methinks the Appian Way should be the only entrance to
Rome, through an avenue of tombs.'

Nathaniel Hawthorne, *Notebooks*

Instead of emancipating Rome politically, or draining the
swamps of the Campagna, Garibaldi himself became
hopelessly 'bogged down'. The General who had, for so
long, placed himself above politics, aloof and absent from
the parliamentary 'talking shop' he so acrimoniously
despised, came to Rome, only to see his pet project sidelined and rebuffed. But many were stirred by his example
and his desire to effect the material regeneration of the land,
inspired to achieve the kinds of outcome that had eluded
him. In the 1870s and beyond, Garibaldi's eldest son,
Menotti, devoted considerable energy to the reclamation of
a huge piece of land in the Campagna, at Carano. He was
also responsible for establishing various health and educational projects. At the age of sixty-three he contracted
malaria, dying in Rome in 1903. On a larger stage, Mussolini
would give priority to land reclamation and the 'war on
malaria' after he passed special legislation for the purpose
in 1928. In the 1930s he went on to create new towns on
previously abandoned, fever-ridden land in the Campagna.
In these endeavours, Mussolini several times referred back
directly to the General's inspiration, and linked this with his

214

own struggle for the salvation of Rome and its surrounding territories.

In a speech in Udine in 1922, Mussolini had asked the crowd to think of Rome and to help him build there a 'city of our spirit, a city well disciplined, disinfected of all the elements which corrupt it and disfigure it . . . the pulsating heart, the agile spirit of that Imperial Italy of which we dream'.[1] There were other influences upon his political thought in general and his projects for health reform and land reclamation in particular, but it is striking how, after his notorious march on Rome in 1922, the Fascist leader came to place great store in those same regenerative projects for the Eternal City and the Campagna that Garibaldi had already taken to heart in the nineteenth century. Garibaldi was to be fêted as a precursor, 'cast in an epic dominated by the divine intuition of Mussolini'.[2] As Il Duce declared: 'If Mazzini, if Garibaldi attempted three times to reach Rome, and if Garibaldi placed before his Redshirts the tragic inexorable dilemma, "Rome or death", that means that among the best men of the Italian Risorgimento, Rome fulfilled an essential function of the first importance to be carried out in the new history of the Italian Nation!'[3]

Mussolini's skilfully fashioned career mimicked aspects of Garibaldi's life and sought to reverse the trajectory of his political defeat. In a speech in 1932, Mussolini insisted on Fascism's special claim on Garibaldi. The blackshirts were the 'legitimate descendants' of the Red Shirts and their great leader: 'Never did he give way, never was he forced to surrender his high ideal – not by men, not by the sects, not by parties or ideologies, nor by the declamation encountered in parliamentary assemblies. These assemblies Garibaldi despised, advocate as he was of an "unlimited" dictatorship in difficult times.' Mussolini noted how Garibaldi had worked on a scheme for draining marshes. And then, speaking of the future moral transformation of the capital, the Fascist leader mused on how current policies would have pleased the old General: 'With what pleasure he would look upon our present-day Rome, luminous, vast, no longer torn by factions, this Rome which he so deeply loved and which from his earliest youth he always identified with Italy!'[4]

Fascism endeavoured to link itself to Garibaldi – that greatest of Risorgimento heroes – and to the illustrious 'volunteers' who had followed him.[5] Now Mussolini would seek to conquer the swamps and fevers that had defeated so many leaders before.[6] Gradually, some previously uninhabitable areas were indeed drained and reclaimed as part of Il Duce's policy of internal colonisation and development.[7] In fact, however, Fascism's anti-malarial achievements were largely confined to the Pontine Marshes, and were also won at the cost of many lives. In the south and the islands, the scourge of malaria remained still largely untouched until after 1945.

Not all of the impetus behind this new 'war on malaria' can be attributed to Fascism, of course; and still less can public awareness of the problem in twentieth-century Italy be ascribed principally to Garibaldi. Despite major anti-malaria works and policies at the turn of the century, the death rate from the disease in Italy had increased during the First World War. Thus malaria was almost bound to have been a political and social priority for any post-war government, and scores of doctors, nurses and scientists continued to devote their lives to the humanitarian tragedy induced by the accursed anopheline mosquitoes. Whereas in 1914 the numbers of deaths were recorded at around 2,000 per annum, by 1918 they had risen to about 11,500. Influenza went on to kill many of those already weakened by the insect's pernicious bite.[8] The Italian dimension of malaria remained very much in the public eye, among health professionals at home and overseas. An article in the journal *The World's Health*, in 1923, went so far as to assert that '[m]alaria is essentially an Italian problem'.[9] Many of the best-known experts on the disease were Italian and the struggle against the fever continued to involve a major political and scientific effort by the national authorities. Seeing the massive Italian campaign to eradicate the disease during the 1920s, Dr Wickliffe Rose, Director of the Rockefeller Foundation in New York, wrote: 'This is the biggest piece of work ever done in malaria; it is Faust's dream realized!'[10] But all that said, Italian malariology in the inter-war period was increasingly to be conceived as, precisely, a triumph for Fascism.[11] Some admiring onlookers and working malariologists celebrated the fact that the re-clamation of marshland dreamed of by Caesar, considered by Napoleon and vainly demanded by Garibaldi, was now actu-ally being realised under Fascism.[12]

Rural reclamation and campaigns against malaria certainly were of enormous political and medical significance, and long-term public gains clearly followed from such endeav-ours, across and beyond the first half of the twentieth century. The aim of producing malaria-free land for internal coloni-sation was extended, building on legislative measures that had already been put in place around 1900. Pumping stations and other land-reclamation measures proliferated. The islands of Sicily and Sardinia, Rome and the Campagna, as well as other mainland black spots, were gradually liberated. New residential quarters were developed on what had once been marshy wastelands. Work proceeded in order to sanitise streets, improve sewers, contain and regularise the flow of the Tiber, remove unwanted ponds and swamps.[13] But in less material ways too, the example of Garibaldi, his aspira-tions, achievements and disappointments, continued to resonate with the hopes and complaints of later generations.

Some contemporaries gave Garibaldi the credit for having provoked action in the long aftermath of the 1870 flood. He had given an important lead and raised urgent questions about urban regeneration, adding to the prestige of the engi-neers of the new Italy. Congresses of specialists were convened to discuss land reclamation and river defence during these years. Welcome advances in sanitation and hygiene were taking place in the Eternal City.[14] Although the General's own scheme was not chosen and the sums allocated were not sufficient for the major undertaking that he first envisaged, the law passed on 6 July 1875 had ordered, partly in deference to him, the further study of the Tiber problem and had established a sum for this purpose. He ensured that the problem would not be ignored.[15] Four options for river defence were closely considered during the 1870s, and the government proceeded in 1876 to the initial stages of the Tiber's repair.[16]

In a letter sent in 1878 to Francesco Crispi, once his chief of staff in Sicily, and by now Minister of the Interior, Garibaldi expressed his disappointment one last time. And then his Tiber correspondence dried up. The General turned to other matters. He was, during his final years, a very frail figure, increasingly confined to his island. Physical pain made walking ever more difficult and meant in the end that he was forced to resort to the use of a wheelchair. He still made occasional appearances in mainland Italy – attending

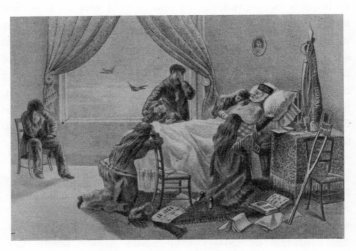

Garibaldi on his death-bed, surrounded by members of his family

events in Milan and Palermo, where observers were shocked by his physical decline. By the early summer of 1882 he lay dying at Caprera, attended by a young doctor from a nearby ship. There was nothing to do. Nonetheless, three days before he died, his mind was still lively; he was to be found occupying himself with astronomical problems and corresponding with the director of the observatory in Palermo, following his last exhausting visit to Sicily.

Close to the end, he expressed anguish about the fate of his children, alive and dead. He passed away on 2 June, leaving behind him plans of remarkable precision for his funeral. His third wife, Francesca, was told to see to his private cremation, on the island, using exactly the materials specified. He stipulated various details, including that he be dressed in his red shirt.[17] 'Make a fire of acacia – it burns like oil – and put me in my red shirt, my face upturned to the sun. When my body is burned put the ashes into an urn – any pot will do – and place it on the wall behind the tombs of Anita and Rosa. I mean to finish so.'[18] Garibaldi also required that the announcement of his death to the authorities be postponed, so as not to interfere with this secret ceremonial event, which was probably inspired in part by the well-known story of the poet Shelley's cremation on an open fire in 1822.[19] During his later years, the General had become a supporter of the practice – attracted to it not only because of its romantic, literary associations, but also, no doubt, because it conflicted with the policy of the Church.★ He wrote various letters to friends and acquaintances, expressing his support for cremation, and specified how he was to be burned and what should happen afterwards: an urn of his ashes was to be left near the remains of his deceased daughters. He even detailed the height of

★ The Catholic Church's policy of outright opposition to cremation was modified in 1963. Although burial is still preferred, cremation is now considered acceptable under certain conditions.

the required pyre and the nature of the wood to be used.

The Ascension of Garibaldi, 1882

In the days that followed his loss, many shops in the major cities were closed; theatres shut their doors; black flags hung in countless windows. Condolences poured in. King Umberto, an old admirer, was among the first to offer his sympathies to the family. Meanwhile, anxious meetings took place about the fate of the body. Some wanted him embalmed, others proposed the transportation of the corpse to the Gianicolo, or even to the Pantheon, in Rome. Practical difficulties were mentioned as arguments against cremation; apparently it might have taken twenty-four hours to incinerate the body in the way Garibaldi had specified. It was quietly pointed out that the visiting dignitaries could hardly be expected to stand respectfully to attention for that length of time. Yet it would be embarrassing for them to turn away prematurely.[20] In fact, Garibaldi's declared wish for cremation was to prove unattainable. Objections were raised: influential voices insisted that the event could not be so drastically screened off from the public; nor could the body be destroyed by fire. Rather, Garibaldi was to be venerated, placed, body intact, in a proper tomb. Such views prevailed. Predictably perhaps, given his colossal national and international symbolic importance, his 'humble' demand was resisted, as Roman dignitaries and other members of his family and entourage moved in. Political bigwigs, including Crispi, emissaries from the King and from the General's family managed to overrule his wife, insisting that religious decency and the sentiments of the entire nation required a quite different kind of arrangement to that originally conceived. Selected representatives of 'the thousand' were to be brought in, to put the coffin on their shoulders and take the General along a final ceremonial path, flanked with flags. Garibaldi was to be buried alongside other members of his family. At the funeral ceremony, there would be speeches by Crispi, Zanardelli and other eminent political figures.

Some superstitious participants and onlookers viewed the violent storm that broke out in the aftermath, and disrupted the return travel plans of the mourners, not merely as an inconvenience, but also as a symbol, even an ominous divine sign.[21] His last resting place was later to become a shrine for some, a casual tourist attraction for others. While vacationing in Sardinia, thousands continue to take time off from the beach, to make the trek to the Garibaldi Museum on Caprera. His rooms, artefacts and tomb are the subject of regular half-hour guided tours in what has proved to be one of the most frequented small museums in Italy.

Even to the end, with his outlandishly low-key funeral instructions to his wife, the General seemed intent on providing a final object lesson in the outrageous deviation of his plans, the politically motivated violation of his private intentions. But what was his will? In those final unrealisable and ostensibly humble instructions, we might see an attempt to retain control, to remain true to the downbeat, idiosyncratic style that was his hallmark. Was there not evidence of his paradoxical character and desire even here? He was a figure who made very large demands but also represented the virtues of extreme simplicity and humility. There was, as ever, a certain flamboyance even in the forceful modesty. He insisted on his own personal entitlement to have things, including the ceremonial arrangements of his own death,

Rome or Death

cast precisely as he liked, even as he criticised the narcissism and self-absorption of less high-minded parties. In asking who should be empowered to conduct the ritual of his death, he focused attention back on the ambiguous question of who pulled the strings during his many years of service to the Italian cause. We might detect here a last-ditch demonstration, even an unconscious enactment, of a scenario of frustration that had so often occurred before, during his youth, maturity and old age. With his self-deprecating 'small funeral', but also his powerful demands for compliance, did he not also seek the best of both worlds, this *'eroe dei due mondi'*? Was it slavish obedience or resistance that he really sought to elicit in his antagonists? We cannot be sure quite how canny he was in this last piece of script, and what desires lay most deeply buried here. But, unsurprisingly, his funeral was orchestrated with the necessary pomp and ceremony of the time. It was said that the public required no less. I rather suspect that he was at least half aware of the prospect that this would happen and thus became a choreographer of his own, posthumous, frustration. The old body was dispatched, the soul released and the nation left to mourn the final departure of Giuseppe Garibaldi.

Notes

1 Roman Fever

1   *Il Secolo*, 26–7 January 1875, p. 1.
2   Speech in Trastevere, 6 February 1875, quoted in Sacerdote 1933, p. 935.
3   By this time Menotti had himself become actively involved in a land-reclamation project in the Campagna Romana; see Chapter 10.
4   Morolli 1982, p. 99.
5   For a report of the line's closure in the terrible flood of 1870, see *L'Unità Cattolica*, 1 January 1871, no. 1, p. 3.
6   *The Times*, 9 February 1875, p. 8.
7   I rely here on the detailed account in Morolli 1982.
8   *Il Secolo*, 26–7 January 1871, p. 1. Garibaldi had most recently been elected a deputy of the first and fifth colleges of Rome for the twelfth legislature of 1875–7.
9   *The Times*, 3 June 1875, p. 5.
10 *The Times*, 9 February 1875, p. 8.
11 Rapisardi 1875.
12 Scirocco 2001, p. 372.
13 The expression was used by George Sand in her admiring account of Garibaldi (1859). On Garibaldi's worldwide fame and influence in the second half of the nineteenth century, see Anon. 1982.
14 Some other ambitious urban schemes in this period were also to fall by the wayside. The politician Quintino Sella, for instance, had advanced a dramatic plan in the 1870s

to move the existing centre of Rome to the east, but this was not adopted. It took until 1883, the year after Garibaldi's death, for the first major urban regulatory plan to be passed by the Italian government. This endorsed, among other things, the construction of a series of city-wide boulevards. In the period between 1870 and 1914, major construction projects did indeed take place; the demolition of substantial areas of housing occurred to enable great thoroughfares to be driven through. The Via Nazionale to the one side of Piazza Venezia, the Corso Vittorio to the other, were both products of this period. For further details of attempts (successful and unsuccessful) to transform Rome, and create a new 'modern' centre, together with plans to commemorate the achievement of unification in suitably colossal fashion, most notably through the controversial Vittoriano monument that dominates central Rome, see Agnew 1995 and Brice 1998.

15   Garibaldi 1983, p. 30.

16   Ibid., p. 36.

17   In Rome, he stayed briefly at the Albergo Costanzi, before transferring to the Villa Severini, and finally to the Villa Casalini; see Morolli 1982, p. 99.

18   Anon. 1882, p. 18.

19   In an address to parliament, Garibaldi pointed out that the Tiber was navigable in many stretches, but because of the impassable section in Rome, the utility of a route that might have been serviceable for some 150 kilometres or more, was vastly curtailed. The deviation of the Tiber from Rome was intended to solve this problem, among others. See the account of Garibaldi's parliamentary presentation, in Depretis's papers at the Archivio di Stato, Rome, fasc. 2, busta 9, serie 1, scatola 9, item 89. For Garibaldi's views about the river's pollution, see Garibaldi 1983, p. 11.

20   In fact, diverse assessments of the Tiber's state, and the diseases that might arise from living in proximity to it, had also been notable features of ancient Roman debate

as well; Sallares 2002, p. 228. For an ancient account of the Tiber's importance for commerce and the transportation of goods to Rome, see Pliny 1991. Pliny also describes the numerous villas overlooking the Tiber; he traces the course of the river back to its source and notes the frequency of the flood problem.

21   Vescovali 1873. For other writings about the floods of the 1870s, see Morolli 1982, p. 109.

22   For suggestive comments on why miasmatic theories of malaria may have been so particularly persuasive in Italy, see Coluzzi and Corbellini 1995; they show that the temperate climate and particular ecological circumstances in which malaria thrived in Italy tended to confirm the assumption that it was caused by the pernicious vapours arising from warm swamps.

2 Engineering the Future

1   I borrow the phrase from this account of the Thames and east London by Henry James: 'the polluted river, the sprawling barges, the dead-faced warehouses, the frowsy people, the atmospheric impurities become richly suggestive. It sounds rather absurd, but all this smudgy detail may remind you of nothing less than the wealth and power of the British Empire at large; so that a kind of metaphysical magnificence hovers over the scene' (quoted in Wilson 2002, p. 42).

2   Filopanti 1875, p. 4.

3   Letter, 12 July 1849, Garibaldi 1889, vol. 3, p. 115.

4   Rome's population grew from 212,000 in 1871, to 660,000 in 1921; see Agnew 1995, p. 11.

5   Letter, 29 April 1875, in Filopanti 1875, p. 112.

6   The Risorgimento Institute that is spectacularly perched at the top of the much lamented 'wedding cake'Vittoriano monument in central Rome, the Library of the Italian Parliament and the Central Archives of the State, at 'EUR'

– that controversial suburb of Rome that was once the architectural inspiration of the Fascist period – yield up their share of books, pamphlets, letters and reports relevant to the present story. The correspondence on the Tiber, contained in the papers of Depretis at the Archivio di Stato, is particularly illuminating. For details of this and other literature consulted, see the bibliography.

7   He used but 'three modest little rooms' inside the great palace; Butler 1901, p. 78.

8   Scirocco 2001, p. 248.

9   These examples are drawn from Hibbert 1987.

10   It was eventually the archaeologist Rosa and the engineer Narducci who succeeded in achieving better drainage for the lower part of the city; major sewer renewals were carried out from 1884 onwards (Celli 1933, pp. 157, 162; cf. Gori 1870, p. 26).

11   Late-nineteenth-century engineering developments and in particular spectacular Alpine demonstrations of the technological ability to pierce hard-rock mountain ranges brought the possibility of a fixed link between England and France to the fore (Travis 1991; Pick 1994).

12   Hunt 2004, p. 194. On the achievement of the chief engineer of the Thames, Sir Joseph William Bazalgette (1819–91), see also Halliday 1999.

13   New pumping techniques enabled ever bolder reclamation efforts. The large Haarlem Lake, between Amsterdam and Leiden, was reclaimed in 1852, and by the 1860s, elaborate plans were made to drain huge areas of the Zuyder Zee. Another possible source of inspiration was the engineering project that transformed the city of Brussels. Between the 1840s and the 1860s, the Senne River became a main sewer running under the wide, straight central boulevards of the inner city.

14   Cosgrove and Petts 1990.

15   Letter, 24 September 1880, Garibaldi 1932–7, p. 306; cf. Mack Smith 1969, p. 174.

16   Ridley 1974, pp. 5, 26.
17   Scirocco 2001, p. 358.
18   Ibid., p. 336.

3 Stagnation and Salvation

1   In practice, different definitions of the Campagna's precise extent have been given at different times; sometimes it is spoken of in a more restricted sense (roughly the area within an arc running to the coast through the Lake of Bracciano, Tivoli, Palestrina and Pomezia); at others, it has been used to signify a larger territory that includes the 'Maremma Laziale' (around Civitavecchia) and the whole of the Pontine Marshes in the south of Lazio, on which the following towns were built in the 1930s: Latina, Sabaudia, Pontinia, Aprilia and Pomezia.

2   The history of malaria in ancient Italy and the changing medical circumstances facing Rome's people have been thoroughly and lucidly discussed in a recent study by Sallares (2002). For compelling, richly illustrated accounts of the shifting cultural image of Rome and the Campagna in the modern age, see Liversidge and Edwards 1996, especially ch. 2.

3   'Rome, devourer of men [*Roma vorax hominum*] . . . Rome, fruitful in fevers [*Roma ferax febrium*]' (quoted in Sallares 2002, p. 231).

4   *Inferno*, canto 17, lines 85–8.

5   See, for instance, Celli 1933, p. 132.

6   Montaigne 1929, p. 149.

7   Gibbon 1981, pp. 688–9.

8   Byron, 'Childe Harolde's Pilgrimage', LXIX and LXXVIII.

9   Naples struck Taine as equally if not more dirty and depraved; he was dismayed by its primitive religion ('pagan Catholicism'), and a sensual reality that lay beneath a façade of asceticism (Taine 1867, p. 27).

10   See Liversidge and Edwards 1996.

11   Taine 1867, p. 269.

12   A feeling of sadness was often the response to the sights of the city and the countryside, a sorrow that was seen in turn to belong to the landscape itself. Chateaubriand, whom Napoleon had appointed to a position at the French Embassy in Rome at the start of the nineteenth century, referred to the silence and melancholy of this fever-stricken territory, a space denuded of trees and birds, in which the traveller encountered such suggestive ruins, lively pointers to the past, but also an overwhelming sense of barrenness and abandonment (Letter to M. de Fontanes, 1804, in Chateaubriand 1844, p. 363). The celebrated intellectual and novelist Madame de Staël drew attention to the poisonous impact of this land in her story of 1807, *Corinne*, neither the first nor the last to highlight the curious, blighted condition of the soil and its people. Here the Campagna was seen as both full of life and death. Rome was a beguiling city, in which the very air threatened the visitor: 'Malaria is the scourge of Rome'; 'you breathe an air which seems pure'; in fact it is anything but (de Staël [1807] 1883, pp. 85, 83). Stendhal also remarks on the dangers of the city and the Campagna in his *Promenades* (1829); see, for instance, p. 46. For the environmental history itself, see Sallares 2002; and for some brief illuminating remarks on the Campagna, see also Braudel 1947, vol. 1, pp. 81–2.

13   Sallares 2002, p. 233.

14   First published in a magazine in 1881, it was reprinted in Verga's *Novelle rusticane* in 1883.

15   Rome was not seen as uniformly dangerous, and malaria clearly was more likely to occur in certain parts of the city. Baedeker's *Handbook for Travellers*, which was reprinted frequently in the late nineteenth century, offered detailed advice on such matters to tourists. It noted that certain districts were practically immune: Via del Babuino, the Via

Sistina, the Via del Quirinale, extending on the south to S. Pietro in Vicoli, the Capitol, the neighbourhood of the Piazza S. Pietro and the quarter between the Ponte Sisto and Ponte Rotto were near exempt. The streets of the Viminal and the area of the Pincio were also found to be relatively safe. On the other hand, the hills of the Esquiline, the Palatine and Caelius were not recommended; the areas around the Coliseum and Monte Testaccio were particularly noted as danger spots (Baedeker 1886, p. xxvi).

16   Hare 1913, p. 9.

17   Sallares 2002, p. 22.

18   Ibid., p. 93. A recent article by Snowden (2002) suggests that the construction of the Rome–Naples railway, as well as increasing deforestation in central Italy, exacerbated malaria.

19   Sallares 2002, p. 215.

20   Hearder 1983.

21   Celli 1933, p. 163.

22   Sallares 2002, p. 4. For descriptions of the topography, climate and hydrological problems of the Pontine Marshes, see Snowden 2002, p. 120.

23   Sallares 2002, p. 190.

24   Celli 1933.

25   Quoted in ibid., p. 164.

26   Ibid., p. 164.

27   Quoted in ibid., p. 165.

28   Grassi 1900.

29   Fantini 1996, p. 14.

30   Anon. 1984, p. 16.

31   Garibaldi 1873, p. 39; cf. pp. 122 and 142. Italy, he wrote, must be seized back from malevolent priestly rule, taken from the control of 'eunuchs'; it needed more robust action, less art, memory and verbose speechifying.

32   Filopanti 1875, p. 5. Filopanti's views are endorsed by Garibaldi at the start and end of the book.

33   Dobson 1997, p. 15.

34   Riley 1987, p. 33, on whom I rely more generally in this section.

35   Quoted in ibid., p. 92. Other leading figures in this new environmentalist medicine were Hoffmann in Germany and Sauvages in France. The Montpellier physician Baumes insisted, a few years later, that 'the existence of marshy miasmas, and the power they have to propagate intermittent and remittent fevers is at present incontrovertibly beyond doubt'.

36   By the thirteenth century, Florence already had a series of regulations on street cleaning; and from the fifteenth century, debate about sewerage and urban waste removal became part of efforts to achieve concerted public health plans in various parts of north and central Italy (Baldwin 1999, p. 6). Policies on drainage, street paving, sewer renewal and so forth were extensively developed in the seventeenth and eighteenth centuries (Riley 1987).

37   Riley 1987.

38   On uses of the term 'malaria' in Italy across earlier centuries, see Sallares 2002, p. 7.

39   Selmi 1870, p. 9.

40   Corti 1984.

41   The social and cultural contexts of miasmatic theory have been considered in an extensive second literature; see, for instance: Parker 1983, Corbin 1986, Goubert 1986, Purseglove 1989, Miller 1989, Giblett 1996.

42   Watson 1921, p. 5. The discovery of the malarial parasite (1880) did not immediately put paid to older theories about miasmas as the cause of the disease. If anything, the parasite became the 'personification' of the miasma itself (Alleori 1967, p. 4). The conviction endured in the early 1890s that the disease might be passed on to the sufferer through the air itself.

43   *The Times*, 22 March 1875, p. 9.

44   See, for instance, Vescovali 1874. It was in fact Vescovali's

ideas, combined with those of another expert, Canevari, which formed the basis of the plan that was finally carried into practice.

45 Dobson 1997.

46 Carlyle 1849, pp. 674–5.

47 For a discussion of social conditions, swamp images and corruption metaphors in Victorian culture, see 'Cesspool City: London', in Wilson 1991, ch. 3.

48 Quoted in Eyler 1979, p. 99.

49 Ibid., p. 156.

50 Anderson 1927, p. 20.

51 Ibid., p. 15.

52 Miller 1989; Purseglove 1989.

53 Miller 1989, p. 9.

54 Giblett 1996.

55 Celli 1910, pp. 64–5.

56 Celli 1900, pp. 15–16.

57 Clark 1996, p. 162.

58 Celli 1900; Clark 1996, p. 21.

59 I rely here on Snowden 2002.

60 DDT was first used commercially in 1940, and then on a mass scale three years later. In 1949, Paris Green replaced DDT; see Snowden 2002.

61 Sallares 2002, pp. 4, 112. Regarding Nazi sabotage, see Snowden 2002. Both of these sources are also illuminating on post-war public health initiatives, led crucially by the Rockefeller Foundation and the WHO. For the history of the Rockefeller Foundation's work in Italy, through the 1920s, 30s and 40s, see Stapleton 2000.

62 *The Times*, 22 March 1875, p. 9.

63 Malissard 2002, p. 271.

64 Ibid., p. 23.

65 Pliny 1991, p. 355.

66 Schama 1995, p. 286.

67 For details of aqueduct construction, and the important role played by Frontinus in regularising Rome's water

system towards the end of the first century AD, see Blackman and Hodge 2001.

68 'All the elements of a new sacred hydraulics were coming together' (Schama 1995, p. 288).

69 Morolli 1982, p. 94.

70 Schama 1995, p. 286.

71 Russo 1979.

72 Celli 1933, p. 104; Morolli 1982, pp. 94ff.

73 Russo 1979, p. 577.

74 Celli-Fraentzel 1934, p. 27.

75 The collaboration between Leonardo da Vinci and Niccolò Machiavelli to move the Arno and make it navigable lasted from 1503 to 1506. Filippo Brunelleschi had a different plan, to swamp the city of Lucca. Various schemes were floated, to deprive Pisa of water and to create a shipping route from Florence to the sea; see Masters 1998.

76 Garibaldi 1983, p. 17.

4 Flood

1 Anon. 1826, p. 172.

2 Davies 1873, p. 3.

3 *The Times*, 3 January 1870, p. 9.

4 On the history of floods and fever in ancient Rome, see Sallares 2002.

5 Cohn 1975, p. 14.

6 Carcani 1875, p. 59.

7 For a wide-ranging discussion of flooding and malaria throughout the Mediterranean plains, and the various drainage schemes proposed to combat flood, in late medieval and early modern Europe, see Braudel [1949], 1972, vol. 1, p. 67.

8 Louis Napoleon had kept a garrison of about five thousand troops in Rome after 1849; the Austrians had a slightly higher number on the Adriatic side of the Papal

States, but they withdrew these without fully alerting the Pope in June 1859; for details, see MacIntire 1983.

9   Carducci 1911, editorial introduction.

10   Dickie, Foot and Snowden 2002, p. 22.

11   *La Civiltà Cattolica*, 1871, vol. 1, p. 367.

12   Garibaldi 1983, p. 5.

13   See, for instance, *L'Unità Cattolica*, 3 December 1870, no. 301, p. 1216, which spoke of a grand punishment falling on the poor city of Rome; cf. *La Civiltà Cattolica*, 1871, vol. 1, p. 368.

14   Cavour had forcefully challenged Church power, first in Piedmont and then more widely in the peninsula. He dissolved monasteries, abolished various clerical privileges and warned the Church about the political risks of civil strife, if his plans were interfered with. He frequently reasserted the mastery of lay over clerical Italy. See Mack Smith 1959, p. 89.

15   On the Po floods, and many other natural calamities and cultural responses, in post-unification Italy, see Dickie, Foot and Snowden 2002. Substantial work to regulate the Po occurred in the Fascist period. The Arno, whose waters had afflicted Florence across the centuries (1547, 1740 and 1844, for instance, were notable years of disaster), continued to threaten the city in modern times, as the devastating flood of 1966 made graphically clear; Batini 1967.

16   Fincardi 1995.

17   Stendhal [1829] 1980, vol. 1, p. 48. He also describes how flood and fever were seen as punishments for transgression.

18   De Cesare 1909, p. 98.

19   Cremonese 1924, p. 8.

20   The history of Vatican attitudes to liberal reform in the nineteenth century is a complex one, however, that is ill-served by blanket descriptions of its ceaseless obscurantism. There had been some signs of dialogue and reform

even before the French occupation under Napoleon. But
the end of the Napoleonic Wars ushered in a severe back-
lash. Those who sought to disseminate new scientific
ideas were to encounter considerable caution and many
obstacles, although not necessarily a brick wall. Scientific
education was carefully monitored in the Papal States,
but there were some attempts at disseminating recent
scientific ideas evident in journals and books published
in Rome in the 1820s and 30s. In 1833, Agostino Capello's
important study of cholera, *Storia medica di colera*, was
published and subsidised by the pontifical government
(Redondi 1980, p. 789). Yet whatever the precise history
of Vatican policy, the image of the Church as timeless
bastion of pure reaction was itself culturally pervasive and
important. The Church saw itself not as fighting science
per se, so much as certain strands of rationalist and posi-
tivist thought. Mechanical materialism and Darwinism
were firmly and consistently opposed.

21 The phenomenon of 'Lourdes' followed the widely publi-
cised visions of a shepherdess, Bernadette Soubirous, in
1858. In the years that followed, thousands would make
their way to this new holy place. In the pilgrimage
phenomenon lay 'the lure of the miraculous and the individual encounter with the supernatural, a vision of
community and of selfhood entirely at odds with secular
creeds' (Harris 1999, p. 11). On related social phenomena
at Marpingen, see Blackbourn 1993.

22 Jefferies [1885] 1939, p. 33.

23 'You, or your fellows, German and French, are at present
busy in vitiating [the air] to the best of your power in
every direction; chiefly at this moment with corpses, and
animal and vegetable ruin in war: changing men, horses,
and garden stuff into noxious gas. But everywhere, and
all day long, you are vitiating it with foul chemical exha-
lations; and the horrible nests, which you call towns, are
little more than laboratories for the distillation into heaven

of venomous smokes and smells, mixed with effluvia from decaying animal matter, and infectious miasmata from purulent disease' (Ruskin 1871–84, p. 91). Cf. Ruskin's 'Storm Cloud of the Nineteenth Century', in Ruskin 1884, where the author produced in his heavy, thundering style and meteorological description, the brooding and ominous darkness that was the unrelenting content of his social message.

24 Burckhardt [1860] 1990, p. 93. In this passage, Burckhardt was describing life in sixteenth-century Rome under Pope Clement VII.

25 The Vatican had been struck in a similar manner in 1846; Smith 1877, p. 81.

26 Ibid.

27 Carcani 1875, p. 60.

28 See the retrospective report in *L'Unità Cattolica*, 4 January 1871, no. 3, p. 11.

29 Carcani 1875, p. 61. Its height was actually 2.34 metres lower than the level reached in the terrible flood of 1598. Stone markers, '*lapide*', still to be seen in Rome, indicate the height the waters have reached in various parts of the city.

30 Smith 1877, p. 82. The present account draws on a plethora of reports that appeared in the final week of 1870 and the first week of 1871 in newspapers such as *La Capitale, Il Secolo, Gazzetta di Roma, Gazzetta Piemontese, L'Unità Cattolica* and *La Civiltà Cattolica*.

31 Smith 1877, p. 121.

32 Carcani 1875, p. 61.

33 *L'Unità Cattolica*, 4 January 1871, no. 3, p. 11.

34 Celli 1933, p. 120.

35 Garibaldi was convinced that the *latifundia* had been formed with deliberate malign intent towards the people by the Popes and Princes (Celli 1933, p. 8).

36 Garibaldi 1870, vol. 1, p. 122.

37 Morolli 1982, p. 94.

38   Dieu 1870, p. 1.

39   An idea of the value of the lira at this time can be gleaned from Baedeker's guide to Rome, published in 1875, which estimated the cost of a dinner in a popular restaurant as between one and a half and three lire; full *pension* in a good hotel might cost between eight and fifteen lire; postage for a letter to Britain cost sixty cents.

40   Dieu 1870.

41   According to one report, public collections (including 200,000 lire donated by the King) brought in a total of 858,640 lire. Some saw such gestures of solidarity as a helpful stimulus to national reconciliation: Rome's population, faced by such sympathetic support, might now see itself as more closely allied to its 'sister' cities and provinces, truly part of the 'national family' it had belatedly joined; see, for instance, Carcani 1875, p. 62.

42   Carcani 1875, p. 62.

43   *Il Secolo*, 5 January 1871, p. 1.

44   Smith 1877, p. 81.

45   Bartoccini et al. 1980, pp. 23–4.

46   Carcani 1875, p. 62. On popular enthusiasm for the King's visit, see Brice 1998, p. 56.

47   '*Le roi était entré dans Rome, mais n'y avait pas dormi!*' (D'Ideville 1878, p. 27).

48   Ibid., p. 25.

49   Garibaldi directly recalled the 1870 flood during his Tiber campaign of 1875; see, for instance, Garibaldi 1932–7, vol. 6, p. 165.

50   Brice 1998.

51   Morolli 1982, p. 96.

52   Ibid., p. 97. For details of the artificial channelling of the river, within the city, after 1880, see the description in Baedeker 1930, p. 10.

53   Letter of 4 December 1875, in Garibaldi 1983, p. 30.

5 Hopes of Italy

1   *The Times*, 5 June 1882, pp. 5–6, reprinted in Mack Smith 1969, pp. 149–52.

2   Scirocco 2001, p. 89.

3   Dumas 1860, p. 89.

4   Gioberti 1844, vol. 1, p. 95. Considering Machiavelli's idea of Italy, however, Gioberti was more critical; he condemned the author of *The Prince* for his scornful and intemperate attacks on the Church.

5   For general reviews of Risorgimento thought and its origins, see, for instance: Hearder 1983, Clark 1998, Banti 2000.

6   Quoted in Mitchell 1980, p. 220.

7   Lammenais, by background a Breton priest, was already influential in the 1820s. He became an eloquent champion for the institutional reform of the Church and his views were decidedly at odds with those of more conservative early-nineteenth-century interpreters of Catholicism such as Joseph De Maistre, who took a more intransigent line on papal supremacy and much else besides. See Hales 1954, pp. 44–5.

8   Balbo 1844, p. 202.

9   Gioberti 1844, vol. 1, pp. 85, 95.

10   He was told by a papal emissary: '*S.S. ringrazia ma non è il caso di profittare dell'offerta*' (quoted in Arpino 1982, p. 28). On the diplomatic and military circumstances surrounding the growing rift between Pius IX and Metternich, see Hearder 1983, p. 112.

11   Mack Smith 1993, p. 38.

12   Valerio 2001, p. 100.

13   Hearder 1983, p. 116.

14   Garibaldi 1889, vol. 1, p. 2.

15   Garibaldi 1870, vol. 1, p. 29.

16   Quoted in Hibbert 1987, p. 254. On Mazzini's invitation to his Young Italy followers, to tour the Campagna

Romana, and to feel the sadness of its dead landscape, see Springer 1987, p. 156.

17 Calabrò 1911, p. 66.

18 Ibid.

19 Mazzini 1849, p. 15.

20 Mazzini 1872.

21 Mazzini, 1850b, p. 18.

22 Despite all the reverence for Garibaldi as a person, his book was not well received. One not untypical review called the adventure almost 'more pitiable than absurd'; for Garibaldi to cast anyone who disagreed with him as a 'black-hearted traitor' struck the *Saturday Review* as naivety in the extreme (quoted in Melena 1887, p. 336; cf. Hibbert 1987, p. 357). Garibaldi was undeterred. The novel was followed by two others, *Cantoni il volontario* and *I Mille*, neither of them translated and both heavily autobiographical. The villainy of the Church and the supine, corrupt nature of Italy's rulers were to loom large in all of these stories.

23 Hibbert 1987, p. 364.

24 Garibaldi's denunciations of the Vatican chimed in with a wider mood of consternation triggered by various scandalous contemporary events, such as the forced removal by the Church authorities of a Jewish child from his distraught parents in Bologna in 1858, after the family's maid had secretly organised his baptism. Garibaldi made direct reference to the outrage of the boy Edgardo Mortara's 'kidnapping' in his fiction. For a good account of these and other similar events together with an analysis of the ensuing cultural impact and international political furore, see Kertzer 1997.

25 Garibaldi 1889, vol. 1, p. 16.

26 Mazzini 1849, p. 5. The preface, written under the auspices of the Italian Refugee Fund Committee, included in its list of sympathisers the names of Dickens, Thackeray and Cobden.

27   Ibid.

28   Tanner 1992.

29   Other badly afflicted areas included the valleys of the Po
        and Adige, the low Veneto, the Maremma and extensive
        parts of Sardinia and Sicily; Cosmacini 1987, p. 14.

30   On cholera, death and desire in the literary representa-
        tion of Venice, see Tanner 1992; for the social and medical
        history of cholera in Naples and more widely in Italy,
        see Snowden 1995.

31   Jones 1909; Celli 1933. Celli was a notable figure within
        the school of researchers from Rome that worked on the
        biological transmission route and medical treatment of
        malaria. He made a substantial contribution to the expla-
        nation and treatment of fevers themselves, but also linked
        his empirical work with calls for radical social reform
        and a more precise historical analysis of the social and
        agricultural neglect of rural Italy. He wrote extensively
        on the problems of the Campagna, past and present. For
        an account of malaria and ancient 'decline and fall', see
        Celli 1933. For a broader historical survey of fever and
        malariology across the globe, see Bruce-Chwatt and de
        Zulueta 1980.

32   For a famous early-nineteenth-century view of the histor-
        ical decline of Italian 'character' (the modern Italian as a
        pale shadow of the ancients), see Sismondi 1832. Here,
        moral decline was principally explained as the product
        of the degradation and dissolution of the Italian idea and
        experience of political freedom.

33   Celli 1933, p. 11.

34   Ibid.

35   Garibaldi 1889, vol. 1, p. 5; cf. Letter, 4 March 1875,
        Garibaldi 1885, p. 99.

36   On 8 September 1847, he wrote to Pius, imploring him
        to unite Italy under Papal command; Mack Smith 1994,
        pp. 51–2.

37   This project was organised by Pietro Sterbini, the Minister

of Public Works, financed through a fund that the Vatican had previously had available for maintaining works of art. The money was used, among other things, to take on unemployed men in road building along the river; Hearder 1983, p. 117.

38   On Easter Day, Mazzini joined foreign diplomats in attending Mass at St Peter's. Some local clergy even rallied to the revolution. At the same time, the Inquisition was abolished and some of its property used to house the poor; the Church monopoly of university teaching was ended and popular education fostered. Newspapers proliferated, the death penalty was removed and various protective tariffs and duties were withdrawn while new taxes designed to aid the poor were introduced.

39   Hibbert 1985, p. 256.

40   De Cesare 1909, p. 22.

41   Hibbert 1987, p. 308.

42   Even midway through his career, Garibaldi's life was being written up by sympathetic followers and journalists. A biography in 1850 by Giovanni Battista Cuneo provided an early indication of the genre, a powerful celebration of the General's special virtues.

43   Sand 1859; Dumas 1860; D'Annunzio 1901; Carducci 1911.

44   Hibbert 1987, p. 314.

45   Venturi 1973, p. 33.

46   Ibid.

47   Garibaldi 1889, vol. 3, p. 354.

48   Monsagrati 1999, p. 325.

49   Venturi 1973, p. 128.

50   Hibbert 1987, p. 337.

51   *The Times*, 23 September 1867, p. 6.

52   Scirocco 2001, p. 348.

53   Quoted in ibid., p. 349.

54   *The Times*, 28 October 1867, p. 6.

55   Trevelyan 1911, p. 51. On Trevelyan's shifting perceptions

of Garibaldi and the Risorgimento, see Cannadine 1992, pp. 68, 69, 82–3.

56   Quoted in Arpino 1982, p. 81.

57   Venturi 1973.

58   Historians have debated how much this later immobility in the Italian parliamentary system owed to the influence of the inert Piedmontese constitution, crafted earlier, under Charles Albert, with the intention of excluding the masses and retaining power tightly within the grasp of the monarch and his immediate advisers, while ostensibly affording legitimacy; see Venturi 1973.

59   Garibaldi 1889, vol. 1, p. 3.

60   Mack Smith 1959, p. 89.

61   Forbes 1861, p. 334; cf. Hibbert 1987, p. 215.

6 Life and Times

1   Morolli 1982, p. 98. A measure of his preoccupation can be gleaned from the fact that nearly a hundred pages of the final volume of his collected writings was given over to the Tiber project (see Garibaldi 1932–7, vol. 6, pp. 126–221).

2   Guerzoni 1882, vol. 1, p. 22; Garibaldi 1888, p. 10; Sacerdote 1933, pp. 66–7.

3   Quoted in Hibbert 1987, p. 45.

4   Colet 1864, vol. 3, p. 13; cf. Hibbert 1987, p. 298.

5   Harriet Meuricoffre, letter of August 1860, in Butler 1901, p. 42.

6   Ibid., pp. 50–1; cf. Hibbert 1987, pp. 291–2.

7   *The Times*, 15 September 1860, p. 11.

8   Forbes 1861, p. 3.

9   Visconti Venosta 1906, p. 544; cf. Hibbert 1987, p. 159.

10   Morolli 1982, p. 103.

11   For these and other examples, see Hibbert 1987.

12   Venturi 1973, p. 1.

13   A biographer records, for instance, how, on first meeting

his bride-to-be Anita, Garibaldi was wearing a grey poncho, blue trousers, black beret and a black silk scarf. A sash held his telescope, pistol and knife. See Valerio 2001, p. 21.

14   Venturi 1973, p. 27.

15   See Mack Smith 1993, p. 225.

16   Ibid., p. 230. Even some sympathisers referred to the lack of a coherent course and a sense of political confusion rivalled only by the 'no less perplexed but ultra-mystical Mazzini' (Anon. 1882, p. 20). There is no evidence that Garibaldi closely studied the details of socialist economics or political theory. Socialism for Garibaldi meant accepting the urgency of the 'social question' in any future political settlement (Scirocco 2001, p. 370).

17   *The Times*, 9 February 1875, p. 8. The personalised 'naming' of canals can also be seen later, when the great drainage ditch that discharged water from the Lepini mountains into the sea was to be named the 'Mussolini canal'. The anti-malarial campaign that was launched in 1928 was known as the 'Mussolini law'. See Snowden 2002, p. 115.

18   For a recent reassessment of the failings of the pre-unification Italian states, see Clark 1998.

19   English opinion was frequently hostile to the *ancien régime* states and particularly to the papacy; the very idea of a state officially subservient to Catholicism was seen as profoundly distasteful. Both Tory and Liberal governments between 1858 and 1861 were unsympathetic to the political position of the Pope; the Liberal government of Lord Palmerston (with Lord John Russell as Foreign Secretary) was the more energetically negative (McIntire 1983). For an example of the indignant counter-attack against Gladstone and accusations of gullibility on his trip to Naples, see Balleydier 1851. For a wider survey of English attitudes in these years, see McIntire 1983.

20   Seton-Watson 1984.

21   Quoted in Beales 1991, p. 188.

22 Sacerdote 1933, p. 26. The German radical Karl Blind, for instance, had indicated that Garibaldi's family might have been descended from the Dukes of Bavaria. One of Garibaldi's secretaries and biographers, Guerzoni, whose two-volume account appeared in 1882, denied this, and suggested that the General was in fact descended from one 'Garibaldo', Duke of Turin in the seventeenth century (Ridley 1974, p. 2). Ridley points out that both stories are far-fetched.

23 Spadolini 1982, p. 47.

24 For useful studies of Fascist aesthetics, and ideas of physical and moral 'regeneration', see Affron and Antliff 1997.

25 Garibaldi 1889, vol. 3, p. 375.

26 A southern doctor and journalist, who was also a friend of Mazzini, Ferdinando Petruccelli della Gattina had spent time in exile in London and Paris. He became a member of parliament in 1861. See Venturi 1973, pp. 72–3.

27 Drake 1980.

28 Freud 1900, vol. 5, p. 429.

29 *The Times*, 5 June 1882, pp. 5–6, reprinted in Mack Smith 1969, pp. 149–152.

30 Hibbert 1987, p. 333; Grévy 2001, pp. 202–19.

31 See Corradini's discourses and speeches, dedicated to Mussolini (Corradini 1923). This influential nationalist attacked materialism and socialism, lamenting Italy's 'torpor' and 'humiliation'. He spoke, in the context of national regeneration, of the problems of 'dwarves', 'apathy', 'sickness', 'corruption', 'pacifism' and 'egotism'.

32 Ridley 1974, p. xi.

33 It was returned to the Savoy Kingdom when Garibaldi was eight.

34 Garibaldi 1889, vol. 1, p. 8.

35 Ibid., p. 9.

36 Bakunin (1871) pointed to Mazzini's fundamental error of idealism, which, he argued, led the Italian back into the embrace of the Church he attacked.

37   Mack Smith 1994, p. 86. Mazzini rejected socialism and communism as excessively preoccupied with material transformation. He favoured free trade, but in other respects rejected liberalism.

38   Hearder 1983, p. 186.

39   Moscheles 1899, pp. 249–50.

40   Quoted in Hibbert 1987, p. 254.

41   Mazzini 1845, p. 6.

42   Mazzini [1860] 1862, p. ix.

43   Ibid., p. 27; cf. 'He who can deny God either in the face of a starlight night, when standing beside the tomb of those dearest to him, or in the presence of martyrdom, is either greatly unhappy or greatly guilty,' p. 31.

44   Valerio 2001.

45   Scirocco 2001, p. 22.

46   Ibid., p. 24.

47   For Garibaldi's Latin American years, see Ridley 1974; Scirocco 2001.

48   Garibaldi fought for the republic of Rio Grande do Sul. In 1842, he became an officer in the Uruguayan Navy; Valerio 2001.

49   Their children, Menotti, Ricciotti, Rosita (who died as a child in 1845) and Teresita, lived for years with their grandmother in Nice, during the period of Garibaldi's second exile. They eventually rejoined him on his return to Caprera during the 1850s. See Valerio 2001.

50   Dumas 1860, p. 96.

51   Valerio 2001.

52   Supplement to Garibaldi's *Autobiography* (1889, vol. 3, p. 93).

53   These are beautifully captured in Gabriel García Márquez's *The General in his Labyrinth* (1989), a novel that tracks Bolívar's meandering course through Latin American history and myth. The title and the story both have resonances for the present discussion.

54   Garibaldi was a great admirer of Bolívar; see Mack Smith

1993, p. 228.

55   Mack Smith 1969, p. 160.

56   Mack Smith 1993, pp. 60, 64.

57   Venturi 1973, p. 24.

58   In 1871, the Vatican had urged the faithful to avoid partici-
      pation in Italian elections.

59   Grew 1986.

7 Via Crucis

1   Knox 1982, pp. 14–15; Valerio 2001. In Garibaldi's auto-
      biography, the figure is given as four or five thousand;
      Dumas 1860.

2   Vecchi 1856, vol. 2, p. 296; cf. Hibbert 1987, p. 94.

3   Scirocco 2001, p. 186.

4   Knox 1982.

5   Quoted in Hibbert 1987, pp. 100, 102.

6   Garibaldi 1889, vol. 2, p. 22.

7   Ridley 1974, p. 326.

8   Quoted in Knox 1982, p. 41.

9   Scirocco 2001, p. 173.

10   Hibbert 1987, p. 110; Valerio 2001, p. 154.

11   Hibbert 1987, p. 104; Ridley 1974, p. 311.

12   The remembrance and myth-making waxed and waned
      in the following century. A notable flurry of commemo-
      rative and celebratory events occurred in the aftermath
      of Garibaldi's death, and again on its fiftieth anniversary.
      Certain images of the General's victories and desperate
      set-backs, such as the paintings of Gerolamo Induno and
      Pietro Bouvier, became iconic. Several film versions of
      these dramatic events of 1849 were also to follow. See
      Garibaldi, Arte e Storia, vol. 2, p. 141; Grévy 2001; cf. the
      suggestive essay by Forgacs in Ascoli and von Henneberg
      2001.

13   Hibbert 1987, p. 108.

14   Ximenes 1907, p. 34.

15   Hibbert 1987, p. 114.

16   Dumas 1860, p. 96.

17   Vecchi 1856, vol. 2, p. 326.

18   Sacerdote 1933, p. 498; Scirocco 2001, p. 186. Anita's racial origins attracted considerable interest and were often stressed in contemporary hagiography, as for instance in the title of a book by Lady Constance Leveson, *The Bride of Garibaldi; or the Creole Beauty of Brazil* (1865).

19   Valerio 2001, p. 156.

20   Scirocco 2001, p. 176.

21   Ximenes 1907, p. 45. On contemporary suspicions that Garibaldi had murdered his wife, see Sacerdote 1933, p. 498. There was further speculation that Garibaldi's friends might have over-hastily buried a dying rather than dead woman, as they anxiously awaited the arrival of the pursuing Austrians; see Scirocco 2001, p. 176.

22   Hibbert 1987, p. 108; Scirocco 2001, p. 172.

23   *The Times*, 19 February 1875, p. 5, and 20 February 1875, p. 9.

24   Monsagrati 1999, p. 325; see also the discussion in Chapter 8, below.

25   Here I refer to the central distinction drawn in Freud's 'Mourning and Melancholia', a paper that remains the indispensable starting point for the psychoanalytic exploration of depression. Faced with the loss of a loved one, wrote Freud, 'we find that the inhibition and loss of interest [in life] are fully accounted for by the work of mourning in which the ego is absorbed ... the inhibition of the melancholic seems puzzling to us because we cannot see what it is that is absorbing him so entirely. The melancholic displays something else which is lacking in mourning – an extraordinary diminution in his self-regard, an impoverishment of his ego on a grand scale. In mourning it is the world which has become poor and empty; in melancholia it is the ego itself' (Freud 1917, pp. 245–6). The self-reproaches of the melancholic 'are

reproaches against a loved object which has been shifted away from it on to the patient's own ego ... Their complaints are really "plaints" in the old sense of the word ... the reactions expressed in their behaviour still proceed from a mental constellation of revolt, which has then, by a certain process, passed over into the crushed state of melancholia' (Freud 1917, p. 248).

26   Guerzoni 1882, vol 2. pp. 585, 589.

27   Mack Smith 1993, p. 100.

28   Melena 1887, p. 315.

29   Psychoanalysis, Freud once sagely observed, in a fascinating attempt to draw the line between 'wild analysis' and the real thing, 'absolutely requires a fairly long period of contact with the patient' (Freud 1910, p. 226).

8 Rome Desired

1   Garibaldi 1870, vol. 1, p. 27.

2   Garibaldi 1889, vol. 1, p. 1.

3   For a detailed analysis of this 'imagined community' and its discursive associations with desecration and the body of the violated woman, see Banti 2000.

4   Serao 1902, p. 8.

5   Ibid.

6   Ibid., p. 12.

7   Ibid., p. 10.

8   Ibid., p. 15.

9   Ibid., p. 29.

10   Letter of 22 December 1818, in Shelley 1905, p. 17.

11   Ibid., p. 72.

12   Ibid., p. 70.

13   Letter of 23 March 1819, ibid., p. 94.

14   Quoted in Hibbert 1985, p. 219.

15   Letter of 1 November 1786, Goethe 1849, p. 350.

16   Ibid., p. 349.

17   The trouble with any utilitarian approach, Mazzini

complained, was that 'souls do not enter into [the] calculation' (Mazzini 1845, p. 6 and *passim*).

18 Cavour was preoccupied by the costs of the separate state administrations within the old Italy, the need for a larger internal market, the inefficiency of tariff barriers, the drag on trade presented by separate coinages and measures (the ducato in Naples, the oncia in Sicily, the scudo in the papal territories, the lira in Piedmont). Such attention to financial constraints was to be of enormous influence and significance in post-unification government, but at the same time, the perceived abuses of such 'accountancy' considerations (in and beyond the policy of Cavour himself) appalled not only Mazzini but also Garibaldi, as when he sought to implement his Tiber initiative of 1875 only to find the government extremely preoccupied by costs. Behind Garibaldi's intense exasperation with the accountants of the government of the right, we detect the shadow of a far longer-running philosophical battle over the appropriate moral language of politics and economics, in which Cavour and Mazzini represented such sharply contrasting approaches. Utility was always an important consideration for the Piedmontese statesman. Cavour's favourite philosopher, at least in his youth, was Bentham. Mack Smith 1959, p. 21.

19 Wolffe 1989.

20 Moore 1988, p. 222.

21 On the other hand, some Protestant organisations railed against his general lack of religiosity; see Hibbert 1997, p. 348. On anti-popery, see McIntire 1983; Wolffe 1989. For details of Garibaldi's visit and popular reactions, see Beales 1991.

22 Quoted in Hilton 1985, p. 58. Dr George Croly was a clergyman and critic, sympathetic to Ruskin's approach to art. He was a prolific reviewer and contributed various pieces to periodicals such as *Blackwood's*.

23   Letter of 31 December 1840, in Ruskin 1903, vol. 1, p. 380; cf. 'anything is better than the *far niente* of Rome'.
24   Ibid., pp. 381–2.
25   Hilton 1985, pp. 54–8.
26   Ibid., p. 58.
27   Quoted in Barzini 1968, p. 56.
28   Ibid., p. 73.
29   Ibid., p. 58.
30   Herzen [1847] 1995, pp. 81–2.
31   Ibid., p. 73.
32   Quoted in Barzini 1968, pp. 57–8.
33   Quoted in Springer 1987, p. 1.
34   Stendhal [1829] 1980, vol. 1, p. 53.
35   James 1909 ['Roman Rides'], p. 158; cf. 'The stern old ramparts of Rome form the outer enclosure of the villa [Ludovisi], and hence a series of "striking scenic effects" which it would be unscrupulous flattery to say you can imagine. The grounds are laid out in the formal last-century manner; but nowhere do the straight black cypresses lead off the gaze into vistas of a melancholy more charged with associations – poetic, romantic, historic; nowhere are there grander smoother walls of laurel and myrtle' (p. 194); or again: 'A drive the other day with a friend to Villa Madama, on the side of Monte Mario; a place like a page out of one of Browning's richest evocations of this clime and civilisation. Wondrous in its haunting melancholy, it might have inspired half "The Ring and the Book" at a stroke' (p. 207).
36   Zola 1896, p. 257.
37   Hawthorne 1860, p. 631.
38   Ibid., pp. 826–7.
39   Ibid., p. 827.
40   In a fine essay on the anxiety evoked by Rome, in the collection *Roman Presences* (Edwards 1999), John Lyon shows how Henry James abandoned any attempt to compete with guidebooks or historical chronicles, and

how the city became an increasingly shadowy and
complicated backdrop to the fiction.

41 Letter of 5 December 1897, Freud 1985, p. 332.

42 Freud 1900, vol. 4, pp. 193ff. He anticipated that for a
long time to come, he would indeed only be able to visit
Rome in his dreams, since the season of the year when
it is possible to travel there is the season when 'residence
in Rome must be avoided for reasons of health' (Freud
1900, vol. 4, p. 194).

43 Ibid., p. 194.

44 This also appears in *The Interpretation of Dreams*; see ibid.,
p. 195.

45 Letter of 5 December 1897, in Freud 1985, p. 285.

46 Hawthorne 1860, p. 826.

47 See the useful discussion of the transformation in Roman
studies fashioned by Gibbon, Niebuhr, Winckelmann and
others in Dowling 1985.

48 An extensive French literature on the future of Rome
and of Roman Catholicism was produced in the 1860s,
as Louis Napoleon continued to defend the papacy from
Italian nationalist incursions. French commentators
offered radically divergent polemics on the future
prospects of the Church. Veuillot's *Le Parfum de Rome* and
various other works in the early 1860s, some sharply crit-
icising Veuillot's pro-papal perspectives, appeared.
Pellerin's *Le Parfum de Rome et M. Veuillot* (Paris, 1862)
was a case in point. Louis François Sosthènes de La
Rochefoucauld's *Rome et les concessions* (Paris, 1862)
explored the compromises required of the Church,
deplored the attack on faith and lamented how the
reformist Pope had been driven back by the anarchy and
extremism of the forces of rationalism. M. le Vte de la
Guéronnière's *L'Abandon de Rome* (Paris, 1862) warned
of the irredentist claims which would lead Italy ever
further into chaos; cf. de Feuillide, *La Papauté selon l'his-
toire* (Paris, 1862).

49   Renan [1859] 1951, p. 181.
50   Renan, quoted in Ternois 1961, p. 70. Renan expected a schism within the Church between the non-Italian and the Italian wings, over how the papacy should relate to the Italian Kingdom. He imagined a 'final decomposition' of the Church with a pope and an anti-pope.
51   Taine 1867, p. 66.
52   Hawthorne 1860, pp. 631–2.
53   Ibid., p. 631.
54   Quoted in McIntire 1983, p. 1.
55   D'Annunzio 1901; cf. Celli-Fraentzel 1931, p. 28.
56   James 1909, p. 173.
57   Ibid., p. 192.
58   Ibid., ['Roman Rides' 1873], p. 156.
59   Ternois 1961, p. 43n.
60   Hemmings 1953, p. 263.
61   2 November 1894, Zola 1958, p. 15.
62   On banking scandals and political corruption in Italy during the late 1880s and early 1890s, see Mack Smith 1959, ch. 22.
63   Zola 1896, p. 257.
64   Ibid., p. 78.
65   Ibid., p. 77.
66   Ibid., p. 221.

9 An Unconcious Contradiction

1   Grévy 2001, p. 55.
2   Mack Smith 1969, p. 175.
3   Garibaldi 1983, pp. 18, 20.
4   '*Infine ci è da impazzire pensando ai colossali vantaggi dell'opera vostra.*' Letter of 12 November 1872, quoted in Morolli 1982, p. 98.
5   Garibaldi's comments were made in the Florentine paper, *L'Opinione*, November 1872; quoted in Morolli 1982, p. 97.

6   Morolli 1982, p. 98.

7   Letter of 6 February 1875, in Garibaldi 1885, p. 97.

8   Morolli 1982; Garibaldi 1983, introduction.

9   A couple of years earlier, a tourist, William Davies, described the weekly steamer that ran from Rome to the coast, run by an Englishman, a certain Mr Welby; Davies 1873, p. 3.

10   Quinterio 1982, p. 111.

11   *The Times*, 22 March 1875, p. 9.

12   Garibaldi 1983, p. 7. Garibaldi had long-standing connections with Freemasonry.

13   See, for instance, *The Times*, 3 March 1875, p. 12; 4 March 1875, p. 5; 22 March 1875, p. 9.

14   The canal's width was to be sixty metres.

15   Among the several competing schemes was one devised by the engineer Rullier, from Marseilles, who had elaborated a plan in 1872, involving the deviation of the Tiber, across Prati di Castello and through the Valle dell'Inferno, along the Gianicolo to Porta Portese. This scheme involved establishing a spectacular boulevard of about seven kilometres that would be flanked by new buildings.

16   Agostino Grattarola, in Garibaldi 1983, p. 5.

17   See the correspondence in Depretis's papers at the Archivio di Stato, Rome; fasc. 2, busta 9, serie I, scatola 9, item 89.

18   Details can be found in the various biographies of the General; see especially Ridley 1974.

19   *The Times*, 5 June 1882, pp. 5–6, in Mack Smith 1969, pp. 149–52. The year given here, 1874, should in fact be 1875.

20   Ridley 1974, p. 596.

21   Having first proposed the total deviation of the Tiber, Amadei, under challenge from other specialists, wavered and changed course. He came up with a new scheme that would involve a canal 'deviation', thereby retaining a suitably pacified Tiber in Rome. The revised version

was also more attentive to the problem of budgeting. See Amadei's letter of 30 April 1875 in Depretis's papers, fasc. 2, busta 9, serie I, scatola 9, item 76. When his proposals finally foundered, Amadei's bitterness emerged into the public domain. He wrote to newspapers, such as the *Monitore di Bologna*, to air his grievances in public.

22 Hibbert 1987, p. 332.

23 Morolli 1982, p. 103.

24 Quoted in ibid., p. 104.

25 Ibid., p. 105.

26 Ibid., p. 103. For the legislative details, see pp. 104–5.

27 Ibid., p. 100.

28 A critical letter from Amadei to Baccarini can be consulted within the Depretis papers, fasc. 2, busta 9, serie I, scatola 9, item 40 (letter of 28 May 1875).

29 Garibaldi's supporters were soon squabbling about who had the most professional and convincing scheme. Professor Filopanti vociferously challenged Colonel Amadei's plans as well as his version of political events surrounding the Tiber deliberations; see Filopanti's letter to the *Monitore di Bologna* (1 June 1875), contained in the Depretis papers, fasc. 2, busta 9, serie I, scatola 9, item 60. For Baccarini's reply to criticism of him, see *Monitore* (letter of 7–8 June 1875), Depretis papers, fasc. 2, busta 9, serie I, scatola 9, item 69.

30 '*L'illustre Garibaldi non ha mai* disapprovato *il mio progetto, non ha mai* veduto *una linea di quella del commendatore Baccarini, non gli ha mai dato alcuna* incombenza. *Questo e quanto so dal Generale. Come avvene dunque l'evoluzione a danno mio?*' Amadei, letter to the director of the *Monitore di Bologna*, 28 June 1875; Depretis's papers, fasc. 2, busta 9, serie I, scatola 9, item 70.

31 Morolli 1982, p. 106.

32 Ibid.

33 Colonna 1925, p. 159. On the debate about the advantages and drawbacks of schemes relying on strengthening

the Tiber walls, see Pecori 1931, p. 618. The author felt that while the walls may have destroyed historic and beautiful villas and artistic scenes, it was a small price to pay for the metamorphosis of the city's health. Compare Augustus Hare's lamentation that fifty years of united Italy had destroyed so much of the charm of Rome and '[t]he Tiber itself has been strait-jacketed all the way along its picturesque course' (Hare 1913, p. 11).

34   For an expression of regret about the deterioration of the beautiful Italian 'race', see, for instance, Garibaldi 1983, p. 45.

35   I rely here on advice received from Professor Marchis, of Turin University, a specialist on the history of engineering, regarding the potential feasibility of the scheme.

36   Knox 1982, p. 86.

37   Cesare Cantù, *Della indipendenza italiana*, Turin 1878, vol. 3, pt 2, pp. 580–3; extract in Mack Smith 1969, p. 153.

38   I borrow this phrase from the title of a seminal book on speech-act theory, by the Oxford philosopher J.L. Austin.

39   See the important study of Cavour and Garibaldi's complex actions and mutual perceptions in 1860 by Mack Smith 1993.

40   Harriet Meuricoffre, in Butler 1901, p. 83.

41   Bent 1881. Many members of the Italian political elite thought Garibaldi had a good heart and a small brain; Grévy 2001, p. 43.

42   Mack Smith 1993, for instance, stresses Garibaldi's rigidity and limitation, while also pointing out how he often outmanoeuvred rivals who had underestimated his political and military abilities. Mack Smith's account deftly captures the mixture of calculated and unforeseen movement, of deliberation and surprise, that informed both Cavour and Garibaldi's behaviour as the opportunity for unification had emerged, and each man sought to realise a personal political vision.

43   Venturi 1973, p. 1; Massobrio 1982.

Notes

44　*The Times*, 5 June 1882, pp. 5–6, reproduced in Mack Smith 1969, pp. 149–52.

45　Ibid.

46　Virgilio Titone, from *Quaderni reazionari*, no. 2, Palermo, February 1963, pp. 52–6, 62–5, quoted in Mack Smith 1969, p. 170.

47　Segal 1981.

48　Valerio 2001, p. 100.

49　Melena 1887, p. 302.

50　Ibid., p. 308.

51　Scirocco 2001, p. 227.

10 Death

1　Speech of 20 September 1922; Pini 1939, p. 114.

2　Gentile 1996, p. 115.

3　Speech of 20 September 1922; Pini 1939, p. 114. Cf. Bondanella 1987, ch. 7.

4　Mack Smith 1969, pp. 166–7.

5　On connections between the social backgrounds of Garibaldi and Mussolini, and subsequent attempts by Il Duce to link his career with the General, see Passerini 1991, pp. 94, 193. Mussolini also followed Garibaldi into fiction. His own salacious, anticlerical tale was evidently inspired in part by Garibaldi's earlier ventures into the genre of the novel. A story by Mussolini, *The Cardinal's Mistress*, dealt with the unhappy love affair of a cardinal and a courtesan from Trent, Claudia Particella, and was set in the 1650s. The narrative proceeded, flamboyantly, towards their respective deaths. Originally serialised in a supplement to *Il Popolo* in 1909, this yarn set up the Church as the symbol of corruption and parasitism. Claudia's rejection of the sexual advances of the libidinous priests aroused their violent hate. The clerics appear as obsessed by the unattainable woman, eaten up by their own passion. Drawing out the lesson of his story, Mussolini wrote of the 'degenerative impulse of Catholicism' which had to be recognised, alongside its moral achievements. The clerics and their quarry, the desirable woman, are tracked by the narrator, as they descend through the various circles of mutual torment and excitement:'Claudia the Woman, offering unimaginable caresses, ineffable voluptuousness, ecstasy to the point of delirium, of exasperation' (Mussolini 1929a, p. 40). The papacy, Mussolini complained, had become a putrid sink of vice. On the relationship of *The Cardinal's Mistress* to Garibaldi's 'equally jejune' novel *Clelia*, see Mack Smith 1981, p. 16.

6   Sallares 2002, p. 4.

7   Baravelli 1935; Longobardi 1936; Turnor 1938. Legislation in the 1880s paved the way for major land-drainage projects.

8   Castiglioni 1927, p. 278.

9   Anon. 1923.

10   Ibid.

11   It has recently been suggested that in many respects Fascism set back the cause of malariology: for the reasons why, see Snowden 2002.

12   Celli-Fraentzel 1931, p. 33.

13   Regis 1889. Financial incentives brought new population movements into the Campagna, during the inter-war years, when over 20,000 people moved from the Paduan area. The reclaimed lands started to rise in value, above all to the benefit of the Latifondisti; Anon. 1984, p. 18.

14   Baedeker's *Handbook for Travellers* charted the progress made. In 1909, for instance, it gave due acknowledgement to the strides taken by the authorities in promoting good sanitation in Rome, and the vital humanitarian work undertaken by the Italian Red Cross that had now come to the aid of the poor, stricken peasants in the Campagna; Baedeker 1909, p. xxviii. For information on the range of educational and health initiatives in the Campagna, after 1900, see Snowden 2002.

15   See Depretis papers, fasc. 50 and 51, for dozens of hand-
      written documents on the Tiber scheme produced from
      within various agencies; there are copious documents here
      that were produced by the Municipality in response to
      government inquiries and decisions; there are also various
      reports from the Ufficio Tecnico Comunale to the Mayor
      of Rome on the precise heights and other technical
      aspects of the proposed Tiber walls. In addition, there are
      surveys from the technical office of the Ministry of Public
      Works as well as from the local authorities in Rome, the
      provincial administration, the Mayor's office, the Ministry
      of the Interior and so on.

16   *Relazione della commissione dei lavori sulle proposte di
      attuazione di alcuni lavori di sistemazione del Tevere*
      [pamphlet], Rome 1876; in the Archivio Centrale dello
      Stato; see Ministero dei Lavori Pubblici, opere governa-
      tive ed edilizie per Roma, fasc. 50, busta 30. For a useful
      summary of engineering works, including the plan by the
      engineer Raffaele Canevari that was adopted, with modi-
      fications, in November 1875, see the following website:
      http://www.isolatiberina.it. This site also provides inter-
      esting maps and photographs, focusing particular atten-
      tion on proposals for the removal of the Isola Tiberina.
      Plans (eventually aborted) during the 1870s, had envis-
      aged the destruction of the island in the Tiber, in order
      to reduce the risk of flood.

17   Garibaldi had also given instructions to his doctor on this
      matter as early as 1877; Scirocco 2001, p. 391.

18   Quoted in Hibbert 1987, p. 368. In this passage, I rely
      heavily on the concluding section of Hibbert's biography.

19   Sacerdote 1933, pp. 943–4. It has been suggested that
      Garibaldi learned the details of Shelley's death from his
      friend Jessie White Mario; Ridley 1974, p. 633.

20   Sacerdote 1933, p. 944.

21   Sacerdote 1933, p. 946.

Acknowledgements

This project would have been much the poorer but for the contribution of a number of colleagues and friends in England and in Italy. I must exempt them all – in customary fashion – from responsibility for the errors and limitations that remain, but I am aware that the book that has finally emerged has been in very many respects a composite enterprise. The notes indicate how much I have drawn here upon the extant literature on Garibaldi, Rome, the politics of nationalism and the history of malaria, but there are other explicit debts to declare that are not set out in those references. I have gained over the years from the advice of a dozen or more librarians and archivists, located, *inter alia*, at the Risorgimento Museums of Bologna and Rome, the university libraries in London, Cambridge and Bologna, the Museum of the History of Science in Florence, the library of the Italian Parliament, the Biblioteca Casanatense, Rome, the National Library (Biblioteca Nazionale) in Florence and Rome, the Biblioteca Nazionale Braidense in Milan, the library of the École de Médicine, Paris, the Central Archives of the State (Archivio Centrale dello Stato) in Rome, the Wellcome Library for the History of Medicine, the London School of Hygiene and Tropical Medicine, and the British Library.

I owe a great personal debt of gratitude to Michael Feldman for his help and insight, before and during the years it took to write this book. Both the late Tony Tanner and the late Roy Porter encouraged me to set off on this particular research in the first place and provided, through their own inimitable written work and conversation, an inspiration. Gareth Stedman Jones has once again been exceptionally generous in his support and has offered astute historical and editorial advice on earlier drafts.

Richard Bourke, Gilberto Corbellini, John Dickie, Felix Driver, Catharine Edwards, Tristram Hunt, Lucy Riall, Lyndal Roper and Jacqueline Rose have also commented patiently and perspicaciously on the manuscript, obliging me to think harder – and sometimes entirely afresh – about various strands of this story. *Rome or Death* would have been considerably less digestible without the timely interventions of Maggie Hanbury, the excellent editorial advice of Will Sulkin and the great amount of trouble taken by his colleagues at Random House, especially Rosalind Porter, Lily Richards, Michael Salu and Alison Worthington who swiftly provided a clear and apposite index.

Mirtide Gavelli, Leonardo Musci and Amanda Russell have been unflaggingly helpful in locating illustrations. For assistance in navigating my way through obscure materials and archives, tracing sources and images or clarifying bio-graphical details, I am also very grateful to Valeria Babini, Chiara Beccalossi, Gianni Carta, Annita Garibaldi Jallet, Maria Flora Giubilei, Ombretta Ingrascì, Elena Lamberti, Pietro Lanzara, Antonello La Vergata, Bruno Leoni, Tracey Loughran and Folco Pasquinelli. For guidance on points of cultural, medical and political history, my thanks to Sally Alexander, Bill Bynum, Laura Cameron, Bernardino Fantini, Stephen Gundle, Vittorio Marchis, Melissa Parker and Miri Rubin.

I have been very much assisted by several institutions. Queen Mary, University of London, has provided an unusually stimulating and facilitating environment for research and teaching. My thanks to the Royal Society for furnishing me with a helpful bursary for my preliminary Italian research. A range of papers given in recent years by colleagues at the British Psychoanalytical Society helped me to ponder anew the vexed question of 'psychobiography'. I am fortunate to have had the chance to present 'work in progress' at research seminars at various universities; the final version of the book has been significantly shaped by ensuing discussions. I am especially grateful to the Leverhulme and the Wellcome Trusts for the award of substantial grants and to the latter a fellowship that enabled me to devote the necessary time to writing this book.

Last, but foremost, my thanks to my family. Irma Brenman Pick closely read this material, and, together with Eric Brenman, very substantially helped me to deepen the argument. My daughters, Anna and Tasha, accompanied me to Rome and other Italian cities. For their humour, forbearance and curiosity, and for the frequent postponements of work that their presence has necessarily brought about, I am equally grateful. I owe a very great deal to Isobel Pick. She has been throughout, a thoughtful reader of − and generous partner in − this drawn-out Roman saga, and I dedicate this book to her with love.

Daniel Pick
November 2004

Bibliography

Affron, Matthew, and Antliff, Mark (eds) (1997), *Fascist Visions: Art and Ideology in France and Italy*, Princeton

Agnew, John (1995), *Rome*, Chichester

Alleori, Sergio (1967), *Lo stato delle conoscenze sulla malaria nel 1831*, Rome

Anderson, Perry (2002), 'Land Without Prejudice', in *London Review of Books* (21 March), vol. 24, no. 6

Anderson, William K. (1927), *Malarial Psychoses and Neuroses with Chapters on History, Race-Degeneration, Alcohol, and Surgery in Relation to Malaria*, London

Anon. ['A Person of Quality, a native of France'] (1706), in *A Comparison between Old Rome in its Glory and London as it is at Present*, London

Anon. (1793), *Discorso sopra la mal'aria, e le malattie che cagiona principalmente in varie spiagge d'Italia e in tempo di estate*, Rome

Anon. (n.d.), *Gladstone, Ireland, Rome: or the Pro-Romish Acts of Mr Gladstone. A Page from Modern History: Being a Clue to Gladstone's Irish Home Rule Bill*, London

Anon. [Anna Jameson] (1826), *Diary of an Ennuyée*, London

Anon. (1882), *Memoir of Giuseppe Garibaldi* [reprinted from *The Times*], London

Anon. (1923), 'Fighting Malaria', in *The World's Health*, 4, no. 12, pp. 7–10

Anon. (1982), *Garibaldi in Parlamento*, 2 vols, Rome

Anon. (1982), *Giuseppe Garibaldi e il suo mito*, Genoa

Anon. [Cooperative Pagliaccetto] (ed.) (1984), *Migrazione e lavoro: storia visiva della campagna romana*, Milan

Arpino, Alberto Maria (1982), 'La Storia', in *Garibaldi: arte e storia* [catalogue of exhibition, Rome, Museo del Palazzo di Venezia and Museo Centrale del Risorgimento, June–December 1982], Florence, pp. 17–91

Ascoli, Albert Russell, and von Henneberg, Krystyna (eds) (2001), *Making and Remaking Italy: The Cultivation of National Identity around the Risorgimento*, London

Ashton, Rosemary (2001), *Thomas and Jane Carlyle: Portrait of a Marriage*, London

Baedeker, Carl (1869), *Italy: Handbook for Travellers*, part 2, *Central Italy and Rome*, Leipzig

Baedeker, Carl (1886), *Italy: Handbook for Travellers*, part 2, *Central Italy and Rome*, 9th edn, Leipzig

Baedeker, Carl (1909), *Central Italy and Rome: Handbook for Travellers*, 15th edn, Leipzig

Baedeker, Carl (1930), *Central Italy and Rome: Handbook for Travellers*, 16th edn, Leipzig

Bakunin, Mikhail (1871), *La Théologie politique de Mazzini et l'Internationale,* Neuchâtel

Balbo, Cesare (1844), *Delle speranze d'Italia*, Capolago

Baldwin, Peter (1999), *Contagion and the State in Europe, 1830–1930*, Cambridge

Balleydier, Alphonse (1851), *La Vérité sur les affaires de Naples: Réfutation des lettres de M. Gladstone*, Paris

Banti, Alberto Mario (2000), *La nazione del Risorgimento: parentela, santità e onore alle origini dell'Italia unita*, Turin

Baravelli, G.C. (1935), *Integral Land-Reclamation in Italy*, Rome

Bartoccini, Fiorella, et al. (1980), *Il decadentismo e Roma*, Rome

Bartoccini, Fiorella (1988), *Roma nell'Ottocento*, 2 vols, Bologna

Barzini, Luigi (1968), *The Italians*, Harmondsworth

Batini, Giorgio (1967), *L'Arno in museo: gallerie, monumenti, chiese, biblioteche, archivi e capolavori danneggiati dall'alluvione*, Florence

Beales, Derek (1991), 'Garibaldi in England: the politics of Italian enthusiasm', in *Society and Politics in the Age of the Risorgimento:*

Bibliography

Essays in Honour of Denis Mack Smith, Cambridge, ch. 8, pp. 184–216

Bent, James Theodore (1881), *The Life of Giuseppe Garibaldi*, London

Blackman, Deane R., and Hodge, Trevor A. (2001), *Frontinus' Legacy: Essay on Frontinus' de Acquis Urbis Romae*, Ann Arbor

Blackbourn, David (1993), *The Marpingen Visions: Rationalism, Religion and the Rise of Modern Germany*, Oxford

Bondanella, Peter (1987), *The Eternal City: Roman Images in the Modern World*, Chapel Hill

Bone, Florence (1914), *The Man in the Red Shirt: The Story of Garibaldi Told for Boys and Girls*, London

Borsa, Giorgio, and Beonio Brocchieri, Paolo (1984), *Garibaldi, Mazzini e il Risorgimento nel risveglio dell'Asia e dell'Africa*, Milan

Bowersock, G.M. (ed.) (1977), *Edward Gibbon and the Decline of the Roman Empire*, Cambridge, Mass.

Braudel, Fernand [1949], (1972), *The Mediterranean and the Mediterranean World in the Age of Philip II* [1949], translated by S. Reynolds, London

Brice, Catherine (1998), *Le Vittoriano: Monumentalité publique et politique à Rome*, Rome

Bruce-Chwatt, Leonard Jan, and Zulueta, Julian de (1980), *The Rise and Fall of Malaria in Europe: A Historico-Epidemiological Study*, Oxford

Bull, Anna Cento, and Gilbert, Mark (2001), *The Lega Nord and the Northern Question*, London

Burckhardt, Jacob (1990), *The Civilization of the Renaissance in Italy* [1860], Harmondsworth

Burdel, Édouard (1875), *De la dégénérescence palustre*, Paris

Butler, Josephine (1901), *In Memoriam, Harriet Meuricoffre*, London

Byrne, Donn (1988), *Garibaldi: The Man and the Myth* [n.p.]

Cacace, Ernesto (1915), *Per la diffusione dell'insegnamento anti-malarico e della profilassi antimalarica scolastica nei paesi malarici*, Rome

Calabrò, Giuseppe Maria (1911), *La dottrina religioso-sociale nelle opere di Giuseppe Mazzini*, Palermo

Rome or Death

Camaiani, Pier Giorgio (1972), 'Il diavolo, Roma e la rivoluzione', in *Rivista di storia e letteratura religiosa*, 8: 485–516

Cannadine, David (1992), *G.M. Trevelyan: A Life in History*, London

Carcani, Michele (1875), *Il Tevere e le sue inondazioni dall' origine di Roma fino ai giorni nostri*, Rome

Carducci, Giosue (1911), *Discorso per la morte di Giuseppe Garibaldi*, Viterbo

Carlyle, Thomas (1849), 'Occasional Discourse on the Nigger Question', in *Fraser's Magazine*, 40: 670–9

Carlyle, Thomas (1850). *Latter-Day Pamphlets*, London

Castiglioni, Arturo (1927), 'Italy's campaign against malaria', in *British Medical Journal*, 13 August 1927, p. 278

Celli, Angelo (1900), *La malaria secondo le nuove ricerche*, 2nd edn, Rome

Celli, Angelo (1900), *Malaria: According to the New Researches*, translated by John Joseph Eyre, London

Celli, Angelo (1910), *La malaria secondo le nuove ricerche*, 4th edn, Rome

Celli, Angelo (1933), *The History of Malaria in the Roman Campagna from Ancient Times*, edited and enlarged by Anna Celli-Fraentzel, London

Celli-Fraentzel, Anna (1931), *La febbre palustre nella poesia (da Virgilio a D'Annunzio)*, Rome

Celli-Fraentzel, Anna, (1932), 'The medieval Roman climate', in *Speculum: A Journal of Medieval Studies*, 7: 96–106

Celli-Fraentzel, Anna (1934), *I riferimenti alla febbre palustre nella poesia*, Rome

Chabod, Federico (1951), 'L'idea di Roma', in his *Storia della politica estera italiana dal 1870 al 1896*, Bari

Chabod, Federico (1961), *L'idea di nazione*, edited by Armando Saitta and Ernesto Sestan, Bari

Chateaubriand, François-René (1844), *Itinéraire de Paris à Jérusalem et de Jérusalem à Paris, suivi des voyages en Italie et en France*, Paris

Clark, Martin (1996), *Modern Italy, 1871–1995*, London

Clark, Martin (1998), *The Italian Risorgimento*, London

Cohn, Norman (1975), *Europe's Inner Demons*, London

Bibliography

Colet, Louise (1864), *L'Italie des italiens*, 3 vols, Paris

Colombo, Cesare, and Sontag, Susan (1988), *Italy: One Hundred Years of Photography*, Florence

Colonna, Gustavo Brigante (1925), *Roma papale: storie e leggende*, Florence

Coluzzi, Mario, and Corbellini, Gilberto (1995), 'I luoghi della malaria e le cause della malaria', in *Medicina nei Secoli*, 7: 575–98

Corbin, Alain (1986), *The Foul and the Fragrant: Odor and the French Social Imagination*, Cambridge, Mass.

Corradini, Enrico (1923), *Discorsi politici, 1902–1923*, Florence

Corti, Paola (1984), 'Malaria e società contadina nel Mezzogiorno', in *Storia d'Italia: annali, malattia e medicina*, vol. 7, edited by Franco Della Peruta, Turin

Cosgrove, Denis, and Petts, Geoff (eds) (1990), *Water, Engineering and Landscape: Water Control and Landscape Transformation in the Modern Period*, London and New York

Cosmacini, Giorgio (1987), 'Campagne e "mal'aria" in Italia tra Cinquecento e Seicento', in *Aspetti storici e sociali delle infezioni malariche in Sicilia e in Italia*, Palermo

Cremonese, Guido (1921), *La malaria Fiumicino e il Prof. Grassi*, Rome

Cremonese, Guido (1924), *Malaria: New Views on Doctrine and Therapeutics*, Rome

D'Annunzio, Gabriele (1901), *La canzone di Garibaldi*, Milan

Davies, William (1873), *The Pilgrimage of the Tiber, from its Mouth to its Source*, London

De Cesare, R. (1907), *Roma e lo Stato del Papa dal ritorno di Pio IX al XX settembre*, 2 vols, Rome

De Cesare, R. (1909), *The Last Days of Papal Rome, 1850–1870*, translated by Helen Zimmern, London

De Staël, Anne-Louise-Germaine Necker (1883), *Corinne; or Italy* [1807], translated by E. Baldwin and P. Driver, London

Depretis, Agostino (n.d.), archivio Depretis, Serie I, b.9, fasc. 27: 'Legge relativa ai lavori di sistemazione del Tevere', Archivio Centrale dello Stato, Rome

Dickie, John (1993), 'Representations of the Mezzogiorno in post-unification Italy (1860–1900)', Ph.D., University of Sussex

Dickie, John (1994), 'La Macchina da scrivere: the Victor Emmanuel monument in Rome and Italian nationalism', in *The Italianist*, 14: 260–85

Dickie, John (1999), *Darkest Italy: The Nation and Stereotypes of the Mezzogiorno, 1860–1900*, London

Dickie, John, Foot, John, and Snowden, Frank M. (2002), *Disastro! Disasters in Italy since 1860: Culture, Politics, Society*, New York

D'Ideville, Cte H. (1878), *Victor Emmanuel II: Sa vie, sa mort: souvenirs personnels*, Paris

Dieu, Hippolyte (1870), *Mémoire sur la demande en concession, faite par MM. le comte Raphaël Ginnasi et consorts d'un canal maritime de la Méditerranée à Rome par la vallée du Tibre, avec un port franc à Rome*, Paris

Dobson, Mary (1997), *Contours of Death and Disease in Early Modern England*, Cambridge

D'Onofrio, Cesare (1980), *Il Tevere: L'Isola Tiberina, le inondazioni, i porti, le rive, i muraglioni, i ponti di Roma*, Rome

Dowling, Linda (1985), 'Roman decadence and Victorian historiography', in *Victorian Studies*, 28: 579–607

Drake, Richard (1980), *Byzantium for Rome: The Politics of Nostalgia in Umbertian Italy, 1878–1900*, Chapel Hill

Dumas, Alexandre (ed.) (1860), *Garibaldi: An Autobiography*, London

Eaton, Charlotte A. (1852), *Rome in the Nineteenth Century* [1820], 5th edn, 2 vols, London

Edwards, Catharine (ed.) (1999), *Roman Presences: Receptions of Rome in European Culture, 1789–1945*, Cambridge

Eyler, John M. (1979), *Victorian Social Medicine: The Ideas of William Farr*, Baltimore and London

Falleroni, Domenico (1921), *La malaria di Trinitapoli (Foggia)*, Rome

Fantini, Bernardino, and Smargiasse, Antonio (1987), 'Le radici scientifiche e sociali della scuola romana di malariologia', in *Aspetti storici e sociali delle infezioni malariche in Sicilia e in Italia*, edited by Calogero Valenti, Palermo

Fantini, Bernardino (1996), unpublished research paper on Roman malariology

Bibliography

Filopanti, Quirico [i.e. Giuseppe Barilli] (1875), *Sulle bonifiche romane proposte dal Generale Giuseppe Garibaldi*, Rome

Fincardi, Marco (1995), '"Ici pas de Madonne": inondations et apparitions mariales dans les campagnes de la vallée du Pô', in *Annales*, 50: 829–54

Fleres, Ugo (1910), *La campagna romana*, Bergamo

Forbes, Charles Stewart (1861), *The Campaign of Garibaldi in the Two Sicilies: A Personal Narrative*, London

Franchetti, Leopoldo, and Sonnino, Sidney (1925), *La Sicilia nel 1876: condizioni politiche e amministrative*, 2nd edn, Florence

Francia, Paolo (1994), *Fini: La mia destra*, Rome

Freud, Sigmund (1900), *The Interpretation of Dreams*, The Standard Edition of the Complete Psychological Works of Sigmund Freud [SE], vols 4 and 5

Freud, Sigmund (1910), '"Wild" Psycho-Analysis', SE, vol. 11

Freud (1917), 'Mourning and Melancholia', SE, vol. 14

Freud, Sigmund (1985), *The Complete Letters of Sigmund Freud to Wilhelm Fliess*, edited by Jeffrey Moussaieff Masson, Cambridge, Mass.

Garibaldi, Giuseppe (1870), *Cantoni il volontario*, Milan

Garibaldi, Giuseppe (1870a), *The Rule of the Monk; or Rome in the Nineteenth Century*, London

Garibaldi, Giuseppe (1870b), *Clelia. Il governo del monaco. Roma nel secolo XIX. Romanzo storico politico*, Milan

Garibaldi, Giuseppe (1873), *Cantoni il volontario. Romanzo storico*, Milan

Garibaldi, Giuseppe (1874), *I Mille*, Bologna

Garibaldi, Giuseppe (1885), *Garibaldi epistolario: con documenti e lettere inedite (1836–1882)*, edited by Enrico Emilio Ximenes, Milan

Garibaldi, Giuseppe (1888), *Memorie autobiografiche*, 4th edn, Florence

Garibaldi, Giuseppe (1889), *Autobiography*, authorised translation by A. Werner, with a supplement by Jessie White Mario, 3 vols, London

Garibaldi, Giuseppe (1932–7), *Edizione nazionale degli scritti di Giuseppe Garibaldi*, 6 vols, Bologna

Garibaldi, Giuseppe (1983), *Il Progetto di deviazione del Tevere e di bonificazione dell'Agro Romano: Scritti e discorsi del 1875–1876*, introduced and edited by Agostino Grattarola, Rome

Gentile, Emilio (1996), *The Sacralisation of Politics in Fascist Italy*, translated by Keith Botsford, Cambridge, Mass.

Gibbon, Edward (1981), *The Decline and Fall of the Roman Empire*, Harmondsworth

Giblett, Rodney James (1996), *Post-Modern Wetlands: Culture, History, Ecology*, Edinburgh

Gibson, Edmund (1848), *A Preservative against Popery*, by eminent divines of the Church of England collected by the Reverend Edmund Gibson, Lord Bishop of Lincoln and London, revised and edited for the British Society for Promoting the Religious Principles of the Reformation by Reverend John Cumming, London

Ginsborg, Paul (ed.) (1994), *Stato dell'Italia*, Milan

Ginsborg, Paul (2001), *Italy and its Discontents, 1980–2001*, London

Gioberti, Vincenzo (1844), *Del primato morale e civile degli Italiani*, 2 vols, Capolago

Gladstone, William (1851), *A Letter to the Earl of Aberdeen on the State Prosecutions of the Neapolitan Government*, London

Gladstone, William (1875), *Rome. Three Tracts. The Vatican Decrees – Vaticanism – Speeches of the Pope*, London

Goethe, Johann Wolfgang von (1849), *Autobiography*, translated by A.J.W. Morrison, 2 vols, London

Gori, Fabio (1870), *Sullo splendido avvenire di Roma capitale d'Italia e del mondo cattolico e sul modo di migliorare l'interno della città e l'aria delle campagne*, Rome

Goubert, Jean-Pierre (1986), *The Conquest of Water: The Advent of Health in the Industrial Revolution*, translated by Andrew Wilson, introduced by Emmanuel Le Roy Ladurie, Cambridge

Gowers, Emily (1995), 'The Anatomy of Rome from Capitol to Cloaca', in *Journal of Roman Studies*, 85: 23–32

Grassi, Battista (1900), *La malaria: propagata esclusivamente da peculiari zanzare*, Milan

Grassi, Battista (1921), *La malaria Fiumicino*, Rome

Bibliography

Grévy, Jérôme (2001), *Garibaldi*, Paris

Grew, Raymond (1986), 'Catholicism and the *Risorgimento'*, in Frank J. Coppa (ed.), *Studies in Modern Italian History: From the Risorgimento to the Republic*, New York, pp. 39–55

Guerzoni, Giuseppe (1882), *Garibaldi*, 2 vols, Florence

Hales, E.E.Y. (1954), *Pio Nono: A Study in European Politics and Religion*, London

Halliday, Stephen (1999), *The Great Stink of London: Sir Joseph Bazalgette and the Cleansing of the Victorian Metropolis*, London

Hare, Augustus (1913), *Walks in Rome* [1871], 20th edn, London

Harris, Ruth (1999), *Lourdes: Body and Spirit in the Secular Age*, London

Hawthorne, Nathaniel (1860), *The Marble Faun, or The Romance of Monte Beni* in *The Complete Novels and Selected Tales of Nathaniel Hawthorne* (1937), New York

Hawthorne, Nathaniel (1871), *Passages from the French and Italian Notebooks of Nathaniel Hawthorne*, London

Hearder, Harry (1983), *Italy in the Age of the Risorgimento 1790–1870*, London

Hemmings, F.W.J. (1953), *Émile Zola*, Oxford

Hemmings, F.W.J. (1977), *The Life and Times of Émile Zola*, London

Herzen, Alexander (1995), *Letters from France and Italy, 1847–1851*, edited and translated by Judith E. Zimmerman, Pittsburgh and London

Hibbert, Christopher (1985), *Rome: The Biography of a City*, London

Hibbert, Christopher (1987), *Garibaldi and his Enemies* [1965], Harmondsworth

Hilton, Tim (1985), *John Ruskin: The Early Years, 1819–1859*, New Haven and London

Hults, Barbara, et al. (1989), *Northern Italy and Rome*, New York

Hunt, Tristram (2004), *Building Jerusalem: The Rise and Fall of the Victorian City*, London

James, Henry (1909), *Italian Hours*, New York

Jefferies, Richard (1939), *After London and Amaryllis at the Fair* [1885], London

Jolivard, Léon (1862), *Victor-Emmanuel et Garibaldi*, Paris

Jones, Tobias (2002), 'Just Because You're Paranoid . . .' [review of
    Michael Dibdin's *And Then You Die*], *Guardian*, 12 January 2002,
    review section, p. 8

Jones, W.H.S. (1907), *Malaria: A Neglected Factor in the History of
    Greece and Rome*, Cambridge

Jones, W.H.S. (1909), *Malaria and Greek History*, Manchester

Kertzer, David (1997), *The Kidnapping of Edgardo Mortara*, New York

Kesterson, David B. (ed.) (1971), *Studies in the Marble Faun*,
    Columbus

Knox, Oliver (1982), *From Rome to San Marino: A Walk in the
    Footsteps of Garibaldi*, London

Laveran, Alphonse (1891), *Du Paludisme*, Paris

Leti, Giuseppe (1909), *Roma e lo Stato Pontifico dal 1849 al 1870*,
    2 vols, Rome

Leveson, Lady Constance (1865), *The Bride of Garibaldi; or the
    Creole Beauty of Brazil*, London

Leynadier, Camille (1860), *Mémoires authentiques sur Garibaldi*, Paris

Liversidge, Michael, and Edwards, Catharine (eds) (1996), *Imagining
    Rome: British Artists and Rome in the Nineteenth Century*, London

Longobardi, Cesare (1936), *Land-Reclamation in Italy*, translated by
    Olivia Rossetti Agresti, London

McIntire, C.T. (1983), *England Against the Papacy 1858–1861: Tories,
    Liberals and the Overthrow of Papal Temporal Power During the
    Italian Risorgimento*, Cambridge

Mack Smith, Denis (1993), *Cavour and Garibaldi 1860: A Study in
    Political Conflict* [1954], Cambridge

Mack Smith, Denis (1959), *Italy: A Modern History*, Michigan

Mack Smith, Denis (ed.) (1969), *Garibaldi*, Englewood Cliffs

Mack Smith, Denis (1981), *Mussolini*, London

Mack Smith, Denis [1958], (1993), *Garibaldi*, Rome

Mack Smith, Denis (1994), *Mazzini*, London and New Haven

Magherini-Graziani, Giovanni (1896), *Aneddoti e memorie sul
    passaggio di Giuseppe Garibaldi per l'alta valle del Tevere nel luglio
    1849*, Città di Castello

Malissard, Alain (2002), *Les Romans et l'eau: fontaines, salles de bains,
    thermes, égouts, aqueducs*, Paris

Bibliography

Mariani,Valerio (1994), *La Campagna nei pittori dell'Ottocento*, Rome

Marx, Karl, and Engels, Friedrich (2002), *The Communist Manifesto* [1848]; reprinted with an introduction and notes by Gareth Stedman Jones, London

Mascanzoni, Irma (1959), *In memoria di Anita Garibaldi nel centenario della traslazione della salma da Mandriole di Ravenna a Nizza, 1859–1959*, Milan

Massobrio, Giovanna (1982), *L'Italia per Garibaldi*, Milan

Masters, Roger (1998), *Fortune is a River: Leonardo da Vinci and Niccolò Machiavelli's Dream to Change the Course of Florentine History*, New York

Mazzini, Giuseppe (1845), *Italy, Austria and the Pope: A Letter to Sir James Graham Bart*, London

Mazzini, Giuseppe (1849), *A Letter to Messrs. De Tocqueville and De Falloux, Ministers of France* (For the Italian Refugee Fund Committee), London

Mazzini, Giuseppe (1850a), *Le Pape au dix-neuvième siècle*, Paris

Mazzini, Giuseppe (1850b), *La santa alleanza dei popoli*, Genoa

Mazzini, Giuseppe (1862), *The Duties of Man*, London

Mazzini, Giuseppe (1872), *The Italian School of Republicanism*, London

Mazzini, Giuseppe (1845), *Italy, Austria and the Pope*, London

Mazzoni, Filippo (1994),'Una problema capitale', in Paul Ginsborg (ed., *Stato dell'Italia*, Milan, pp. 108–14)

Melena, Elpis (Baroness von Schwartz) (1887), *Garibaldi: Recollections of his Public and Private Life*, London

Merello, Faustino (1945), *Mazzini. Il pensiero religioso*, Geneva

Miller, David C. (1989), *Dark Eden: The Swamp in Nineteenth-Century American Culture*, Cambridge

Missiroli, Alberto (1934), *Lezione sulla epidemiologia e profilassi della malaria*, Rome

Mitchell, David (1980), *The Jesuits: A History*, London

Moe, Nelson (2002), *The View from Vesuvius: Italian Culture and the Southern Question*, Berkeley and London

Monestès, J.L. (1896), *La Vraie Rome, réplique à M. Zola*, Paris

Monsagrati, Giuseppe (1999), 'Giuseppe Garibaldi', in *Dizionario biografico degli Italiani*, Catanzaro, pp. 315–31

Montaigne, Michel Eyquem de (1929), *The Diary of Montaigne's Journey to Italy in 1580 and 1581*, edited by E.J. Trechmann, London

Moore, James (ed.) (1988), *Religion in Victorian Britain*, vol. 3, *Sources*, Manchester

Morolli, Gabriele (1982), 'Garibaldi e l'ultima "difesa" di Roma: quattro progetti per il Tevere', in *Garibaldi: arte e storia* [catalogue of exhibition, Rome, Museo del Palazzo di Venezia and Museo Centrale del Risorgimento, June–December 1982], Florence, pp. 95–112

Moscheles, Felix (1899), *Fragments of an Autobiography*, London

Mussolini, Benito (1929a), *The Cardinal's Mistress*, translated by H. Motherwell, London [originally serialised as *Claudia Particella, l'amante del Cardinale: grande romanzo dei tempi del Cardinale Emmanuel Madruzzo*, in *La vita trentina*, a supplement to *Il Popolo*, 1909]

Mussolini, Benito (1929b), *La dottrina del fascismo*, edited by A. Marpicati, M. Gallian and Z. Contu, Milan

Nielsen, Fredrik (1906), *History of the Papacy in the Nineteenth Century*, London

North, William (1896), *Roman Fever: The Results of an Inquiry during three years' Residence on the Spot into the Origin, History, Distribution and Nature of the Malarial Fevers of the Roman Campagna, with especial reference to their supposed connection with Pathogenic Organisms*, London

Parker, Robert (1983), *Miasma: Pollution and Purification in Early Greek Religion*, Oxford

Parks, Tim (2001), 'Berlusconi's Way', in *New York Review of Books*, 18 October 2001, 63–7

Passerini, Luisa (1991), *Mussolini immaginario*, Bari

Pecori, Giuseppe (1931), 'Come Roma città fu liberata dalla malaria poco dopo la sua annessione al Regno d'Italia', in *Atti del I° Congresso Nazionale di Studi Romani*, Rome, pp. 612–21

Peschi, Ugo (1907), *I primi anni di Roma capitale (1870–1878)*, Firenze

Bibliography

Petty, William (1867), *Observations upon the Cities of London and Rome*, London

Pick, Daniel (1994), 'Pro Patria: Blocking the Tunnel', *Ecumene: A Geographical Journal of Environment, Culture and Meaning*, vol. I, pp. 77–93

Pini, Giorgio (1939), *The Official Life of Benito Mussolini*, translated by Luigi Villari, London

Pliny the Elder (1991), *Natural History: A Selection*, London

Purseglove, Jeremy (1989), *Taming the Flood: A History and Natural History of Rivers and Wetlands*, Oxford

Quinterio, Franceso (1982), 'La sistemazione del Tevere e dell'Agro Romano nel carteggio di Garibaldi', in *Garibaldi: arte e storia* [catalogue of exhibition, Rome, Museo del Palazzo di Venezia and Museo Centrale del Risorgimento, June–December 1982], Florence, pp. 110–12

Rapisardi, Giovanni (1875), *Garibaldi al Tevere: poemetto lirico*, Rome

Redondi, Pietro (1980), 'Aspetti della cultura scientifica negli stati pontifici', in 'Cultura e scienza dall'illuminismo al positivismo', section III, *Storia d'Italia: annali 3, scienza e tecnica*, edited by Gianni Micheli, Turin, pp. 782–811

Reed, T.J. (1984), *Goethe*, Oxford

Regis, Angelo (1889), *Gli argini del Tevere e la loro influenza sulle acque sotterranee di Roma*, Rome

Renan, Ernest (1951), 'Essai de morale et de critique' [1859], in *Oeuvres complètes*, vol. 2, Paris

Riall, Lucy (1994), *The Italian Risorgimento: State, Society and National Unification*, London

Ridley, Jasper (1974), *Garibaldi*, London

Riley, James (1987), *The Eighteenth-Century Campaign to avoid Disease*, Basingstoke

Rocco, Fiammetta (2003), *The Miraculous Fever-Tree: Malaria, Medicine and the Cure that Changed the World*, London

Romano, Pietro (1943), *Ottocento romano*, Rome

Ross, Ronald (1924), 'Private note' (3 typed pages, dated 10 March 1924), [Ross Papers, 65/051, pp. 1–2, London School of Hygiene and Tropical Medicine]

Ross, Ronald (1925), 'The Mosquito Theory of Malaria and the Late Prof. G.B. Grassi' (pamphlet), extracted from *Science Progress*, 78: 311–20, [Ross Papers, 65/167, p. 319, London School of Hygiene and Tropical Medicine]

Ruskin, John (1871–84), *Fors Clavigera: Letters to the Workmen and Labourers of Great Britain* in *The Works of John Ruskin*, edited by E.T. Cook and Alexander Wedderburn, 1903–12, London, vol. 27

Ruskin, John (1884), *The Storm Cloud of the Nineteenth Century: Two Lectures Delivered at the London Institution*, Orpington

Russo, Maria-Teresa Bonadonna (1979), 'Appunti sulle bonifiche pontine', in *Rinascimento nel Lazio*, edited by Renato Lefevre, Rome, pp. 575–97

Sacerdote, Gustavo (1933), *La Vita di Giuseppe Garibaldi*, Milan

Saint-Cyr, Charles de (1939), *Garibaldi contre Mussolini*, Paris

Saint-Simon, Henri de (1975), *Selected Writings on Science, Industry and Social Organisation*, translated and edited by Keith Taylor, London

Saint-Simon, Henri de (1969), *Le Nouveau Christianisme* [1825], *et les écrits sur la religion*, edited by Henri Desroche, Paris

Sallares, Robert (2002), *Malaria and Rome: A History of Malaria in Ancient Rome*, Oxford

Sand, George (1859), *Garibaldi*, Paris

Savelli, Giulio (1992), *Che cosa vuole la Lega*, preface by Umberto Bossi, Milan

Scardozzi, Mirella (1976), 'La bonifica dell'Agro Romano nei dibattiti e nelle leggi dell'ultimo trentennio dell'Ottocento', in *Rassegna storica del Risorgimento*, 63: 181–208

Schama, Simon (1995), *Landscape and Memory*, London

Schneidel, Walter (2003), 'Germs for Rome', in C. Edwards and G. Woolf, *Rome the Cosmopolis*, Cambridge, ch. 8, pp. 158–76

Scirocco, Alfonso (2001), *Garibaldi: battaglie, amori, ideali di un cittadino del mondo*, Rome and Bari

Segal, Hanna (1981), *The Work of Hanna Segal: A Kleinian Approach to Clinical Practice*, New York

Selmi, Antonio (1870), *Il miasma palustre: lezioni di chimica igienica*, Padua

Bibliography

Serao, Matilde (1902), *The Conquest of Rome*, London

Seton-Watson, Christopher (1984), 'Garibaldi's British image', in *Giuseppe Garibaldi e il suo mito*, Rome, pp. 247–58

Shelley, Percy Bysshe (1905), *With Shelley in Italy: Being a Selection of the Poems and Letters*, edited by Anna Benneson McMahan, Chicago

Sismondi, J.C.L. (1832), *A History of the Italian Republics, being a View of the Origin, Progress and Fall of Italian Freedom*, London

Smith, S.A. (1877), *The Tiber and its Tributaries*, London

Snowden, Frank (1995), *Naples in the Time of Cholera, 1884–1911*, Cambridge

Snowden, Frank M. (2002), 'From Triumph to Disaster: Fascism and Malaria in the Pontine Marshes, 1928–1946', in John Dickie, John Foot and Frank M. Snowden, *Disastro! Disasters in Italy since 1860: Culture, Politics, Society*, New York, ch. 4

Spadolini, Giovanni (ed.) (1982), *Il mito di Garibaldi nella Nuova Antologia: 1882–1982*, Florence

Springer, Caroline (1987), *The Marble Wilderness: Ruins and Representation in Italian Romanticism*, Cambridge

Stapleton, D.H. (2000), 'Internationalism and Nationalism: The Rockefeller Foundation, Public Health, and Malaria in Italy, 1922–1951', in *Parassitologia*, vol. 42, pp. 127–34

Stendhal (1980), *Promenades dans Rome* [1829], 2 vols, Paris

Sternberg, George M. (1884), *Malaria and Malarial Diseases*, New York

Strachey, Lytton (1948), *Eminent Victorians* [1918], Harmondsworth

Taine, Hippolyte (1867), *Italy: Naples and Rome*, translated by John Durand, London

Taine, Hippolyte (1869), *Italy: Florence and Venice*, translated by John Durand, New York

Tanner, Tony (1992), *Venice Desired*, Oxford

Ternois, René (1961), *Zola et son temps: Lourdes-Rome-Paris*, Paris

Ternois, René (1967), *Zola et ses amis italiens*, Paris

Toscanelli, Nello (1927), *La malaria nell'antichità e la fine degli Etruschi*, Milan

Trambusti, Arnaldo (1910), *La lotta contro la malaria in Sicilia nel 1910*, Palermo

Travis, Anthony (1991), 'Engineering and Politics: The Channel Tunnel in the 1880s', in *Technology and Culture*, 32: 461–97

Trevelyan, George Macaulay (1907), *Garibaldi's Defence of the Roman Republic*, London

Trevelyan, George Macaulay (1909), *Garibaldi and the Thousand, May 1860*, London

Trevelyan, George Macaulay (1911), *Garibaldi and the Making of Italy, June–November 1860*, London

Turnor, Christopher (1938), *Land-Reclamation and Drainage in Italy*, London

Valerio, Anthony (2001), *Anita Garibaldi: A Biography*, Westport

Vecchi, C. Augusto (1856), *La Italia: storia di due anni, 1848–1849*, 2 vols, Turin

Venturi, Alfredo (1973), *Garibaldi in Parlamento*, Milan

Verga, Giovanni (1979), 'Malaria' [1881], in *Tutte le novelle*, edited by Carla Riccardi, Milan, pp. 262–70

Verga, Giovanni (1883). *Novelle rusticane*, Turin

Vescovali, Angelo (1874), *Esecuzione pei lavori di sistemazione del tronco urbano del Tevere. Relazione spiegativa*, Rome

Vidotto, Vittorio (ed.) (2002), *Roma capitale*, Rome

Visconti Venosta, Giovanni (1906), *Ricordi di gioventù: cose vedute o sapute, 1847–1860*, Milan

Vitelleschi, Francesco (1877), *Atti Parlamentari: sessione del 1876–7, documenti, progetti di legge e relazioni*, Rome

Watson, Malcolm, et al., (1921), *The Prevention of Malaria in the Federated Malay States: A Record of Twenty Years' Progress*, 2nd revised edn, Preface by Sir Ronald Ross, London

Wilson, A.N. (2002), *The Victorians*, London

Wilson, Elizabeth (1991), *The Sphinx in the City: Urban Life, the Control of Disorder, and Women*, Berkeley

Wolffe, John (1989), 'Evangelicalism in mid-Nineteenth-Century England', in Raphael Samuel (ed.), *Patriotism: The Making and Unmaking of English National Identity*, London, 3 vols, vol. 1, pp. 188–202

Bibliography

Ximenes, Enrico Emilio (1907), *Anita Garibaldi*, Bologna

Zola, Émile (1894), *Lourdes*, translated by E.A. Vizetelly, London

Zola, Émile (1896), *Rome*, translated by E.A. Vizetelly, London

Zola, Émile (1958), *Mes Voyages: journaux inédits*, edited and introduced by René Ternois, Paris

Zuccagni-Orlandini, Attilio (1870), *Roma e l'Agro Romano*, Florence

Index

Page numbers in *italics* refer to illustrations.

Index

Index

Index